# Literacy in Human Development

# Literacy in Human Development

edited by

Marta Kohl de Oliveira
University of São Paulo, Brazil

and

Jaan Valsiner
Clark University, Worcester, Massachusetts

Ablex Publishing Corporation
Stamford, Connecticut
London, England

Permission to reprint chapter 1 granted by the *Journal of Russian and East European Psychology,* M.E. Sharpe, Inc.



Printed in the United States of America

**Library of Congress Cataloging-in-Publication Data**

Literacy in human development / edited by Marta Kohl de Oliveira and Jaan Valsiner.
p. cm.
Includes bibliographic references and index.
ISBN 1-56750-366-7 (cloth). — ISBN 1-56750-367-5 (paper)
1. Literacy—Social aspects. 2. Literacy—Psychological aspects. 3. Reading. 4. Writing. I. Oliveira, Marta Kohl de. II. Valsiner, Jaan.
LC149.L49916 1998
302.2′244—dc21 97-35105
CIP

Ablex Publishing Corporation
100 Prospect Street
Stamford, CT 06901-1640

Published in the U.K. and Europe by:
JAI Press Ltd.
38 Tavistock Street
Covent Garden
London WC2E 7PB
England

# Contents

Preface vii

Introduction: To Be or Not to Be . . . Literate
*Marta Kohl de Oliveira & Jaan Valsiner* 1

*Part I. Literacy Processes: Access to a Symbolic System*

1. The Development of Writing in the Child
*Alexander Romanovich Luria* 15

2. Parallels Between the Perspectives of Alexander Luria and Emilia Ferreiro
*Maria Thereza Fraga Rocco* 57

3. Educational Tendencies in the Beginning of Reading and Writing Instruction
*Berta P. de Braslavsky* 79

*Part II. Learning and Meaning in Childhood*

4. Approaching Knowledge and Meaning Elaboration in the Classroom: Some Theoretical and Methodological Issues
*Ana Luiza B. Smolka* 107

5. Why There Might Be Several Ways to Read Storybooks to Preschoolers in Aotearoa/New Zealand: Models of Tutoring and Sociocultural Diversity in How Families Read Books to Preschoolers
*Stuart McNaughton* 123

6. Literacy and Language Processes: Orthographic and Structural Effects
*Prathibha Karanth* 145

*Part III. Literacy and Activity Contexts in Adulthood*

7. Illiterate Adults in Literate Societies: Interactions With a Social World
   *Ann Hagell & Jonathan Tudge* 163

8. Schooling, Literacy, and Social Change: Elements for a Critical Approach to the Study of Literacy
   *Angela B. Kleiman* 183

9. Conceptual Organization and Schooling
   *Marta Kohl de Oliveira* 227

10. Learning to Write Letters: Semiotic Mediation in Literacy Acquisition in Adulthood
   *Simone Gonçalves De Lima & Maria Helena Fávero* 247

Author Index 281

# Preface

The editing of this book took a very long time, yet it is with a feeling of accomplishment that we look back at the tedious process of getting the contributions together, and some of them translated. The editors are grateful to Barbara Rae Swem for translating chapters 3 (Rocco) and 4 (Braslavsky) from Portuguese and Spanish into English. Michael Cole's support to the project is gratefully acknowledged, as he took care of the permission to reprint the seminal article by Alexander Luria, from M.E. Sharpe, Inc. Publishers.

Much of the work on editing this book was facilitated by the support of the Fulbright Foundation to the second author. The serial grant that brought him to Brazil in the course of three consecutive years (1995, 1996, and 1997) proved very helpful for this book, among other objectives.

introduction

# To Be or Not to Be...Literate

Marta Kohl de Oliveira
University of São Paulo, Brazil

Jaan Valsiner
Clark University, Worcester, Massachusetts

Issues of literacy have been explored in the literature on human development and education both in terms of social achievement and the individual benefits of the possession of such cultural skills as reading and writing. The literature on literacy is also fragmented into a number of thematic domains—so, for instance, aside from the basic distinctions of literacy as the capability to read (and/or write) versus the lack of such capacities, we can observe talk about "computer literacy," "math literacy," "science literacy," and so on. Yet, there are limits to such construction of meaning. For instance, we rarely (if ever) encounter the term "literacy" linked with some relevant activities of everyday life, such as "cooking literacy," "driving literacy," "gossiping literacy," or "gardening literacy." Without doubt, inter-individual differences in these relevant everyday activities are recognized by language use (e.g., statements like "he is a good cook" and "she is a better driver than he"). Yet such recognition of qualities and differences need not immediately lead to the construction of an essentialistic literacy for such activities.

In other terms, *literacy is a concept selectively applied to some domains of our socio-mental activities* and ways of reflection about them. In this respect, the talk about something in terms of literacy (versus "illiteracy") is a socio-cultural result of some form of social highlighting of an activity domain by institutions. Such institutional definition of literacies is often linked with nonneutral orientation to these. "Literacy in X" is necessarily positively valued, and its opposite ("illiteracy in X") viewed as an undesirable state. This valuation indicates how social institutions use the determination of what the labelling of something by "literacy" entails. In the social world at large, there are many domains where ordinary persons are purposefully kept ignorant or unskilled in some domains—for the benefit of those who are informed and skilled. If one were to apply the label illiteracy to those, it would entail positive social value. (For example, buyers' illiteracy in the area of knowing the profit margins of sellers would be hailed positively by the sellers, or otherwise the whole economic system might collapse under the challenge of social discussion of what is a fair price for the buyers to pay.)

In the psychology of literacy and its social use, both researchers and policy makers are usually very emotional about literacy. We tend to be sure that it would solve many of our pressing social, educational, economic, or personal problems, and we create narratives of disapproval of the conditions where illiteracy dominates. Discourse about literacy is thus also discourse of social change in a society—necessarily inheriting the intellectual baggage involved in any construction of social utopia (see Valsiner, 1996).

## THE FOCUS IN THIS BOOK

The focus of the present volume is on the developmental processes involved in the acquisition of literacy, and on the novel psychological possibilities that the newly acquired literacy makes possible for people, through a multiplicity of perspectives on the role of literacy in human development. An internationally representative cast of authors has been brought together, in order to give justice to the wide international coverage of the topic in contemporary research groups.

The notion of human development covers the whole of human life span, rather than merely childhood years. Furthermore, the development of literacy (and the corresponding discourse about literacy/illiteracy issues) is taken as a historical phenomenon, linked with the histories of particular societies, and with social transformations within those societies.

All of the contributions to this book refer to societies with long histories of literacy. The societies involved are not moving from a state of lack of writing systems to their presence (in contrast to other books that are explicitly dealing with the emergence of writing systems, e.g., Goody, 1968; Bottéro et al., 1995). Rather, in all of the contributions to this book the authors deal with literacy as a socially stratified and stratifying phenomenon within their respective societies. Some social (or age) groups, or classes, in a given society possess the literacy skills and define the meanings of literacy and its opposite (illiteracy), in conjunction with the social practices of the given society at the given time.

## RELATIVITY OF LITERACY/ILLITERACY DISTINCTIONS

It will be seen in this book that different authors use different connotations of literacy in their specific papers. All in all, we may be left with a largely relativistic view—literacy can mean anything from being able to sign one's name to the ability to read and write in Latin (see chapter 7, by Hagell & Tudge). Nevertheless, there is some unity in this diversity—it seems that all authors consider literacy as a positive state of affairs (in a society, or in the life of a person), and illiteracy is seen as a negative phenomenon, from the viewpoint of social or personal "progress." It is assumed that formal schooling leads to such progress in the development of literacy, and the escape from the dungeon of illiteracy.

This optimistic view of schooling need not be so absolute (see Tulviste, 1991), since the buildup of literacy in school can be of varied nature, and can disappear if the social practices after schooling do not support it. The present concerns about the so-called "functional illiterates" are visible both in countries where rates of absolute lack of literate or schooled abilities are traditionally very high (in Latin America, for example, where UNESCO is presently carrying out an extensive survey on functional illiteracy [Infante, 1994; see also Londono, 1991]) and in countries where universality of schooling would supposedly warrant a minimum level of literacy in the population (see Cook-Gumperz, 1986). Besides, the very insertion of literate and schooled practices into a wider cultural environment presupposes interactions among different social phenomena and the production of different meanings for literacy and schooling. A good example of this possible diversity is given by Ginzburg (1987), when he explores the interaction between the written word and other elements of a nonliterate culture by studying the thought of a mill worker of the 16th century who, different from the majority of the members of his social group, knew how to read and write and dealt with written texts. In this work the author discusses, on one hand, the way by which a particular individual, from his specific cultural place, articulates (and may "distort") the information given by the written word and, on the other hand, how the access to the written word outlines new possibilities of dealing with knowledge. Still another phenomenon that challenges the unquestionability of the value of literacy is the substantial unemployment of very literate persons, which is becoming a serious social problem in many contemporary societies. This problem is of general nature—achievements in education may not be a panacea nor even a guarantee of regular income for a person in a society.

We are not trying to change the emotional valence that is habitually linked with literacy, nor will we try to unify the various definitions of literacy. Rather, in order to think about the contributions to this book, it may be of use to try to elaborate possible connections between the social systems that promote different ways of making sense of literacy (and illiteracy). By doing this we hope to provide a framework for organization of the different perspectives included in this book, as well as in the literature on literacy at large. The heterogeneity of the discourse about literacy must have some good reasons to exist.

## SOCIAL INSTITUTIONS, THEIR GOALS, AND THE MAKING OF LITERACIES

As was mentioned above, issues of literacy are value-laden in a given society. Any society at any time is a heterogeneous—or *polyphonic*, to use a Bakhtinian term—(see also Smolka, chapter 4 in this volume) system of constant goal-oriented activities of different social institutions. Societies cannot be viewed as homogeneous entities; instead, they are heterogeneous systems of mutually discordant social institutions. These institutions attempt to define social role expectations for particular roles that are to be assumed by persons. The role of literacy as a cultural-historical phenomenon starts in conjunction with such roles. In countries where the history of schooling is relatively recent we can observe how the instructional level required for a certain job rapidly changes along history: For a job that could be at first fullfilled by a person with no schooling at all (a janitor in an industrial plant, for example), the employers start to require a minimum literacy level, then education to the fourth grade of elementary school, and later eighth grade. The capacity for performing the same tasks becomes associated with higher and higher levels of schooling as the population becomes more and more educated. For example, elementary school teachers themselves, who are by definition representatives of the literate culture, may be recruited among barely literate persons to teach in public schools in remote rural areas of Brazil. At the same time, other teachers are selected among university-level professionals by the owners of private schools that serve the upper classes in the metropolitan areas of the same country. Both of these kinds of teachers may work hard on the task of promotiong literacy, yet the kind of literacy that is actually established would be profoundly social-class-specific.

This heterogeneity of literacy education renders general talk about the "needs of society" mute. In whatever might be called "our modern society" (note that even in this expression we find a tendency towards overlooking the heterogeneity of any particular society and of different societies), the background role of social institutional regulation of the meanings of literacy is clearly demonstrable. First, let us consider the categorical distincton "literacy" *versus* "illiteracy." This dichotomy itself constitutes a social distinction. Interestingly, we do not encounter in pertinent societal discourse a *three*-part categorization (i.e., in addition to the two opposites, their transitional form of "no longer illiterate but not yet literate"). Such distinction could be made if a social institution were oriented towards the promotion of human development (and not towards selection of persons who have developed to their present state). This distinction is made when research is oriented towards the understanding of human development; in this volume it is made by many of the authors, particularly the ones that direct their work to the question of literacy among adults (see especially Hagel & Tudge in chapter 7, Kleiman in chapter 8, and Lima & Fávero in chapter 10).

Second, the positively value-laden nature of literacy is a socio-cultural construction. Some social institutions can construct the desirability of illiteracy in many ways. First, the state of illiteracy can be glorified for purposes of ideological attachment to a social group (group loyalty), in opposition to the educated classes. During turmoil in a society, the lower social classes may be coerced to eradicate the upper ones by revaluing their state of illiteracy to that of positive characteristic.

Furthermore, relative illiteracy in specific domains of social languages may be a desired state of affairs for the social "outsiders" of the group of "insiders." Thus, universal literacy in the sense of reading (and writing) in the language of the legal or medical professions may eradicate the basis of the social prestige (and the exclusionary practice) for the specific profession within a society. Professions that carefully defend their boundaries within a society may do that through setting limits upon access to literacy of the general population in the sense of their social language. Even if the general population may be considered fully literate in terms of some general (minimal—e.g., "writing one's name") criterion, only some persons from that population may be given possibilities to enter into specifically restricted professions. Reasons for their rejection may be precisely their insufficient literacy in terms of the specific social language of the professional group. Once accepted for special preparation for the given profession, the selected few are carefully prepared in the use of the language of the given profession—be this law, medicine, or psychology. Clinical psychologists, for instance, master the literacy of writing clinical case reports in their professional trade training. This makes them acceptable role-enactors in the system of clinical psychology of a given country. Thus, the interaction of social institutions and their goal-oriented selection of persons for the social roles defined by the institutions, together with the subsequent cultivation of the persons for such social roles, is based on access to specific social languages.

To summarize: Societies at any historical time are hierarchical systems of social institutions, the relations of which are organized by the divergence and convergence of their particular goal orientations. This hierarchical organization sets up the heterogeneity of the issue of literacy in the given society at the time. The social institutions create their appropriate social languages, which become hierarchically organized "voices" (following Bakhtin—see Wertsch, 1991; Smolka, 1994; and chapter 4 in this volume), functioning both in social interaction between persons, and within individuals' minds. This hierarchy of social languages may include specific social expectations for literacy at some level of the hierarchy (e.g., requirement for "universal basic literacy" in society X), together with social restrictions against the proliferation of literacy to the other (higher) levels of the hierarchy of social languages. The latter restriction is not contradictory to the former expectation. The socio-institutional system merely works to provide frameworks for inclusion and exclusion at different levels of the hierarchy.

We can see, for example, that social campaigns for literacy are often about the regulation of access for one or another social stratum of a population to one or another level of social language hierarchy. Thus, the orientation towards universal literacy of populations that was started by the Protestant Reformation in Europe in the 16th century was linked with the socio-political goal of delegating the cultural control over persons' socio-moral selves to the internalized social control mechanisms. In order to achieve that goal, parts of the population who had previously not had access to reading and writing were guided to gain such access, together with the kind of literature (the Bible) that they were expected to read, in ways that were in line with the socio-political goals of the social institutions that made achievement of literacy their goal. In the history of the former Soviet Union in the 20th century, we can observe the politically guided promotion of literacy in Central Asia in the 1920s and 30s, together with the introduction of alternative writing systems. Thus, the first wave of literacy promotion (in the late 1920s) in these areas was meant to limit the newly literate persons from reading the Islamic religious texts (written in Arabic script) by giving the local (mostly Turkic) local languages a new (Latinized) script. However, in the further effort to limit the access of the newly literate Central Asian people to non-Soviet texts in the 1930s, the Latinized writing system was replaced by a Cyrillic one. That effectively blocked the possibility to read "foreign" modern text of non-Russian origin. In the early 1920s Turkey had introduced a Latinized script to Turkish, and Turkish texts would have been easy reading for the Central Asians, since the Latinized script of their new literacy was very similar.

## LITERACY AS A PROPOSED ROUTE TO DEMOCRATIZATION

It may become clear in this context why generic, non-contextualized talk about literacy as a solution to social problems is misguided. "Social problems" themselves are defined as such by some social institution, and linking the promotion of literacy with the stated goals of changing society may merely be discursive vehicles for social talk, rather than goals themselves. Each promotion of literacy—access to a social language—entails the possibility that the newly acquired tool may be turned against the goals of the providing institution. Hence we can see the careful orchestration (by social institutions) of the promotion of literacy together with the expected and desired objects to which this new skill is to be applied. Learning to read in one's native language (rather than Latin) in post-Reformation Europe was coordinated with the focus on reading the Bible (and its didactic versions—"catechisms"; see Sommerville, 1983); likewise learning to read in Soviet Central Asia in the 1930s (using the Cyrillic alphabet) was coordinated with the reading of Soviet-provided texts (and not of the Islamic religious texts).

Democratization of societies may be a stated goal in many efforts to promote literacy. Yet specific literacy by itself merely creates a socially situated activity setting. While the newly literate person has access to sources of information in an "open society," some way of presenting that information by the communicating social institutions can begin to limit the access to such information. In many societies, specific books—often classics of world literature—are banned from local school libraries because of the feared "negative effects" that students' reading them might entail. Hence open access to information is an appealing idea which nevertheless is unrealistic in social conditions where that information itself can be a value exactly because of lack of access to it by some persons, to the benefit of others. Thus, fees paid to copyright owners and purchases of databases indicate the reality behind the overwhelming slogan of "democratization" via literacy-based access to texts.

## MECHANISMS OF LITERACY PROMOTION: PROCESSES IN EDUCATION

In this book, the specific focus of most authors is on the mechanisms of literacy promotion and acquisition. By and large, the participating authors do not make the socio-institutional construction of literacy education a goal of their analyses. This is due to an editorial decision to concentrate the volume on issues of literacy processes, rather than literacy programs. Still, different socio-institutional aspects of the guidance of literacy are covered in the description of processes of human development.

Furthermore, the divergence of socio-institutional goals can be traced in the dialogue between "Vygotskian" and "Piagetian" perspectives on the development of literacy. The contrast between these perspectives may itself be an institutional construction—despite many scholarly analyses pointing to the contrary (Saxe, 1991; Castorina, 1995; Rocco, chapter 2 in this volume), the counterpositioning of these two schools of thought remains widespread. Supposedly the Piagetian school emphasizes child-based discovery of the nature and structure of the writing system, while the Vygotskian school requires the active and eminently helpful teacher to lead the student to acquire the relevant skills. Traces of this ideological dialogue can be seen in this book (see Braslavsky, chapter 3, and Rocco, chapter 2, in this volume), and are widespread in the literature.

## CONTENTS OF THIS VOLUME

The articles that constitute this volume are organized in three parts, which represent different aspects of the literacy issue. Part 1, "Literacy Processes: Access to a Symbolic System," focuses on writing as a representational system and the processes of literacy development as related to this conception about writing. In order to start the reflection about these questions, we reproduce here the classic text written by Luria in 1929. The main reason for this choice is that the central ideas explored in this work are extremely contemporary and still provoke intense dialogue with present-day authors and ideas. He treats writing not as a code that allows for transcription of oral language to the graphic mode, but as a system of representation of reality.

In accordance with his cultural-historical perspective, Luria conceptualizes writing as a symbolic system that has a mediating role in the subject/object relationship; as a cultural artifact that functions as a support for certain psychological actions, specially related to memory; and as an instrument that allows for the amplification of human capabilities for registering, transmitting, and recovering information. He also postulates that the process of becoming literate starts much before the beginning of schooling: The child that grows up in a literate society develops early conceptions about writing, a cultural object much present in his everyday life.

Approximately 50 years after the first publication of Luria's work, a Piagetian approach to the psychogenesis of literacy came about, with great penetration in the educational milieu, specially in Latin America (Ferreiro & Teberosky, 1982). In spite of the important differences between the two approches, given their diverse theoretical points of departure, there are strong similarities between them, particularly regarding the idea of writing as a representation system and the conception of the "illiterate" child as a subject that does have hypotheses about writing and that has already started to, somehow, master this system. The confrontation of Luria's and Ferreiro's work on literacy is as natural an enterprise as the contrast between Vygotsky and Piaget, and has produced many pieces of work in the last years, particularly in Brazil (Azenha, 1995; Ferreiro, 1994 and 1995; Oliveira, 1995; Rocco, 1990; Setúbal, 1993). Chapter 2 of this volume, by Maria Thereza Fraga Rocco, analyzes this confrontation, exploring some of its theoretical possibilities, and in a certain sense, represents the atmosphere of the discussions developed in these recent works.

Another kind of atmosphere is conveyed in the chapter "Educational Tendencies in Beginning Reading and Writing Instruction". As a pragmatic counterpart of the aforementioned theoretical discussions, Berta Braslavsky's chapter (3) approaches the differences between Ferreiro and Vygotsky based on an experimental project that took place under the Department of Education of the City of Buenos Aires, Argentina. After giving a brief panoramic view of beginning reading and writing instruction in Latin America, the author describes that project, which involved teacher training and continuous analysis of the students' production in reading and writing, and its relationship with Vygotskian postulates. Her view of the confrontation between Piaget and Vygotsky is marked by the point of view of the actor immersed in decision-making situations of educational practice, clearly differing from the intended exemption of the theoretical analysts.

In Part 2 of the book, "Learning and Meaning in Childhood," the articles deal with empirical data collected among children, explicitly relating literacy with development. Ana Luiza Smolka (chapter 4) explores language as event and object of knowledge in school, discussing an episode taken from observations made in a first grade classroom, where initial reading and writing instruction was taking place. The focus of the analysis is the dynamics of the interlocutory processes in the classroom, revealing an apparent "chaos" in a situation where the production of meaning is not necessarily transparent to the observer.

The two other articles included in this second part explore the effects of cultural practices in development. Stuart McNaughton (chapter 5) studies different modes of storybook reading to preschoolers in New Zealand, analyzing different configurations in tutorial patterns. This variety of configurations relates to the function of storyreading within particular socializing environments, making clear the importance of understanding literacy practices within the socialization settings where they become meaningful. Prathiba Karanth (chapter 6) explores literacy processes, specially meta-linguistic abilities, in speakers of the Kannada language—a language spoken in southern India whose script is nonalphabetical. Data obtained in various empirical studies are used to discuss the relationship between script and meta-linguistic abilities, leading to the conclusion that different scripts enhance different types of meta-linguistic abilities. In that sense, the linguistic and cognitive consequences of literacy need to be related to the particular kind of script of the written language being learned and used.

Part 3, "Literacy and Activity Contexts in Adulthood," includes four articles that deal with the issue of illiteracy (or very low instructional level) among adults in literate societies and its relationships with psychological functioning. The first two articles of this part focus on conceptual questions about literacy and illiteracy, emphazising the idea of literacy as social construction, where individual processes interact with cultural processes in the constitution of the phenomenon of illiteracy in literate societies. Both of the texts question the so-called "autonomous model" of literacy, which carries the idea of a universal effect of the process of learning how to read and write that would be independent of cultural practices. While Ann Hagell and Jonathan Tudge's chapter (7) is a theoretical discussion and focuses mainly on the case of the "poor readers" in highly schooled societies, Angela Kleiman (chapter 8) directs her discussion to the case of illiterate adults who had never learned how to read and write, using empirical data collected among adults who attend adult literacy courses.

The issue of literacy practices as co-construction and the consequent questioning of postulations about the general effects of schooling and/or literacy, which would lead to the contrast between literate and illiterate groups as homogeneous entities, are prominent in the last two chapters of the book. Marta Kohl de Oliveira (chapter 9) explores the question of conceptual organization among low-instructional-level adults, showing how their involvement in situations of dense verbal interaction and collaborative reflective activity promotes the emergence of cognitive processes usually associated with higher levels of schooling. Simone Gonçalves de Lima and Maria Helena Fávero (chapter 10) present a case study of an adult's acquisition of the written language, focusing on the analysis of his text production. Taking the written text as a generator of meaning, the authors discuss how the increase in the socio-communicative complexity of the text is related to its transformation from oral dialogic forms to written monologic forms.

Speaking from different cultures and analyzing different aspects of the complex and multilinear phenomenon of literacy, the texts in this volume explore the topic with an explicit developmental approach, where the very process of the joint construction of meaning can be considered the main object for investigation in psychology and education. Making graphic signs on paper, facing the classroom practices of literacy tutoring, listening to stories read by more competent readers—that is, getting involved in all kinds of literate practices—children and adults are shown to build their relationships to literate society through complex interactional patterns that take place within meaningful social practices. The school setting is a privileged place for these meaningful practices to occur, and the relationship of schooling processes to literacy processes, explored by most of the authors, shows a very strong connection between these two realms of human activity, the complexity of which must be better understood.

## REFERENCES

Azenha, M. G. (1995). *Imagens e letras: Ferreiro e Luria, duas teorias psicognéticas [Images and letters: Ferreiro and Luria, two psychogenetic theories]*. São Paulo, Brazil: Ática.

Bottéro, J., Morrison, K., Vandermeersch, L., Lapacherie, J., Fraenkel, B., & Herrenschmidt, C. (1995). *Cultura, pensamento e escrita [Culture, thought and writing]*. São Paulo, Brazil: Ática.

Castorina, J. A. (1995). O debate Piaget-Vygotsky: A busca de um critério para sua avaliagão [The Piaget-Vygotsky debate: The search for a criterion for its evaluation]. In J. Castorina, E. Ferreiro, D. Lerner, & M. K. de Oliveira (Eds.), *Piaget-Vygotsky: Novas contribuicões para o debate* (pp. 7-50).

Cook-Gumperz, J. (1986). Literacy and schooling: An unchanging equation? In J. Cook-Gumperz (Ed.), *The social construction of literacy* (pp. 16-44). Cambridge: Cambridge University Press.

Ferreiro, E. (1994). Luria e o desenvolvimento da escrita na criança [Luria and the development of child's writing]. *Cadernos de Pesquisa*, *88*, 72–77.

Ferreiro, E. (1995). Sobre a necessária coordenação entre semelhanças e diferenças [About the necessary coordination between similarities and differences]. In J. Castorina, E. Ferreiro, D. Lerner, & M. K. de Oliveira (Eds.), *Piaget-Vygotsky: Novas contribuições para o debate*. São Paulo, Brazil: Ática.

Ferreiro, E., & Teberosky, A. (1982). *Literacy before schooling*. Exeter, NH: Heinemann.

Ginzburg, C. (1987). *O queijo e os vermes: O cotidiano e as idéias de um moleiro perseguido pela Inquisição [The cheese and the worms: Daily life and ideas of a mill worker persecuted by the Inquisition]*. São Paulo, Brazil: Companhia das Letras.

Goody, J. (Ed.). (1968). *Literacy in traditional societies*. Cambridge: Cambridge University Press.

Infante R. (1994). *Investigacion regional sobre analfabetismo funcional [Regional investigation about functional illiteracy]*. (mimeographic report). Santiago, Chile: UNESCO/OREALC.

Londono, L. O. (1991). *El analfabetismo funcional: Un nuevo punto de partida [Functional illiteracy: A new starting point]*. Lima, Peru: Tarea.

Oliveira, M. K. de. (1995). Pensar a educação: Contribuições de Vygotsky [Thinking about education: Vygotsky's contribution]. In J. Castorina, E. Ferreiro, D. Lerner, & M. K. de Oliveira (Eds), *Piaget-Vygotsky: Novas contribuições para o debate* (pp. 51-83). São Paulo, Brazil: Ática.

Rocco, M. T. F. (1990). Acesso ao mundo da escrita: os caminhos paralelos de Luria e Ferreiro [Access to the world of writing: The parallel roads of Luria and Ferreiro]. *Cadernos de Pesquisa, 75*, 25–33.

Saxe, G. (1991). *Culture and cognitive development: Studies in mathematical understanding*. New Jersey/London: Erlbaum.

Setúbal. M. A. (1993). A língua escrita numa perspectiva interacionista: embates e similaridades [Written language in an interactionist perspective: Confrontations and similarities]. *Idéias 20—Construtivismo em revista,* 95–104. São Paulo, Brazil: FDE.

Smolka, A. L. B., Fontana, R. A. C., & Laplane, A. L. F. (1994). The collective process of knowledge construction: Voices within voices. In A. Rosa & J. Valsiner (Eds.), *Explorations in sociocultural studies, Vol. 1: Historical and theoretical discourse* (pp. 109-119). Madrid, Spain: Fundación Infancia y Aprendizaje.

Sommerville, C. J. (1983). The distinction between indoctrination and education in England, 1549-1719. *Journal of the History of Ideas, 44*, 387–406.

Tulviste, P. (1991). *Cultural-historical development of verbal thinking: A psychological study.* Commack, NY: Nova Science Publishers.

Valsiner, J. (1996). Social utopias and knowledge construction in psychology. In V. A. Koltsova, Y. N. Oleinik, A. R. Gilgen, & C. K. Gilgen (Eds.), *Post-Soviet perspectives on Russian psychology* (pp. 70–84). Westport, CT: Greenwood Press.

Wertsch, J. (1991). *Voices of the mind*. Cambridge, MA: Harvard University Press.

part I

# Literacy Processes: Access to a Symbolic System

chapter 1

# The Development of Writing in the Child

Alexander Romanovich Luria

## I

The history of writing in the child begins long before a teacher first puts a pencil in the child's hand and shows him how to form letters.

The moment a child begins to write his first school exercises in his notebook is not actually the first stage in the development of writing. The origins of this process go far back into the pre-history of the development of the higher forms of a child's behavior; we can even say that when a child enters school, he has already acquired a wealth of skills and abilities that will enable him to learn to write within a relatively short time.

If we just stop to think about the surprising rapidity with which the child learns this extremely complex technique, which has thousands of years of culture behind it, it will be evident that this could come about only because during the first years of his development, before reaching school age, a child has already learned and assimilated a number of techniques leading up to writing that have already prepared him and made it immeasurably easier for him to grasp the concept and technique of writing. Moreover, we may reasonably assume that even before reaching school age, during this individual "prehistory," as it were, the child has already developed a number of primitive techniques of his own that are similar to what we call writing and perhaps even fulfill similar functions, but that are lost as soon as the school provides the child with the culturally elaborated, standard, and economical system of signs, but that these earlier techniques served as necessary stages along the way. The psychologist is faced with the following important and intriguing problem: to delve deeply into this early period of child development, to ferret out the pathways along which writing developed in its prehistory, to spell out the circumstances that made writing possible for the child and the factors that provided the motive forces of this development, and, finally, to describe the stages through which the development of the child's primitive writing techniques pass.

The developmental psychologist therefore concentrates his attention on the preschool period in the child's life. We begin where we think we shall find the beginnings of writing, and leave off where educational psychologists usually begin: the moment when the child begins to learn to write.

If we are able to unearth this "prehistory" of writing, we shall have acquired a valuable tool for teachers, namely, knowledge of what the child was able to do before entering school, knowledge on which they can draw in teaching their pupils to write.

## II

The best way to study this prehistory of writing and various tendencies and factors involved in it is to describe the stages we observe as a child develops his ability to write and the factors that enable him to pass from one stage to another, higher stage.

In contrast to a number of other psychological functions, writing may be described as a culturally mediated function. The first, most fundamental condition required for a child to be able to "write down" some notion, concept, or phrase is that some particular stimulus or cue, which in itself has nothing to do with this idea, concept, or phrase, is employed as an *auxiliary signs* whose perception causes the child to recall the idea, etc., to which it referred. Writing therefore presupposes the ability to use some cue (e.g., a line, a spot, a point) as a functional auxiliary sign with no sense or meaning in itself but only as an auxiliary operation. For a child to be able to write or note something, two conditions must be fulfilled. First, the child's relations with the things around him must be differentiated, so that everything he encounters will fall into two main groups: either things that represent some interest of the child's, things he would like to have, or with which he play; or instrumental objects, things that play only a utilitarian, or instrumental, role and have sense only as aids for acquiring some object or achieving some goal and therefore have only functional significance for him. Second, the child must be able to control his own behavior by means of these aids, in which case they already function as cues he himself invokes. Only when the child's relationships with the world around him have become differentiated in this way, when he has developed this functional relationship with things, can we say that the complex intellectual forms of human behavior have begun to develop.

The use of material tools, the rudiments of this complex, mediated adaptation to the external world, is observable in apes. In his classic experiments, Köhler (1921) demonstrated that under certain conditions things may acquire a functional significance for apes and begin to play an instrumental role. When an ape takes a long stick to get at a banana, it is quite obvious that the banana and the stick are psychologically of different orders for the animal: Whereas the banana is a goal, an object toward which the animal's behavior is directed, the stick has meaning only in relation to the banana, that is, throughout the entire operation it plays only a functional role. The animal begins to adapt to the given situation not directly, but with the aid of certain tools. The number of such instrumental objects is still few, and in the ape their complexity is minimal; but as behavior becomes more complex, this instrumental inventory also becomes richer and more complex, so that by the time we reach man, the number of such objects playing an auxiliary functional role in the life of a human being, who is a cultural animal, is enormous.

At a certain stage in evolution, external acts, handling objects of the external world, and internal acts as well, that is, the utilization of psychological functions in the strict sense, begin to take shape indirectly. A number of techniques for organizing internal psychological operations are developed to make their performance more efficient and productive. The direct, natural use of such techniques is replaced by a cultural mode, which relies on certain instrumental, auxiliary devices. Instead of trying to size up quantity visually, man learns to use an auxiliary system of counting; and instead of mechanically committing things to, and retaining them in, memory, he writes them down. In each case these acts presuppose that some object or device will be used as an aid in these behavioral processes, that is, that this object or device will play a functional auxiliary role. Such an auxiliary technique used for psychological purposes is writing, which is the functional use of lines, dots, and other signs to remember and transmit ideas and concepts. Samples of florid, embellished, pictographic writing show how varied the items enlisted as aids to retaining and transmitting ideas, concepts, and relations may be.

Experiments have shown that the development of such functional devices serving psychological ends takes place much later than the acquisition and use of external tools to perform external tasks. Köhler (1921) attempted to set up some special experiments with apes to determine whether an ape could use certain signs to express certain meanings, but was unable to find any such rudiments of "record keeping" in apes. He gave the animals paint, and they learned how to pain the walls, but they never once tried to use the lines they drew as signs to express something. These lines were a game for the animals; as objects they were ends, never means. Thus, devices of this sort develop at a much later stage of evolution.

In what follows we shall describe our efforts to trace the development of the first signs of the emergence of a functional relation to lines and scribbles in the child and his first use of such lines, etc., to express meanings; in doing so we shall hopefully be able to shed some light on the prehistory of human writing.

## III

The prehistory of writing can be studied in the child only experimentally, and to do this the skill must first be brought into being. The subject must be a child who has not yet learned to write; he must be put into a situation that will require him to use certain external manual operations similar to writing to depict or remember an object. In such a situation we should be able to determine whether he has acquired the ability to relate to some device that has been given to him as a sign or whether his relation to it still remains "absolute," that is, unmediated, in which case he will be unable to discover and use its functional, auxiliary aspect.

In the ideal case the psychologist might hope to force a child to "invent" signs by placing him in some difficult situation. If his efforts are more modest, he can give the child some task that is easier for the child to cope with and watch the successive stages the child goes through in assimilating the technique of writing.

In our preliminary experiments we followed this second course. Our method was actually very simple: We took a child who did not know how to write and gave him the task of remembering a certain number of sentences presented to him. Usually this number exceeded the child's mechanical capacity to remember. Once the child realized that he was unable to remember the number of words given him in the task, we gave him a sheet of paper and told him to jot down or "write" the words we presented. Of course, in most cases the child was bewildered by our suggestion. He would tell us that he did not know how to write, that he could not do it. We would point out to him that adults wrote things down when they had to remember something and then, exploiting the child's natural tendency toward purely external imitation, we suggested that he try to contrive something himself and write down what we would tell him. Our experiment usually began after this, and we would present the child with several (four or five) series of six or eight sentences that were quite simple, short, and unrelated to one another.

Thus, we ourselves gave the child a device whose intrinsic technique was unfamiliar to him and observed to what extent he was able to handle it and to what extent the piece of paper, the pencil, and the scribbles the child made on the paper ceased being simple objects that appealed to him, playthings, as it were, and became a tool, a means for achieving some end, which in this case was remembering a number of ideas presented to him. We think our approach here was correct and productive. Drawing on the child's penchant for imitation, we gave him a device to use that was familiar to him in its outward aspects but whose internal structure was unknown and strange. This allowed us to observe, in its purest form, how a child adapts spontaneously to some device, how he learns how it works and to use it to master a new goal.

We assumed that we would be able to observe all the stages in a child's relationship to this device, which was still alien to him, from the mechanical, purely external, imitative copying of an adult's hand movements in writing to the intelligent mastery of this technique.

By giving the child merely the external aspects of the technique to work with, we were able to observe a whole series of little *inventions* and discoveries he made, within the technique itself, that enabled him gradually to learn to use this new cultural tool.

It was our intention to provide a psychological analysis of the development of writing from its origins and, within a short period, to follow the child's transition from the primitive, external forms of behavior to complex, cultural forms. Let us now examine our results. We shall try to describe how children of different ages responded to this complex task and to trace the stages of development of writing in the child from its beginnings.

## IV

Not surprisingly, at the outset we encountered a problem that could have presented a considerable obstacle. It turned out that 4-5 year olds were totally unable to understand our instructions. On closer analysis, however, we found that this "negative" finding actually reflected a very essential and fundamental characteristic of this age group: 3-, 4-, and 5-year-old children (it was impossible to fix a definite dividing line: These

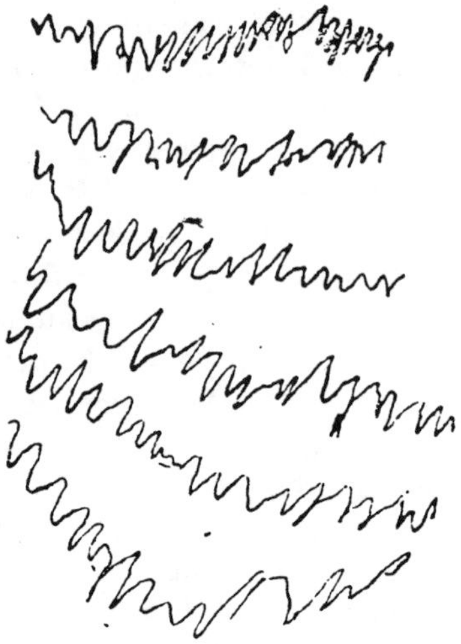

FIGURE 1.1

age demarcations depend on a multitude of dynamic conditions having to do with the child's level of cultural development, his environment, etc.) were still unable to relate to writing as a tool, or means. They grasped the outward form of writing and saw how adults accomplished it; they were even able to imitate adults; but they themselves were completely unable to learn the specific psychological attributes any act must have if it is to be used as a tool in the serve of some end.

If we asked such a child to note (or write) on paper the sentences presented to him, in many instances the child would not even refuse with any special insistence, simply referring to his inability to perform the task.

Little Vova N. (5 years old), for the first time in our laboratory, in response to the request to remember and write down the sentence "Mice have long tails," immediately took a pencil and "wrote" a number of scrawls on the paper (Figure 1.1). When the experimenter asked him what they were, he said, quite confidently, "That's how you write."

The act of writing is, in this case, only externally associated with the task of noting a specific word; it is purely imitative. The child is interested only in "writing like grownups;" for him the act of writing is not a means of remembering, or representing some meaning, but an act that is sufficient in its own right, an act of play. But such an act is by no means always seen as an aid to helping the child later remember the sentence. The connection between the child's scrawls and the idea it is meant to represent is purely external. This is especially evident in cases in which the "writing" is sharply and noticeably divorced from the sentence to be written and begins to play a completely independent and self-sufficient role.

We frequently observed one peculiar phenomenon in small children: A child whom we had asked to write down the sentences we gave him would not limit himself to ordinary "writing down," as in the case just described; he would sometimes invert the normal order of writing and begin to write without hearing out what we had to say.

In these cases the function of "writing" had become dissociated from the material to be written; understanding neither its meaning nor its mechanism, the child used writing in a purely external and imitative way, assimilating its outer form, but not employing it in the right way. Here is a graphic example from an experiment with Lena L., 4 years old. Lena was given some sentences and told to remember them, and to do this she had to "write them down." Lena listened to the first three sentences and after each began to write down her scribbles, which were the same in each case, that is, they were indistinguishable from one another. Before the fourth sentence I said to her: "Listen, this time write...." Lena, without waiting until I finished, began to write. The same thing happened before the fifth sentence.

The results are the undifferentiated scrawls in Figure 1.2, characteristic of this phase of development. There are two points that stand out especially clearly here: "Writing" is dissociated from its immediate objective, and lines are used in a purely external way; the child is unaware of their functional significance as auxiliary signs. That is why the act of writing can be so completely dissociated from the dictated sentence; not understanding the principle underlying writing, the child takes its external form and thinks he is quite able to write before he even knows what he must write. But a second point is also clear from this example: The child's scrawls bear no relationship to the meaningful sentence dictated to him. We have deliberately presented an example with quite explicit features that would be reflected in the mere outward form of writing if only the child understood the actual purpose and mechanism of writing things down, and its necessary connection with the meaning of what is to be written. Neither the number of items (five pencils, two tablets), the size factor (large table, small table), nor the shape of the object itself had any influence on the jottings; in each case there were the same zigzag lines. The "writing" had no connection with the idea evoked by the sentence to be written; it was not yet instrumental or functionally related to the content of what was to be written. Actually, this was not writing at all, but simple scribbling.

This self-contained nature of the scrawls is evident in a number of cases: We observed scribbling in children from 3 to 5 years old, and

**FIGURE 1.2. 1. There are five pencils on the table. 2. There are two plates. 3. There are many trees in the forest. 4. There is a column in the yard. 5. There is a large cupboard (written prematurely). 6. The little doll (written prematurely).**

sometimes even as old as 6 (although in these older children it was not as invariant, as we shall show further on). In most children in kindergarten, scribbling on paper is already an accustomed activity, although its functional, auxiliary significance has not yet been learned. Hence, in most children of this age, we observed a similar, undifferentiated scrawling, which had no functional significance and surprisingly easily became simple scribbling on paper merely for fun. We cannot refrain from the pleasure of relating a typical example of this total dissociation between writing and its primary purpose and its transformation into the mere fun of scribbling on paper.

Experiment 9/III, series III, Yura, age 6 (middle kindergarten group).

After Yura discovered in the first series that he was unable to remember by mechanical means all the sentences dictated to him, we suggested he note them down on paper; and in the second series we obtained results like those shown in Figure 1.2. Despite the undifferentiated nature of what he wrote down, Yura remembered more words in the second series than in the first, and was given a piece of candy as a reward. When we went on to the third series and again asked him to write down each word, he agreed, took the pencil, and began (without listening to the end of one sentence) to scribble. We did not stop him, and he continued to scribble until he had covered the whole page with scrawls that bore no relation to his initial purpose, which was to remember the sentences. These scrawls are shown in Figure 1.3. Everything on the right side (A) was done before the sentences were presented; not until later, after we stopped him, did he begin to "write down" the sentences shown on the left side (Nos. 1-7).

Complete lack of comprehension of the mechanism of writing, a purely external relation to it, and a rapid shift from "writing" to self-contained fun bearing no functional relation to writing are characteristic of the first stage in the prehistory of writing in the child. We can call this phase the prewriting phase or, more broadly, the pre-instrumental phase.

One question remains that has a direct bearing on this first phase in the development of writing and has to do with its formal aspects: Why did most of the children we studied choose to write zigzags in more or less straight lines?

There is considerable literature on the first forms of graphic activity in the child. The scrawling stage is explained in terms of physiological factors, the development of coordination, etc. Our approach to the phenomenon was more straightforward. The drawings that interested us were the scribbles. Hence, the most crucial factor here was unquestionably the one that brought these scribbles most closely, albeit only outwardly, to adult writing, namely, the factor of outward imitation.

Although the child at this stage does not yet grasp the sense and function of writing, he does know that adults write; and when given the task of writing down a sentence, he tries to reproduce, if only its outward form, adult writing, with which he is familiar. This is why our samples actually look like writing, arranged in lines, etc., and why Vova immediately said, "This is how you write."

We can persuade ourselves of the crucial role of pure, external imitation in the development of this process by a very simple experiment: If we reproduce the experiment in the presence of a child with another subject (a different one) who is asked to write signs, not words, we shall see how this immediately alters the way the child's "writing" looks.

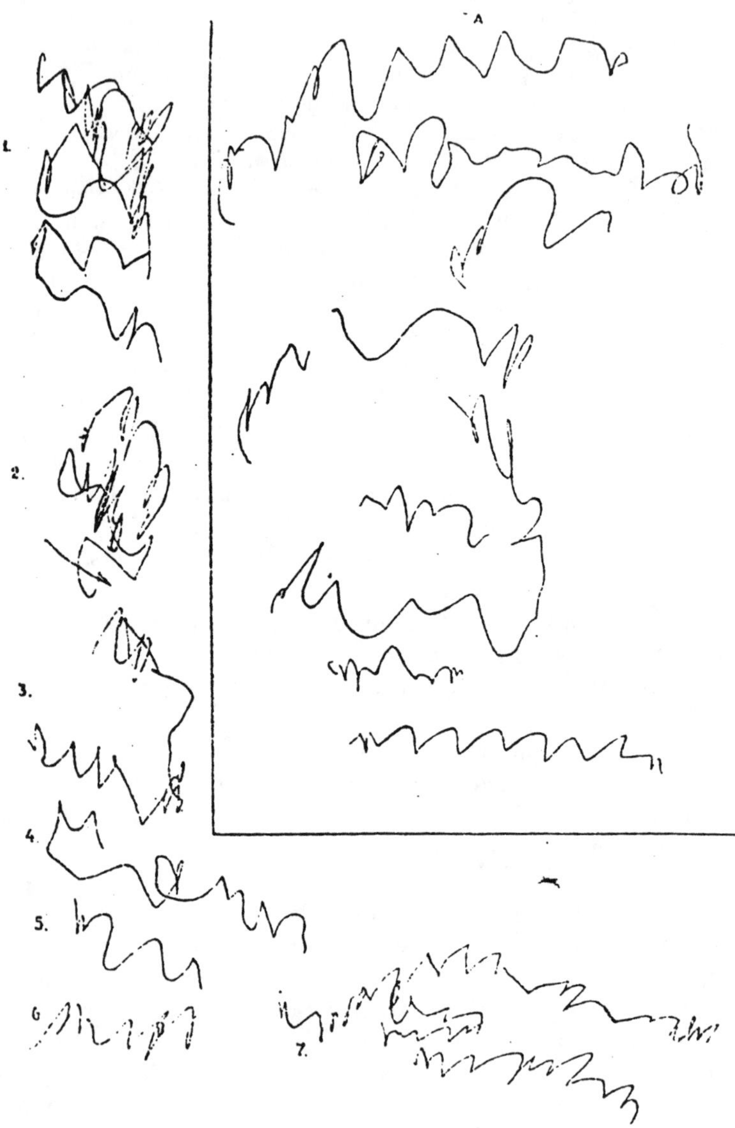


**FIGURE 1.3.** **1. There are many stars in the sky. 2. There is one moon. 3. I have thirty teeth. 4. Two hands and two legs. 5. A large tree. 6. The car runs.**

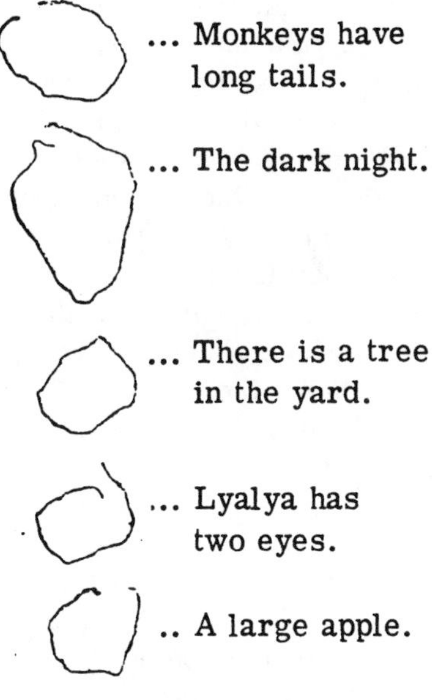
... Monkeys have
long tails.
... The dark night.
... There is a tree
in the yard.
... Lyalya has
two eyes.
.. A large apple.

**FIGURE 1.4**

Lena, 4 years old, who gave us the typical scribbles (see Figure 1.2), in the break after the session noticed that her friend Lina, age 7, "wrote down" the dictated sentences with a system of "marks" (one mark for each sentence). This was enough to induce her, in the next session, after the break, to produce scrawls that looked completely different. Adopting the manner of her friend, she stopped writing lines of scribbles and began to note each dictated sentence with a circle.

The result is shown in Figure 1.4. Despite its uniqueness of form, this specimen is not fundamentally different from those presented above. It, too, is undifferentiated, random, and purely externally associated with the task of writing; and it, too, is imitative. Just as in the previous examples, the child was unable to link the circles she drew with the ideas conveyed in the sentences and then to use this circle as a functional aid. This phase is the first phase of direct acts, the phase of pre-instrumental, precultural, primitive, imitative acts.

## V

Does "writing" help a child, at this stage, to remember the meaningful message of a dictated sentence? We can answer "no" in almost all cases, and that is the characteristic feature of this prewriting stage. The child's writing does not yet serve a mnemonic function, as will become obvious if we examine the "sentences" written by the child after dictation. In most cases the child remembered fewer sentences after "writing" them down in this way than he did without writing; so writing did not help, but actually hindered, memory. Indeed, the child made no effort to remember at all; for in relying on his "writing," he was quite convinced that it would do his remembering for him.[1]

Let us, however, take a case in which the child remembered several sentences even in a writing experiment. If we observe how these sentences were recalled, we shall see clearly that "writing" had nothing at all to do with this remembering, that it took place independently of the child's graphic efforts.

The first thing a psychologist studying memory notices is that a child mobilizes all the devices of direct mechanical memory, none of which are found in reading. The child fixes and recalls; he does not record and read: Some of his jottings are quite beside the point, and without effect. In our experiments we frequently observed that a child would repeat the sentence after writing it down, to nail it down, as it were; when we asked him to recall what he had written, he did not "read" his jottings from the beginning, but would go right to the last sentences, to catch them while they were fresh in his memory—a procedure very typical of the phenomenon of making a mental note.

Finally, the most instructive observation was how a child would behave in recalling. His behavior was that of someone remembering, not of someone reading. Most of the children we studied reproduced the sentences dictated to them (or rather, some of them) without looking at what they had written, with their gaze directed toward the ceiling questioningly; quite simply, the entire process of recall took place completely apart from the scribbles, which the child did not use at all. We recorded some cases of this sort on film; the child's total disregard of his writing and his purely direct form of remembering are clearly evident from his facial expressions recorded on film.

Thus, the way children in our experiments recalled the dictated sentences (if they did at all) clearly demonstrates that their graphic efforts at this stage of development are actually not yet writing, or even a graphic aid, but merely drawings on paper, quite independent of, and unrelated to, the task of remembering. The child does not yet relate to writing as a tool of memory at this stage of development. This is why in our experiments the children almost always cut a poor figure: Of a total of six to eight sentences, most of which they were able to remember by mechanical means, they could remember only two or three at most if asked to write them down, which indicates that if a child has to rely on writing without the ability to use it, the efficiency of memory is considerably reduced.

Nevertheless, our findings also include some cases that at first glance are rather surprising in that they are completely at variance with all we have just described. A child would produce the same undifferentiated nonsense writing as we have described, the same meaningless scribbles and lines, yet he would still be able to recall perfectly all the sentences he had written down. Moreover, as we observed him, we had the impression that he was actually making use of his writing. We checked this and indeed discovered that these scribblings actually were more than just simple scrawls, that they were in some sense real writing. The child would read a sentence, pointing to quite specific scrawls, and was able to show without error and many times in succession which scribble signified which of the dictated sentences. Writing was still undifferentiated in its outward appearance, but the child's relation to it had completely changed: From a self-contained motor activity, it had been transformed into a memory-helping sign. The child had begun to associate the dictated sentence with his undifferentiated scribble, which had begun to serve the auxiliary function of a sign. How did this come about?

In some sessions we noted that the children would arrange their scribblings in some pattern other than straight lines. For instance, they would put one scribble in one corner of the paper and another in another, and in so doing begin to associate the dictated sentences with their notations; this association was further reinforced by the pattern in which the notations were arranged, and the children would declare quite emphatically that the scribble in one corner meant "cow," or that another at the top of the paper meant "chimney sweeps are black." Thus, these children were in the process of creating a system of technical memory aids, similar to the writing of primitive peoples. In itself no scribble meant anything; but its position, situation, and relation to the other scribbles, that is, all these factors together, imparted to it its function as a technical memory aid. Here is an example:

> Brina, age 5 (first time in our laboratory), was asked to write down a number of sentences dictated to her. She quickly learned how to proceed and after each word (or sentence) had been dictated, she would make her scribble. The results are shown in Figure 1.5. One might think that our little subject had made these marks without any connection with the task of remembering the dictated sentences, just as most of the children discussed above. But to our surprise, she not only recalled all the dictated sentences (true, there were not many, only five) but also correctly located each sentence, pointing to a scribble and saying: "This is a cow" or "A cow has four legs and a tail," or "It rained yesterday evening," etc. In other words, she recalled the dictated sentences by "reading" them. It is clear that Brina

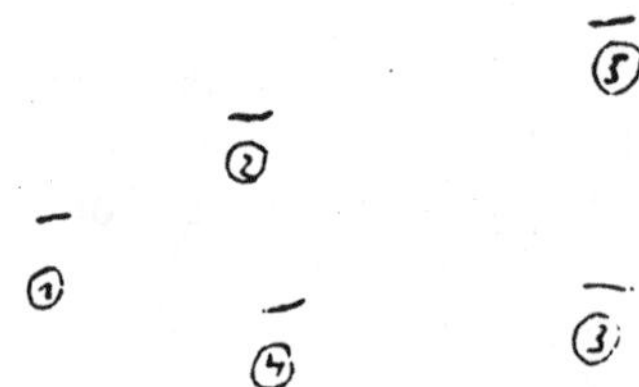

**FIGURE 1.5. 1. Cow. 2. A cow has legs and a tail. 3. Yesterday evening it rained. 4. Chimney sweeps are black. 5. Give me three candles.**

> understood the task and employed a primitive form of writing, writing by means of topographical markings. These markings were quite stable; when she was questioned directly, she did not mix them up, but rigorously distinguished one from the other, knowing exactly what each one meant.

This is the first form of "writing," in the proper sense. The actual inscriptions are still undifferentiated, but the functional relation to writing is unmistakable. Because the writing is undifferentiated, it is variable. After using it once, a child may a few days later have forgotten it, and revert back to mechanical scribbling unrelated to the task. But this is the first rudiment of what is later to become writing in the child; in it we see for the first time the psychological elements from which writing will take shape. The child now recalls the material by associating it with a specific mark rather than just mechanically, and this mark will remind him of the particular sentence and help him to recall it. All this and the presence of certain techniques of undifferentiated topographical writing in primitive peoples spurred our interest in this undifferentiated technical aid to memory, the precursor of real writing.

What role actually is played by the little mark the child makes on a piece of paper? We saw that it had two main features: It organized the child's behavior, but did not yet have a content of its own; it indicated the presence of some meaning, but did not yet tell us what this meaning was. We could say that this first sign plays the role of an ostensive sign or, in other words, the primary sign to "take note" (see Vygotsky, 1929). The mark jotted down by the child creates a certain set and serves as an additional cue that some sentences have been dictated, but provides no hints as to how to discover the content of those sentences.

An experiment demonstrated that this interpretation of a primary sign was unquestionably the right one. We can describe a number of cases to prove this. A child at this stage of development in his relationship to a sign tries to use the marks he has made to guide him in recalling. Frequently, these "sentences" have nothing in common with those dictated, but the child will formally fulfill his assignment and for each cue find the "matching word."

Here is an example of this relation of the child's to a primitive sign (we omit the actual drawing as it is very similar in structure to the preceding illustrations). We gave a child 4 years, 8 months old a series of words: "picture—book—girl—locomotive."

The child noted each of these words with a mark. When she had finished her writing, we asked her to read it. Pointing to each mark in succession, the girl "read": "girl—doll—bed—trunk."

We see that the words recalled by the child have nothing in common with the words given; only the number of words recalled was correct; their content was determined completely by the emotional sets and interests of the child (R. E. Levin's experiment).

This illustration enables us to get to the psychological structure of such a primary graphic sign. It is clear that a primary, undifferentiated, graphic sign is not a symbolic sign, which discloses the meaning of what has been written down; nor can it yet be called an instrumental sign in the full sense of the word, as it does not lead the child back to the content of what was written down. We should rather say that it is only a simple *cue* (although one artificially created by the child) that conditionally evokes certain speech impulses. These impulses, however, do not necessarily direct the child back to the situation he has "recorded;" they can only trigger certain processes of association whose content, as we have seen, may be determined by completely different conditions having nothing at all to do with the given cue.

We might best describe the functional role of such a cue as follows:

Let us imagine the process of writing (alphabetic, pictographic, or conventionally agreed on) in an adult. A certain content A is written with the symbol X. When a reader looks at this symbol, he immediately thinks of the content A. The symbol X is an instrumental device to direct the reader's attention to the initial written content. The formula:

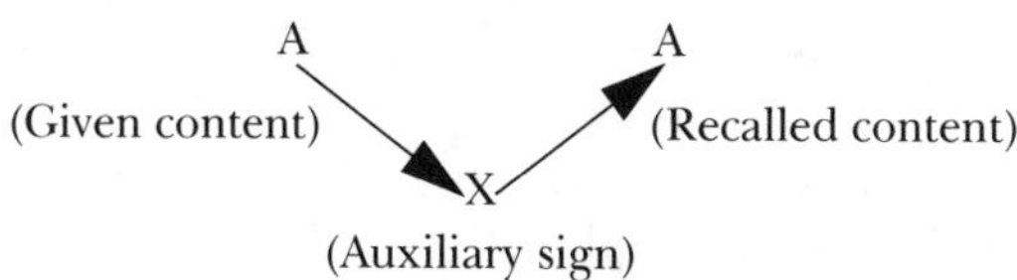


is the best expression of the structure of such a process.

The situation with respect to a primitive mark such as we have just been discussing is completely different. It only signals that *some* content written down by means of it exists, but does not lead us to it; it is only a cue evoking some (associative) reaction in the subject. We actually do not have in it the complex instrumental structure of an act, and it may be described by the following formula:

(Given content) A ——▶ X
X ——▶ N (Recalled association)
(Primitive mark)

where N may not have any relation to the given content A, or, of course, to the mark X.

Instead of an instrumental act, which uses X to revert attention back to A, we have here two direct acts: (1) the mark on the paper, and (2) the response to the mark as a cue. Of course, in psychological terms this is not yet writing, but only the forerunner of it, in which the most rudimentary and necessary conditions for its development are forged.[2]

## VI

We have already discussed the insufficient stability of this phase of undifferentiated, memory-helping writing. Having taken the first step along the path of culture with it, and having linked, for the first time, the recalled object with some sign, the child must now go on to the second step: He must differentiate this sign and make it really express a specific content; he must create the rudiments of literacy, in the truest sense of the word. Only then will the child's writing become stable and independent of the number of elements written down; and memory will have gained a powerful tool, capable of broadening its scope enormously. Finally, only under these conditions will any steps forward be taken along the way toward objectivization of writing, that is, toward transforming it from subjectively coordinated markings into signs having an objective significance that is the same for everyone.

Our experiments warrant the assertion that the development of writing in the child proceeds along a path we can describe as the transformation of an undifferentiated scrawl into a differentiated sign. Lines and scribbles are replaced by figures and pictures, and these give way to signs. In this sequence of events lies the entire path of development of writing in both the history of nations and the development of the child.

We are psychologists, however, and our task is not confined to simple observation and confirmation of the sequence of individual phases: We should like also to describe the conditions that produce this sequence of events and to determine empirically the factors that facilitate for the child the transition from a stage of undifferentiated writing to the level of meaningful signs expressing a content.

Actually, one can say there are two pathways by which differentiation of the primary sign may take place in a child. On the one hand, the child may try to depict the content given him without going beyond the limits of arbitrary, imitative scrawling; on the other hand, he may make the transition to a form of writing that depicts content, to the recording of an idea, that is, to pictograms. Both paths presuppose some jump that must be made by the child as he replaces the primary, undifferentiated sign with another, differentiated one. This jump presupposes a little invention, whose psychological significance is interesting in that it alters the very psychological function of the sign by transforming the primary sign, which merely establishes ostensively the existence of a thin, into another kind of a sign that reveals a particular content. If this differentiation is accomplished successfully, it transforms a sign-stimulus into a sign-symbol, and a qualitative leap is thereby effected in the development of complex forms of cultural behavior.

We were able to follow the elementary inventions of a child along both these paths. Let us examine each of them separately.

The first signs of differentiation we were able to observe in the small child occurred after several repetitions of our experiment. By the third or fourth session, a child of 4 or 5 years would begin to link the word (or phrase) given him and the nature of the mark with which he distinguished the word. This meant that he did not mark all the words in the same way: The first differentiation, as far as we could judge, involved reflection of the rhythm of the phrase uttered in the rhythm of the graphic sign.

The child quite early begins to show a tendency to write down short words or phrases with short lines and long words or phrases with a large number of scribbles. It is difficult to say whether this is a conscious act, the child's own invention, as it were. We are inclined to see other, more primitive mechanisms at work in this. Indeed, this rhythmic differentiation is by no means always stable. A child who has written a series of sentences given him in a "differentiated" manner in the next session (or for that matter even in the same session) will revert to primitive, undifferentiated writing. This suggests that in this rhythmically reproductive writing some more primitive mechanisms, not an organized and conscious device, are at work.

But what are these mechanisms? Are we not dealing here with simple coincidence, which leads us to see a pattern where there is only the play of chance?

An example drawn from one of our experiments may serve as material for a concrete analysis of this problem.

> Lyuse N., age 4 years, 8 months. We gave her a number of words: mama, cat, dog, doll. She wrote them all down with the same scrawls, which in no way differed from one another. The situation changed considerably, however, when we also gave her long sentences along with individual words:

> (1) girl; (2) cat; (3) Zhorzhik is skating; (4) Two dogs are chasing the cat; (5) There are many books in the room, and the lamp is burning; (6) bottle; (7) ball; (8) The cat is sleeping; (9) We play all day, then we eat dinner, and then we go out to play again.
>
> In the writing the child now produced, the individual words were represented by little lines, but the long sentences were written as complicated squiggles; and the longer the sentence, the longer was the squiggle written to express it.

Thus, the process of writing, which began with an undifferentiated, purely imitative, graphic accompaniment to the presented words, after a period of time was transformed into a process that on the surface indicated that a connection had been made between the graphic production and the cue presented. The child's graphic production ceased being a simple accompaniment to a cue and become its reflection—albeit in very primitive form. It began to reflect merely the rhythm of the presented phrase: Single words began to be written as single lines, and sentences as long, complicated scribbles, sometimes reflecting the rhythm of the presented sentence.

The variable nature of this writing suggests, however, that perhaps this is no more than a simple *rhythmic* reflection of the cue presented to the subject. Psychologically, it is quite comprehensible that every stimulus perceived by a subject has its own rhythm and through it exerts a certain effect on the activity of the subject, especially if the aim of that activity is linked to the presented stimulus and must reflect and record it. The primary effect of this rhythm also produces that first rhythmic differentiation in the child's writing that we were able to note in our experiments.

Below we shall discuss the very intimate relationship that we believe exists between graphic production and mimicry. Functionally, graphic activity is a rather complex system of cultural behavior, and in terms of its genesis may be regarded as expressiveness materialized in fixed form. It is just this sort of reflection of mimicry we see in the example given above. The rhythm of a sentence is reflected in the child's graphic activity, and we quite frequently encounter further rudiments of such rhythmically depictive writing of complex speech clusters. It was not invention, but the primary effect of the rhythm of the cue or stimulus that was at the source of the first meaningful use of a graphic sign.

## VII

This first step along the way of differentiation of primitive, imitative, graphic activity is still very weak and impoverished, however. Although a child may be able to reflect the rhythm of a sentence, he is still unable to mark the content of a term presented to him graphically. We must await the next step, when his graphic activity begins to reflect not only the external rhythm of the words presented to him but also their content; we await the moment when a sign acquires meanings. It is then that we shall doubtless be dealing with inventiveness.

Actually when undifferentiated, imitative, graphic activity first acquires expressive content, is this not a tremendous step forward in the child's cultural behavior? But even here, again, it is not enough merely to show invention. Our task must be to ascertain what factors are responsible for the shift to a meaningful, depictive sign; and to show what they are means to discover the internal factors determining the process of invention of expressive signs in the child.

The task of the experimenter in this case is consequently to test certain inputs into an experiment and determine which of them produces the primary transition from the diffuse phase to the meaningful use of signs.

In our experiments there was one serious factor that could influence the development of writing in the child: This was the content of what was presented to him; and in varying this, we might ask, what changes in the content we presented were conditions for inducing a primary transition to differentiated, depictive writing?

Two primary factors can take the child from an undifferentiated phase of graphic activity to a stage of differentiated graphic activity. These factors are number and form.

We observed that number, or quantity, was perhaps the first factor to break up that purely imitative, unexpressive character of graphic activity in which different ideas and notions were expressed by exactly the same sort of lines and scribbles. By introducing the factor of number into the material, we could readily produce differentiated graphic activity in 4-5-year-old children by causing them to use signs to reflect this number. It is possible that the actual origins of writing are to be found in the need to record number, or quantity.

Perhaps the best thing to do is to reproduce a protocol showing the process of differentiation of writing as it took place under the influence of the factor of quantity.

> Lena L., 4 years old, in her first attempt to write sentences produced an undifferentiated scrawl for each sentence, with completely identical scribbles (see Figure 1.2). Of course, since these scribbles were totally unrelated to the ideas, they did not even give the effect of writing, and we concluded that this kind of mechanical graphic production hindered rather than helped memory.

We then introduced the factor of quantity into a number of experiments to determine how the altered conditions would affect the development of graphic activity. We were immediately able to note the beginnings of differentiation.

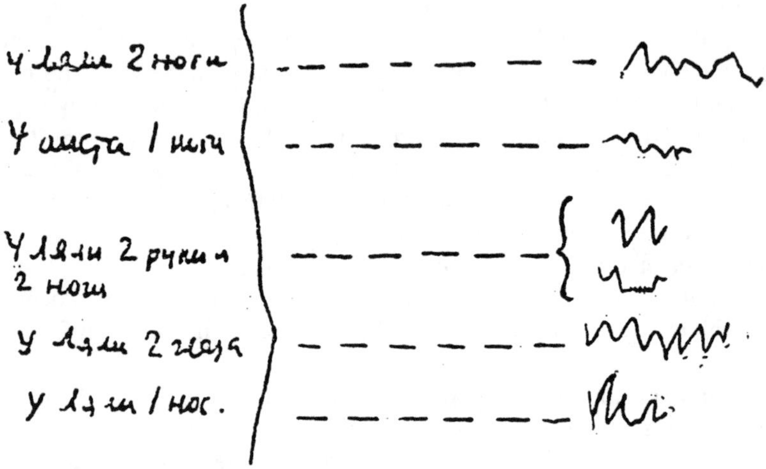

Indeed, graphic production changed sharply under the influence of this factor (especially if one compares it with the sample in Figure 1.2). We now see a clear differentiation, linked to the particular task. For the first time each scrawl reflects a particular content. Of course, the differentiation is still primitive: What differentiates "one nose" from "two eyes" is that the scribbles representing the former are much smaller. Quantity is still not clearly expressed, but relations are. The sentence "Lilya has two hands and two legs" was perceived and recorded in a differentiated fashion: "Two hands" and "two legs" each had their own scribble. But most important, this differentiation appeared in a child who had just produced some totally undifferentiated scribblings, not betraying even the least indication that they might have anything at all to do with the sentences dictated.

This example brings us to the following observation: Quantity was the factor that broke up the elementary, mechanical, undifferentiated, graphic production and for the first time opened the way toward its use as an auxiliary device, hence raising it from the level of merely mechanical imitation to the status of a functionally employed tool.

Of course, the graphic production itself is still muddled; and the technique has not yet assumed precise, constant contours: If we again dictated material having no reference to quantity, we would again obtain an undifferentiated scribbling by the same child, with no attempt on her part to represent a particular content with a particular mark. But now that the first step had been taken, the child was, for the first time, able really to "write" and, what is most important, to "read" what she had written. With the transition to this primitive but differentiated graphic activity, her entire behavior changed: The same child who had been unable to recall two or three sentences was now able to recall all of them confidently and, what is more, for the first time was able to read her own writing.

Thanks to the quantity factor, this differentiation was achieved in children 4-5 years old. The influence of the factor of quantity was especially strong in cases in which the factor of contrast was added—when, for example, the sentence "There are two trees in the yard" was followed by the sentence "There are many trees in the forest," the child tried to reproduce the same contrast, and hence could not write both sentences with the same markings and instead was forced to produce differentiated writing.

Having noted this, let us go on immediately to the second factor defining and accelerating the transition from undifferentiated play writing to real, differentiated, expressive, graphic activity.

In our experiments we observed that differentiation of writing could be considerably accelerated if one of the sentences dictated concerned an object that was quite conspicuous because of its color, clear-cut shape, or size. We combined these three factors into a second group of conditions that would promote the child's learning to put a specific content into his writing and make it expressive and differentiated. In such cases we saw how graphic production suddenly began to acquire definite contours as the child attempted to express color, shape, and size; indeed, it began to have a rough resemblance to primitive pictography. Quantity and conspicuous shape lead the child to pictography. Through these factors the child initially gets the idea of using drawing (which he is already quite good at in play) as a means of remembering, and for the first time drawing begins to converge with a complex intellectual activity. Drawing changes from simple representation to a means, and the intellect acquires a new and powerful tool in the form of the first differentiated writing.

Here is a protocol illustrating the guiding role played by the factor of form in the child's discovery of the mechanism of writing; this protocol also shows clearly the process of differentiation as it progresses.

> Vova N., 5 years old, first time in our laboratory. The subject was asked to write sentences dictated to him in order to remember them. He began immediately to produce scribbles, saying, "This is how you write" (see Figure 1.1). Obviously, for him the act of writing was purely an external limi-

tation of the writing of an adult without any connection with the content of the particular idea, since the scribbles differed from one another in no essential way. Here is the record:

| | |
|---|---|
| 1. The mouse with a long tail. | Subject (writes): This is how you write. |
| 2. There is a high column. | Subject (writes): Column...This is how you write. |
| 3. There are chimneys on the roof. | Subject (writes): Chimneys on the roof...This is how you write.... |

Now we give the subject a picture in bright colors, and the reaction immediately changes.

| | |
|---|---|
| 4. Very black smoke is coming out of the chimney. | Subject: Black. Like this! (Points to the pencil and then begins to draw very black scribbles, pressing hard.) |
| 5. In the winter there is white snow. | Subject: (Makes his usual scribbles, but separates them into two parts, apparently unrelated to the idea of "white snow.") |
| 6. Very black coal— | Subject: (Again draws heavy lines.) |

Both the protocol and the writing itself in Figure 1.6 show that the generally undifferentiated writing acquires an expressive character in only two cases (4 and 6), in which "black smoke" and "black coal" are depicted with heavy black lines. For the first time the scrawls on paper assume some of the features of true writing.

The effect becomes clear when we see how the subject recalls what he has written. When asked to recall what he has written, he refuses to recall anything at all. It seems that he has forgotten everything, and his scribblings tell him nothing. But after examining the scrawls, he suddenly stops at one of them and says, spontaneously: "This is coal." This is the first time such spontaneous reading occurs in this child, and the fact that he had not only produced something differentiated in his graphic activity but also was able to recall what it represented fully confirms that he had taken the first step toward using writing as a means of remembering.

This sort of differentiation was achieved in 4 and 5 year olds, and it is quite possible that in some cases it can occur even much earlier. The most important thing about all this is that the emergence of the conditions necessary for writing, the discovery of pictographic writing, the first use of writing as a means of expression, occurred before our eyes. We can say with assurance that after observing with our own eyes, in our laboratory, how a child gropingly repeated the first primitive steps of culture, many elements and factors in the emergence of writing became incompa-

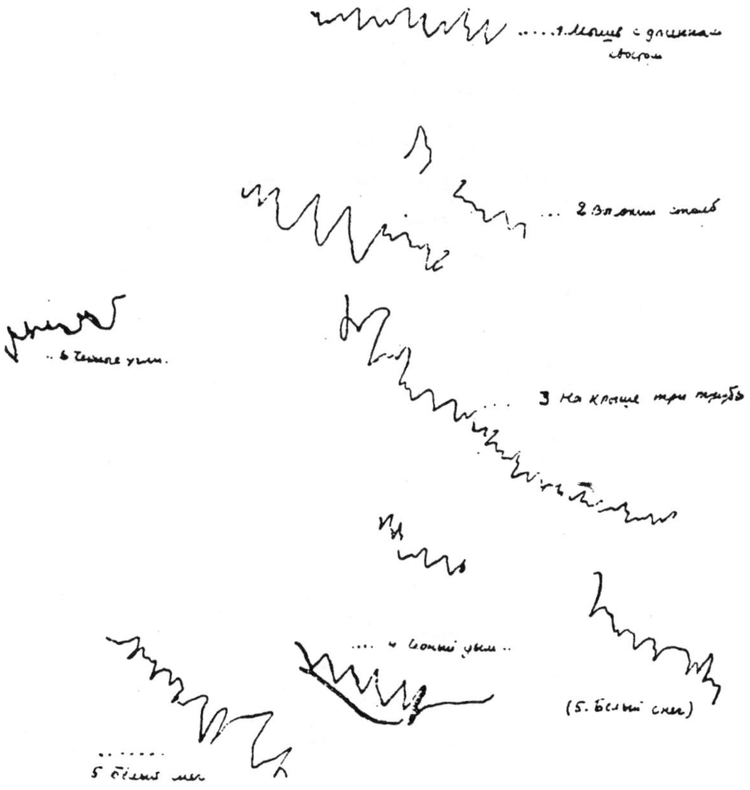

**FIGURE 1.6**

rably clearer for us. Sometimes, in the same experiment, we were able to observe the sequence of a whole series of inventions carrying the child forward to one new stage after another in the cultural use of signs.

The best thing to do, perhaps, is to present a protocol from one of our experiments in its entirety. We have therefore selected a record for a 5-year-old girl in which we may follow step by step her discovery of cultural signs. We have purposely chosen a subject whose undifferentiated, mnemotechnical writing we have presented earlier (Figure 1.5).

> Brina Z., age 5. The experiment was done in a number of consecutive sessions, in each of which five or six sentences were dictated with the instruction to write them down in order to remember them.
>
> 1st session. The experimenter dictated five sentences: (1) The bird is flying. (2) The elephant has a long trunk. (3) An automobile goes fast. (4) There are high waves on the sea. (5) The dog barks.

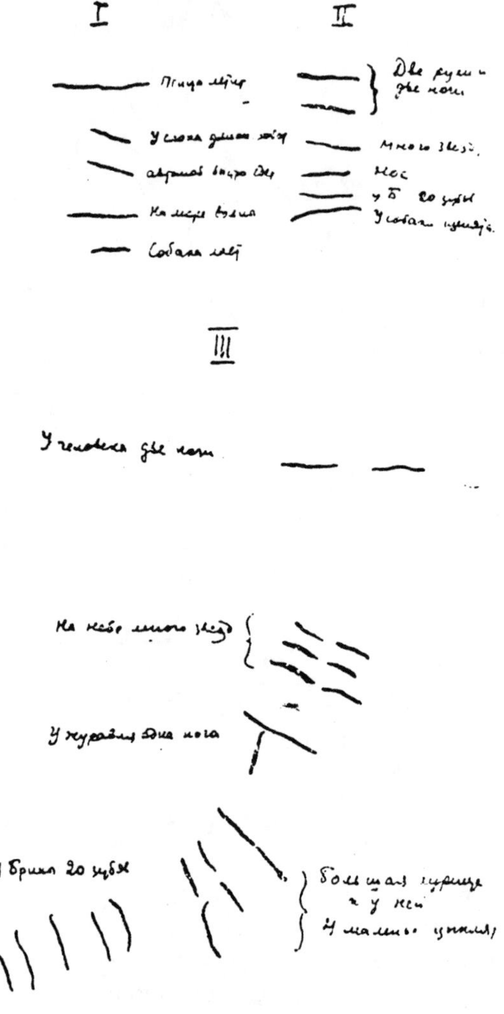


**FIGURE 1.7A**

The subject made a line for each sentence and arranged the lines in columns (see Figure 1.7A, I). The lines were identical. In the recall test, she remembered only three sentences, that is, the same number she remembered without writing anything down. She recalled spontaneously, that is, without looking at her scribblings.

2nd session. The experimenter dictated five sentences, which included quantitative elements: (1) A man has two arms and two legs. (2) There are many stars in the sky. (3) Nose. (4) Brina has 20 teeth. (5) The big dog has four little pups.

The subject drew lines arranged in a column. Two arms and two legs were represented by two discrete lines; the other sentences were represented by one line each (Figure 1.7A, II). In the recall test the subject declared that she had forgotten everything and refused to try to remember.

3rd session. The experimenter repeated the second series "to help her write down and remember what was dictated a little better." He then dictated the second series again with a few changes: (the subject's scribblings are given in Figure 1.7A, III):

| | |
|---|---|
| 1. Here is a man, and he has two legs. | Subject: Then I'll draw two lines. |
| 2. In the sky there are many stars. | Subject: Then I'll draw many lines. |
| 3. The crane has one leg. | (Makes a mark)...The crane is on one leg...There you are...(Points) The crane is on one leg. |
| 4. Brina has 20 teeth. | (Draws several lines.) |
| 5. The big hen and four little chicks. | (Makes one big line and two small ones; thinks a little, and adds another two.) |

In the recall test, she remembered everything correctly except for sentence number 2. When the experimenter dictated this sentence to her and asked, "How can you write this so as to remember it?" she answered, "Best with circles."

4th session. The experimenter again dictates sentences and the subject writes them down.

| | |
|---|---|
| 1. The monkey has a long tail. | Subject: The monkey (draws a line) has a long (draws another line) tail (yet another line). |
| 2. The column is high. | Okay, so I'll draw a line. The column came broken. |
| 3. The bottle is on the table. | Now I can draw the table and then the bottle. But I can't do it right. |
| 4. There are two trees. | (Draws two lines.) Now I'll draw the branches. |
| 5. It's cold in winter. | Okay. In the winter (draws line) it's cold (draws line). |
| 6. The little girl wants to eat. | (Draws a mark.) [Experimenter]: Why did you draw it like that? [Subject]: Because I wanted to. |

In the recall test she remembered correctly numbers 2, 3, 5, and 6 (see Figure 1.7B). About number 4 she said: "This is the monkey and the long tail." When the experimenter pointed out that this sentence was number 1, she objected: "No, these two long lines are the monkey with the long tail. If I hadn't drawn the long lines, I wouldn't have known."

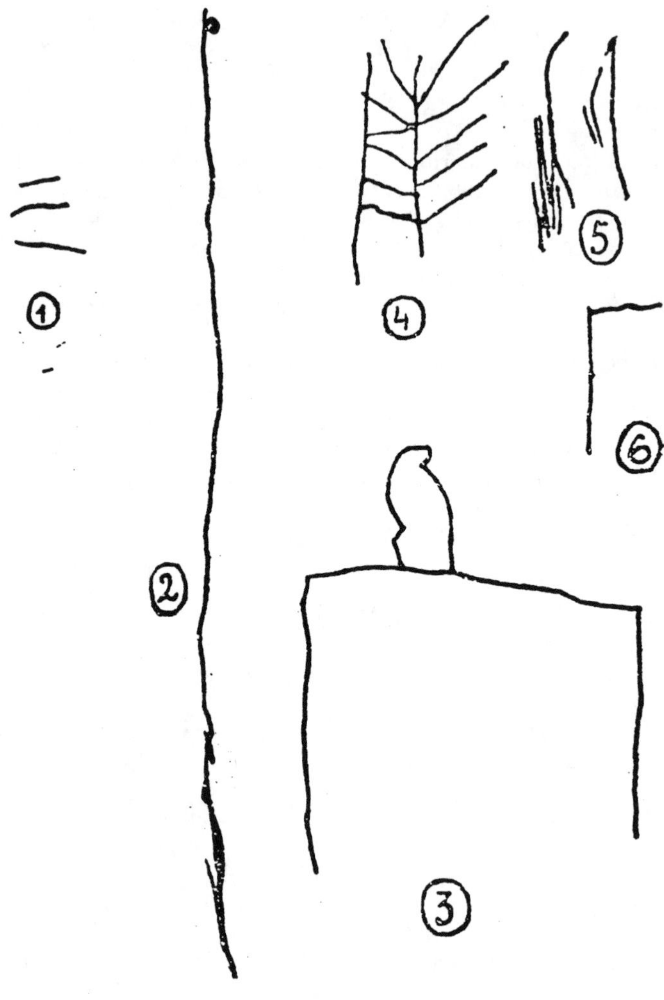


**FIGURE 1.7B**

This experiment began with completely undifferentiated writing. The subject would jot down lines without relating to them in any way as differentiated signs referring to something. In the recall test she did not use these lines and recalled directly, as it were. It is understandable that the failure in the first two experiments depressed her somewhat, and she tried to refuse to go on, declaring that she couldn't remember anything and that she didn't "want to play anymore." At this point, however, a sudden change occurred, and she began to behave completely differently. She had discovered the instrumental use of writing; she had invented the sign. The lines she had drawn mechanically became a differentiated, expressive tool, and the entire process of recall for the first time began to be mediated. This invention was the result of a confluence of two factors: the interjection of the factor of quantity into the task, and the experimenter's insistent requirement that she "write so that it would be understood." Perhaps even without this last condition the subject would have discovered the sign, maybe a little later; but we wanted to accelerate the process and restore her interest. This we were able to do; and the subject, after switching to a new technique and finding it successful, continued to cooperate for another hour and a half.

In the third session, which we shall now discuss, she discovered for the first time that a sign, by means of numerical differentiation, had an expressive function: When asked to write "The man has two legs" Brina immediately declared, "Then I'll draw two lines;" and once having discovered this technique, she continued to use it. She then combined this device with a rough schematic representation of the object: The crane with one leg she depicted with a line with another meeting it at right angles; the large dog with four pups became a large line with four smaller ones. Thus, in the recall test she no longer proceeded completely from memory, but read what she had written, each time pointing to her drawing. The only case of failure was "There are many stars in the sky." In the test session this was replaced with a new drawing in which the stars were represented by circles, not lines.

Differentiation continued in the fourth session, in which the length of the column was represented by a long line and the tree and bottle were drawn directly. Of particular interest is her attempt to differentiate her writing in another direction, mentioned above: When Brina had difficulty expressing a complex formulation, she wrote down the dictated sentence semimechanically, rhythmically breaking it down into words, each of which was represented by a line (monkey—long—tail, winter—cold). She continued to use this technique for some time; we have observed the same technique in 7–8-year-old children. This technique was less successful than the technique of real, differentiated writing, however, and hence is a special case. After writing "It is cold in winter" with two long lines, the subject began to recall them as the "monkey with the long tail," declaring that she had purposely drawn the long line and that without it she would have been unable to remember the monkey's long tail. We see here how a technique that has been used ineffectively is reworked and acquires an attribute corresponding to one of the ideas; the line is then interpreted differently and is transformed into a sign.

After having started with undifferentiated play writing, before our very eyes the subject discovered the instrumental nature of such writing and worked out her own system of expressive marks, by means of which she was able to transform the entire remembering process. Play was transformed into elementary writing, and writing was now able to assimilate the child's representational experience. We have reached the threshold of pictographic writing.

## VIII

The period of picture writing is fully developed by the time a child reaches the age of 5 or 6 years; if it is not fully and clearly developed by that time, it is only because it already begins to give way to symbolic alphabetic writing, which the child learns in school—and sometimes long before.

If it were not for this factor, we should have every reason to expect that pictography would achieve a flourishing development; and this is what we actually see everywhere that symbolic writing is not developed or does not exist: Pictography flourishes among primitive peoples (there have been many interesting studies of pictography). The richest development of pictography is found in retarded children, who are still preliterate; and we should, without reserve, recognize that their fine and colorful pictographic writing is one of the positive accomplishments of retarded children. (In Figure 1.8 we show some drawings by a retarded child that are quite impressive in their vividness and grace.)

The pictographic phase in the development of writing is based on the rich experience of the child's drawings, which need not in themselves serve the function of mediating signs in any intellectual process. Initially drawing is play, a self-contained process of representation; then the perfected act can be used as a device, a means, for recording. But because the direct experience of drawing is so rich, we often do not obtain the pictographic phase of writing in its pure form in the child. Drawing as a means is very frequently blended with drawing as a self-contained, unmediated process. Nowhere in such material can one discern any sign of the difficulties the child experiences in going through the differentiation of all these processes into means and ends, objects and functionally related techniques, which, as we saw above, are the necessary conditions for the emergence of writing.

Wed shall not dwell in detail on all the characteristic features of this pictographic phase in the development of writing in the child, since this phase has been studied much more than all the others. We shall merely underscore the distinction between pictographic writing and drawing, and once again draw on an actual experimental record to illustrate our point.

**FIGURE 1.8**

Marusya G., 8 years old, is a mentally retarded child. She cannot write, and has poor command of speech. Her Binet-Bert IQ is 60. Despite this handicap, however, she has remarkable representational gifts. Her drawings are an excellent example of how drawing may not be an indicator of intellectual aptitude, but may in compensation develop in people whose intellectual (especially verbal) aptitudes are impaired.

We performed our usual experiment with Marusya. In the first natural series, she remembered only one of the six words. After nothing this, we went directly on to the writing experiment. Here is the record:

Experimenter: Now I shall tell you a number of things, and you should write them down on the paper so you can remember them better. Here is a pencil.

Subject: How should I write it? House and girl, right? (Begins to write "girl"; see Figure 1.8, 1.)

| | |
|---|---|
| Experimenter: (1) Listen. Write that a cow has four legs and a tail. | Subject: A little cow, a real little cow. I think I'd better draw the girl instead. |
| (Experimenter repeats the instructions.) | I don't know how (draws the girl). |
| (2) Chimney sweeps are black. | Black. A little box. I don't know how to draw a chimney (draws a box, then begins to draw a flower). (Figure 1.8, 2 and 2a ["This is a flower."]) |
| (3) Yesterday evening it rained. | It was wet. I put on my galoshes. There was a little drizzle. Here it is (makes a few light lines on the paper [Figure 1.8, 3]). I can draw snow, too. Here it is (draws a star, Figure 1.8, 3a). |
| (4) We had a tasty soup for lunch. | Soup, tasty (Figure 1.8, 4); they go together. |
| (5) The dog is running about the yard. | Dog, little (draws a dog). |
| (6) The boat is sailing the sea. | Here's the boat (draws). |

At this point a bright light was turned on so that we could film the process, and the experimenter called the subject's attention to it: "Look at our little sun." The subject then proceeded to draw a circle and declared: "Here is the sun" (Figure 1.8, 2a).

In the recall test, the subject named all the figures she had drawn, regardless of whether they depicted what had been dictated or were spontaneous drawings: (1) Girl, (2) Soup, (3) The boat is sailing, (4) The black box, (5) Here is a flower, (6) The dog.... She then took the pencil and drew a road and said, "Here is a road" (Figure 1.8, 7).

Our record gives a good, detailed description of the development of pictographic writing in the child. What is especially noteworthy is the extraordinary ease with which the child took up this kind of writing yet dissociated the depicted figures from the writing task and turned it into spontaneous, self-contained drawing. It was with this tendency to draw pictures, not to write with the aid of pictures, that our experiment began, when Marusya at our request to pay attention to everything said to her immediately answered: "How should I write it? House and girl, right?" The process of the functional use of writing was incomprehensible to her; and if she learned it later, it would remain a shaky acquisition. Several times during the course of the experiment, Marusya reverted to spontaneous drawing, with no function related to remembering the dictated material.

This dual relationship to drawing remained with our subject throughout all the following experiments, and the agility with which she would switch from pictographic writing back to spontaneous drawing was something observed in many preschools and, especially, in older retarded children. The more outstanding the pictography, the easier it was for these two principles of picture writing to be mixed.

A child may draw well but not relate to his drawing as an auxiliary device. This distinguishes writing from drawing and sets a limit to the full development of pictographic literacy in the narrow meaning of the term. The more retarded the child, the more marked is his inability to relate to drawing other than as a kind of play and to develop and understand the instrumental use of a picture as a device or symbol, though his drawing skills may be well developed.

But now we have come to the problem of the development of the symbolic phase of writing; and in order not to lose the connection with what has been said, we should pause for a moment on a very important factor at the borderline between pictography and symbolic writing in the child.

## IX

Let us imagine a case in which a child who can write pictographically must put down something that is difficult (or even impossible) to express in a picture. What does the child then do?

This situation, of course, forces the child to find ways around the problem, if he does not simply refuse to perform the task. Two such detours, very similar to each other, are possible. On the one hand, the child instructed to record something difficult to depict may instead of object A put down object B, which is related in some way to A. Or, he may simply put down some arbitrary mark instead of the object he finds difficult to depict.

Either way leads from pictographic writing to symbolic writing, except that the first still operates with the same means of pictographic representation whereas the second makes use of other qualitatively new devices.

In experiments with mentally retarded children we often observe the development of indirect means of the first type; school and school instruction provide ample opportunities for the second type.

Let us imagine that a small child or a retarded child is able to draw well, and we suggest to him some picture that, for some reason, he finds difficult to draw. How does he proceed in this case?

**FIGURE 1.9**

We can analyze the indirect means a child devises in such a case in their purest form on the basis of one of our experiments. Let us first take a subject whom we have already discussed earlier—Marusya G.

In a fourth session we again gave her a series of sentences that were not all equally easy to write down. Here is an extract from the record (see Figure 1.9).

| | |
|---|---|
| 1. Two dogs on the street. | Subject: Two dogs (draws)...and a cat (draws a cat). Two big dogs. |
| 2. There are many stars in the sky. | What stars...here is the sky (draws a line). Here is some grass below (draws)...I see them from the window (draws a window). |

What does the extract tell us? The subject has difficulty in representing pictographically the sentence "There are many stars in the sky," and she creates her own unique way to get around the problem: She does not draw the image given her, but instead portrays an entire situation in which she saw the stars, and so on. Instead of the part, she reproduces the entire situation, and in this way solves the problem.

A similar situation was encountered with another subject, Petya U., 6½ years old. Here is an extract from the record.

| | |
|---|---|
| Session III, (2) There are 1,000 stars in the sky. | Subject: I can't draw 1,000 stars. If you want, I'll draw an airplane. This is the sky (draws a horizontal line)...Oh, I can't.... |

We see here the difficulty of an image that does not lend itself well to graphic representation, so that the subject tries to get around the problem by depicting other, related objects.

These children had insufficient ability to use drawing as a sign or a means, and this was complicated by their attitude toward drawing as a self-contained game. Hence, the representation is extended from a single image to a whole situation in which this image was perceived; it is given new roots. In this situation, however, the indirect path is purely of the most primitive sort. The whole instead of the part is the first indirect device used in early childhood; we shall be able to understand it if we take into account the diffuse, holistic, poorly differentiated nature of a child's perceptions (Werner, 1925). At the very last stages, these indirect means acquire another, more differentiated and more highly developed nature.

It is hardly necessary to present all the instances in which a child chooses an indirect means and, instead of a whole that he finds difficult to depict, draws some part of it, which is easier. These features of all infantile drawing that is already at a more differentiated stage have been described many times, and are well known to all. Two tendencies are characteristic of the pictographic writing of a child at a relatively advanced stage: The object to be depicted may be replaced either by some part of it or by its general contours or outline. In either case the child has already gone beyond the aforementioned tendency to depict an object in its entirety, in all its details, and is in the process of acquiring the psychological skills on whose basis the last form, symbolic writing, will develop. Let us give just one more example of the first appearance of this kind of representational drawing in a child. This is the "part instead of the whole" device we observed in the experiments involving writing a number.

Shura N., 7½ years old. The child is instructed to write the sentence we presented above: "There are 1,000 stars in the sky." The subject first draws a horizontal line ("the sky"), then carefully draws two stars, and stops. Experimenter: "How many do you still have to draw?" Subject: "Only two. I'll remember there are 1,000."

Clearly, the two stars here were a sign for a large quantity. It would be wrong, however, to assume that such a small child was capable of using the "part for the whole" device. We had occasion to observe a number of children who wrote the sentence about 1,000 stars with so many "stars," that is, marks, that after demurring several minutes, we finally had simply to stop this procedure, which looked as though it were going to end with a thousand stars. A considerable degree of intellectual development and abstraction are necessary to be able to depict a whole group by one or two representatives; a child who is capable of this is already at the verge of symbolic writing.

Let us consider briefly some experiments we ran in this regard on adults. An adult audience was asked to represent concrete or abstract concepts graphically; these adults invariably depicted one attribute of the whole (e.g., "stupidity" was represented as donkey ears, "intelligence" by a high forehead, "fear" by raised hair or big eyes, etc.). Graphic representation by means of a particular attribute, however, is not at all easy for a child, whose discriminating and abstracting powers are not very well developed.

We have arrived at the question of a child's symbolic writing, and with this will have reached the end of our essay on the prehistory of a child's writing. Strictly speaking, this primitive period of infantile literacy, which is so interesting to the psychologist, comes to an end when the teacher gives a child a pencil. But we should not be completely correct in saying such a thing. From the time a child first begins to learn to write until he has finally mastered this skill is a very long period, which is of particular interest for psychological research. It is right at the borderline between the primitive forms of inscription we have seen above, which have a prehistoric, spontaneous character, and the new cultural forms introduced in an organized fashion from outside the individual. It is during this transitional period, when the child has not completely mastered the new skills but also has not completely outgrown the old, that a number of psychological patterns of particular interest emerge.

How does a child write who, although he is still unable to write, knows some of the elements of the alphabet? How does he relate these letters, and how does he (psychologically) try to use them in his primitive practice? These are the questions that interest us.

Let us first describe some extremely interesting patterns we observed in our material. Writing by no means develops along a straight line, with continuous growth and improvement. Like any other cultural psychological function, the development of writing depends to a considerable extent on the writing techniques used, and amounts essentially to the replacement of one such technique by another. Development in this case may be described as a *gradual improvement in the process of writing, within the means of each technique, and sharp turning points marking a transition from one such technique to another*. But the profoundly dialectical uniqueness of this process means that the transition to a new technique initially sets the process of writing back considerably, after which it then develops further at the new and higher level. Let us try to see what this interesting pattern means, since without it, in our opinion, it would be impossible for such cultural psychological functions to develop.

We saw the prehistory of infantile writing traces a path of gradual differentiation of the symbols used. At first the child relates to writing things without understanding the significance of writing; in the first stage, writing is for him not a means of recording some specific content, but a self-contained process involving imitation of an adult activity but having no functional significance in itself. This phase is characterized by undifferentiated scribblings; the child records any idea with exactly the same scrawls. Later—and we saw how this develops—differentiation begins: The symbols acquire a functional significance and begin graphically to reflect the content the child is to write down.

At this stage the child begins to learn how to read: He knows individual letters, and he knows that these letters record some content; finally, he learns their outward forms and how to make particular marks. But does this mean that he now understands the full mechanics of their use? Not at all. Moreover, we are convinced that an understanding of the mechanisms of writing takes place much later than the outward mastery of writing, and that in the first stages of acquiring this mastery the child's relation to writing is purely external. He understands that he can use signs to write everything, but he does not yet understand how to do this; he thus becomes fully confident in this writing yet is still totally unable to use it. Believing completely in this new technique, in the first stage of development of symbolic alphabetic writing the child begins with a stage of undifferentiated writing he had already passed through long before.

Here are some examples from our records for different subjects obtained under different conditions.

> Little Vasya G., a village boy 6 years old, could not yet write, but knew the individual letters A and I. When we asked him to remember and write down some sentences we dictated, he easily did so. In his movements he showed total confidence that he would be able to write down and remember the dictated sentences. The results are shown in the following record.

| | |
|---|---|
| 1. A cow has four legs and a tail. | Subject: I know he has four legs, and this (writes) is "I." |
| 2. Chimney sweeps are black. | (Writes) And this is "A." |
| 3. Yesterday evening it rained. | Here's rain. Here's "I" (writes). |
| 4. There are many trees in the woods. | Subject: (writes) Here is "u." |

| | |
|---|---|
| 5. The steamer is sailing down the river. | The steam goes like this (makes a mark). Here's "I." |

The result was a column of alternate I's and A's having nothing to do with the dictated sentences. Obviously, the subject had not yet learned how to make such a connection, so that in the task in which he was to read what he wrote, he read the letters (I and A) without relating them at all to the text.

In this case the letters were completely nonfunctional; the child was at a stage fully analogous with the stage studied earlier.

But one may object: The child had obviously not yet learned the function of writing, and psychologically the letters were totally analogous to the earlier scribbles. He had not yet gone beyond the stage of primary, undifferentiated, graphic activity. This observation is quite true, but it does not vitiate the law we wished to demonstrate. We can present data showing that this inability to use letters, this lack of understanding of the actual mechanism of alphabetic writing, persists for a long time. To study the psychological underpinnings of automated writing skills rather than these skills themselves we selected a somewhat different approach; the children were instructed not to write each word in a sentence completely. The results of this test gave us a deeper insight into a child's attitude toward writing. Here is an example:

Vanya Z., 9 years old, a village boy, wrote the letters well, and willingly participated in our experiment. The results, however, showed a very unique attitude toward his writing. Here is the record:

| | |
|---|---|
| 1. Monkeys have long tails. | Subject writes first "n" and then crosses it out and writes "i" (saying to himself: u obezyan-*i*). |
| 2. There is a tall tree. | "v" |
| 3. It's dark in the cellar | "v" |
| 4. The balloon soars. | "v" |
| 5. The big dog gave birth to four pups. | "u" |
| 6. The boy is hungry. | "m" |

[Translator's note: Each of the Russian sentences begins with the letter the boy wrote down.]

Of course, the subject was able to recall very little of the written words on the basis of what was written here. The way he wrote three different sentences (2, 3, and 4) induced us to do the following test.

In a second session we gave the boy six sentences beginning with the preposition "u." All six sentences were written down as six completely identical letters "u" (see Figure 1.11).

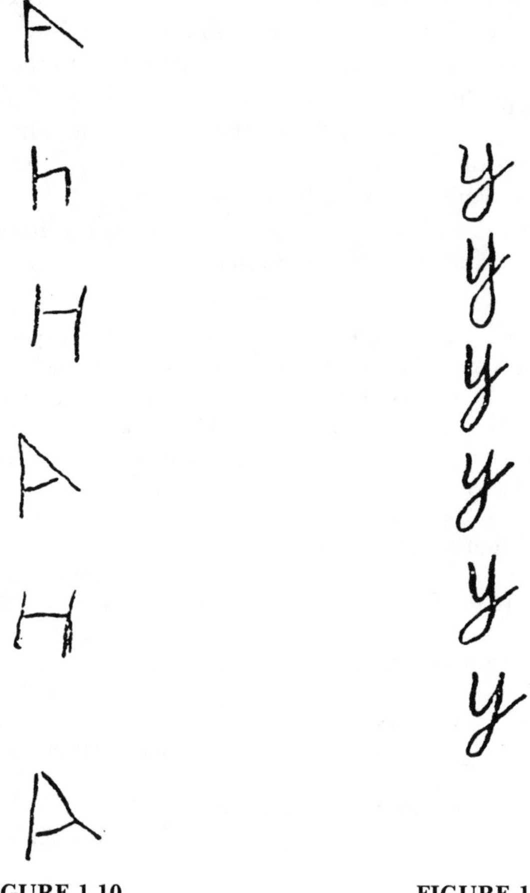

FIGURE 1.10

FIGURE 1.11

These data show that the ability to write does not necessarily mean that the child understands the process of writing, and that a child who can write may, under certain conditions, display a totally undifferentiated attitude toward writing and a lack of comprehension of the basic premises of it, namely, the need for specific distinctions to record different contents.

We obtained even clearer results when we asked a schoolchild who had recently learned how to write to write some idea with any marks (or graphic designs); he was forbidden only to use letters. The most conspicuous result of these experiments was the surprising difficulty the child had in reverting to the phase of pictorial, representational writing through which he had already passed. Our expectation, which seemed quite reasonable, that given the conditions of our experiment, the child would immediately revert to simple drawings proved wrong. The child whom we had forbidden to use letters did not revert to the picture stage, but remained at the level of symbolic writing. He worked out his own signs and, using them, tried to do the assignment. Finally, what was most interesting of all was that in using these signs he started with the same undifferentiated phase with which he began the development of writing in general, only now he gradually developed differentiated techniques for this higher level of development.

> Here is a record of an experiment done with Shura I., a city schoolboy 8½ years old. We asked him to note each sentence we dictated with marks to remember it. The subject quickly consented to the experiment, and in the first session used a very simple system. He marked each sentence with crosses, each element of the sentence being noted by one cross. Here is what he produced:
>
> 1. A cow has four legs and a tail. XXX
> (Cow—four legs—tail.)
> 2. Negroes are black. XXX
> (Negroes—are—black.)
> 3. It rained yesterday evening. XXX
> (It rained —yesterday—evening.)
> 4. There are many wolves in the forest. XXX
> (There are—many wolves—in the forest.)
> 5. House. X
> 6. Two dogs, a large one and a small one. XXX
> (Two dogs—large one and—small one.)

The completely undifferentiated nature of this writing shows with graphic clarity that the subject had not yet grasped the mechanisms of symbolic writing and used it only externally, thinking that these marks in themselves would be of assistance to him.

The effect of such writing was quite expected; the subject remembered only three of the six sentences, and moreover was completely unable to indicate which of his markings represented which sentence.

To follow the process in its purest form, we forbade our subject to make crosses. The result was a transition to a new form, marks that were not as undifferentiated by that he continued to use in a purely mechanical fashion. In this second trial, however, we were already able to achieve some differentiation; the subject discovered pictographic writing and resorted to it after a number of failures with his marks. Here is the record (see Figure 1.12).

**FIGURE 1.12**

Session II:

| | | |
|---|---|---|
| 1. | Monkeys have long tails. | (Makes two marks.) |
| 2. | There is a high column on the street. | (Two marks.) |
| 3. | The night is dark. | (Two marks.) |
| 4. | There is one bottle and two glasses. | (I'll write down a bottle.) |
| 5. | One big dog and one small dog. | (Makes two marks.) |
| 6. | Wood is thick. | (I'll write down wood.) |

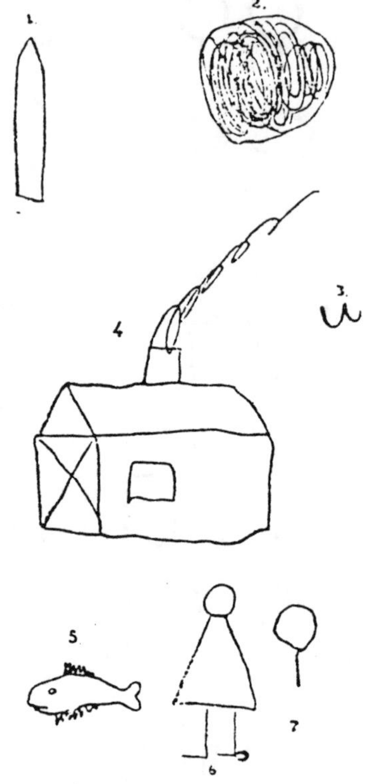


**FIGURE 1.13**

We see that at first this writing was undifferentiated; but then, in cases that were especially conducive to pictography, the subject went over to a graphic depiction of the objects. He was not consistent in this, however, and at even the slightest difficulty in depicting something would again revert to undifferentiated use of signs.

But in this case, we were able to advance one step in our inquiry into the most difficult problem of our study, namely, the mechanisms by which this arbitrary conventional sign is created. Session III shows this mechanism.

We gave the subject a number of concrete images with a word between them identifying the situation. Figure 1.13 shows the interesting process of generation of a sign to identify an abstract term.

Session III:

| | |
|---|---|
| 1. There is a column. | (The subject draws something.) |
| 2. The night is dark. | I'll put a circle for the night (draws a filled-in circle). |
| 3. The bird is flying. | (The subject draws something.) |

| | |
|---|---|
| 4. Smoke is coming from the chimney. | I'll draw a house with smoke (draws). |
| 5. The fish is swimming. | Fish...fish.... I'll draw a fish. |
| 6. The girl wants to eat. | I'll draw a girl.... She wants to eat (makes a mark)—there it is—she wants to eat (Figure 1.13, 6,7). |

The last is very characteristic. The subject, unable to draw "hunger," reverted to his system of signs and, next to the figure of the little girl, placed a mark meant to signify that the girl wanted to eat. Pictography here is combined with arbitrary symbolic writing, and a sign is used where pictographic means are not sufficient.

Our example clearly shows that a child initially assimilates school experience purely externally, without yet understanding the sense and mechanism of using symbolic marks. Over the course of our experiment, however, a positive aspect of this assimilated experience emerged; when conditions were restricted, the child reverted to a new, more complicated form of pictographic writing, in which the pictographic elements were combined with symbolic marks used as technical means for remembering.

The further development of literacy involves the assimilation of the mechanisms of culturally elaborated symbolic writing and the use of symbolic devices to simplify and expedite the act of recording. This takes us beyond our topic, and we shall explore the psychological fate of writing further in another study of adults who are already cultural beings. We have come to the end of our essay, and may sum up our conclusions as follows.

One thing seems clear from our analysis of the use of signs and its origins in the child: It is not understanding that generates the act, but far more the act that gives birth to understanding—indeed, the act often far precedes understanding. Before a child has understood the sense and mechanism of writing, he has already made many attempts to elaborate primitive methods; and these, for him, are the prehistory of his writing. But even these methods are not developed all at once: They pass through a number of trials and inventions, constituting a series of stages with which it is very useful for an educator working with school-age children and preschoolers to be acquainted.

The 3 or 4 year old first discovers that his scribblings on paper can be used as a functional aid to remembering. At this point (sometimes much later) writing assumes an auxiliary instrumental function, and drawing becomes sign writing.

At the same time as this transformation takes place, a fundamental reorganization occurs in the most basic mechanisms of the child's behavior; on top of the primitive forms of direct adaptation to the problems imposed by his environment, the child now builds up new, complex, cultural forms. The major psychological functions no longer operate through primitive natural forms and begin to employ complex cultural devices. These devices are tried to succession, and perfected, and in the process transform the child as well. We have observed the engrossing process of the dialectical development of complex, essentially social forms of behavior that after traversing a long path, have brought us finally to the mastery of what is perhaps the most priceless tool of culture.

## NOTES

[1]This is yet another example of a purely external relation to writing that does not take into account its sense. We could say that the child's relation to writing assumes a primitive, logical character. We shall take up this point in more detail elsewhere.

[2]It is difficult to enumerate on the spur of the moment all the factors that allow the child to enter this phase of primary utilization of some undifferentiated sign. The topography and integral perception of the entire surface of the paper and the relationships among the signs on it probably play an essential role here. Werner (*Einführung in die Entwicklungspsychologie*) gives the example of the graphic production of primitive peoples, some of which signifies nothing whatever and acquires meaning only through its topographical position.

## REFERENCES

Koehler, W. (1921). *Intelligenzpruefungen an menschenaffen* [*Intelligence in apes*]. Berlin: Julius Springer.

Vygotsky, L. (1929/1976). Razvitie aktivnogo vnimania v detskom vozraste [Development of active attention in childhood]. In *Khrestomatia po vnimaniyu* [*Readings on attention*]. Moscow: Moscow State University Press.

Werner, H. (1925). *Einführung in der entwicklungspsychologie* [*Introduction to developmental psychology*]. Leipzig: J. A. Barth.

chapter 2

# Parallels Between the Perspectives of Alexander Luria and Emilia Ferreiro

Maria Thereza Fraga Rocco
University of São Paulo, Brazil

The twentieth century witnessed a shift in the epistemological focus of research in several sciences. If previously the foundations of knowledge were sought in a realm external to human beings, in the last three decades of the century we observe a tendency to research specific topics basically in terms of relationships between persons and their environments. Language uses constitute such relations. While speaking and writing, a person simultaneously shapes one's activity as a special object of his knowledge—yet one that is continuously further questioned by language uses. When producing speech and using the symbolism of writing to represent it, human beings create multiple interfaces that constitute the specific conditions within which speaking and writing occur. These same conditions must also be investigated by those scholars who attempt to understand the complexity inherent in the stages of the process of production of "the verbal," despite the apparent simplicity of the final product.

Focusing on the question of writing among children who have not yet had any contact with school, it is of interest to analyze the work of two authors—Alexander Luria and Emilia Ferreiro. Although they are distant from one another in the times and places where they lived, and differ in respect to some of the circumstances that guided their research, they nevertheless reveal points in common. Their general concerns bring them close together—both in the theoretical questions they pose (and which are the origin of their experiments), and in respect to the very manner in which they conducted their research.

## BACKGROUND OF THE COMMON CONCERNS: PIAGET AND VYGOTSKY

Both Luria and Ferreiro build upon their mentors—Vygotsky and Piaget. It is not possible to discuss Luria's work without thinking about Vygotsky, in the same manner that we cannot deal with Ferreiro's work without alluding to Piaget.

In one of his finest pieces of work, *The Making of Mind,* Luria (1979, pp. 189-225) described the path followed by Vygotsky, Leontiev, and himself, as well as other scholars of Soviet psychology in the decades of the 1920s and 30s. In his account, Luria began with his youth—he was still in his early twenties when he met Vygotsky, who was of similar age. While jointly working in the Institute of Psychology in Moscow, Vygotsky organized a study group among people who were exceptional in their efforts to make sense of complex issues of psychology. The group would meet for 5 or 6 hours daily, several times a week. They shared a common objective, that of trying to resolve the crisis faced by psychology in the 1920s, and to propose a new basis for psychology, now conceived with the help of Marxist inspiration.

In his lucid reflections, written at nearly 70 years of age, Luria points to the difficulty of the endeavor to which they dedicated themselves, shaped as it was by the ideas of persons who, while very serious, were also very young. Thus, although the proposal for a new psychology was of socialist-Marxist derivation, and was not fully realized, the group led by Vygotsky left behind remarkable research which extended in multiple, important directions. Whereas Leontiev dedicated himself to studies of memory, Levina looked at the role of speech, and Luria attempted to analyze the development of writing among small children, in conjunction with the functions of attention and also of memory.

Vygotsky was the source of ideas for this research. Like Luria, Vygotsky had a good command of several languages—Latin, French, English, German, and Spanish—which made it possible for both to maintain continuous contact with the greatest members of the intelligentsia of both the East and the West. Luria (1979) mentioned that the group of young intellectuals read everything—from the German Romanticists to the texts of Lenin and Marx. In keeping with this program of a very high intellectual level, during the systematic weekly encounters, they discussed, among others, the works of Brentano, Dilthey, and above all, the writings of the young and already famous biologist from Geneva, Jean Piaget.

Half a century later Piaget would become the intellectual mentor of many scholars, including Emilia Ferreiro. In order to speak of Emilia Ferreiro's work, it is essential that we reflect upon certain positions held by Vygotsky and Piaget. In recent decades, the heritages of these two thinkers have almost always been considered as if they were conflicting, especially the former in relation to the latter. This tendency to establish an opposition and even force a choice between one theory or the other, between one author or the other, as though they were a topic of dispute and mutually exclusive, leads to a reductionist vision of the work of both, thus depriving the body of research of their essential theoretical contributions. Oliveira observes that in the Brazilian context,

> Piaget has been the predominant reference in the area of psychology of education and that the growing penetration of Vygotsky's thought seems to bring with it the need to choose between him and Piaget, which could be translated as a form of opposition between the two theoreticians. (1993, p. 103)

Even if differences do exist between the ideas of Piaget and Vygotsky (and are considerable in some domains), it is possible to verify that Piaget and Vygotsky have many points in common, beginning with the cognitive-interactionist approach encountered at the theoretical basis of the works of each. In regard to interactionism, Claudia Lemos maintains that

> the term interactionism (in the psychological literature) has for many decades now served to designate an epistemological position distinct from rationalism and from empiricism, insofar as it assumes the *interaction* between the human organism and the environment to be the source of the *qualitative transformations* of this organism. Thus, it is capable of explaining the genesis of superior mental activities and of knowledge.... although the term [interactionism] appears to be as applicable to the works of Vygotsky and Wallon as to that of Piaget, traditionally it is the latter who has been referred to when speaking of interactionism in psychology of development. (1986, pp. 1–2)

Although, as Lemos claims, the term has been traditionally linked to the work of Piaget, we believe that it is not importune to apply it to the theoretical positions of Vygotsky and Luria. Here it obviously refers to a socio-interactionism whose principal focus is of the historical-dialectical nature envisioned under Marxist theory.

In his memoirs, Luria (1979) mentioned the enormous importance of the works of Piaget for the studies that they were developing in Moscow under the leadership of Vygotsky. On this occasion, he describes how the work by the young scholar from Geneva was received by the group in Moscow:

> When Piaget's *Language and Thought of the Child* became known to us, we studied it carefully. A fundamental disagreement with the interpretation of the relation between language and thought distinguished our work from that of this great Swiss psychologist. But we found the style of his research, especially his use of the clinical method in the study of individual cognitive processes, highly compatible with our goal of discovering the qualitative differences that distinguish children of different ages. (1979, pp. 42–43)

In turn, in the postface of the Argentinian edition of Vygotsky's *Language and Thought,* Piaget (1981) makes unusual "critical observations," as he himself called them, on the work of the Russian author. These observations show that, despite their differences, they probably would have been in agreement on many issues, had life brought them into contact earlier. It is worth remembering that Piaget and Vygotsky were both born in the year 1896, and Vygotsky died prematurely in 1934 at the age of 38.

Piaget began his text—which were his comments to the first English edition of Vygotsky's *Thought and language* in 1962—by saying,

> It is with great sorrow that an author discovers the work of a deceased colleague twenty-five years after its publication, above all when he takes into account the fact that it contains so many aspects of immediate interest to him, to the extent that he thinks they could have discussed them personally and in detail. Although my friend A. Luria has informed me of the position Vygotsky held in relation to my work, at one and the same time, favorable and critical, I was never able to read his work or have any contact with him. Today, upon reading his book, I profoundly lament this since, had a greater approximation been possible, we could have come to understand one another's positions on a great number of points (1981, p. 199)

Piaget continues by commenting that Vygotsky's book of 1934 referred to his own works of 1923 and 1924. In an attitude of great respect for the intellectual production of the other author, at that time Piaget decided to verify whether Vygotsky's criticisms were justified in light of his later studies. Piaget (1981, p. 199) concluded that the answer would be *yes* and *no* since, as he states, "on certain aspects I am more in agreement with Vygotsky today than I would have been in 1934, and on other questions I believe I would now have better argumentations to use in responding to him."

Scholars of the Piagetian school, in addition to Ferreiro herself, point to the fact that crucial theoretical incompatibilities between the works of Piaget and the Russian psychologists—above all Vygotsky—do not exist. Consequently, we find some statements that reiterate this viewpoint in the work organized by Ferreiro and by Margarita G. Palacio (1987), where they summarize the discussions at the International Symposium on New Perspectives in the Processes of Reading and Writing, held in Mexico in 1981:

> Cazden emphasized the importance of comparing the theoretical viewpoints of Piaget and Vygotsky, insofar as some of the work presented at the symposium utilized one or the other as theoretical references. Hermine Sinclair pointed out that it was impossible to do so within the limitations of the discussion, but added that the two are probably very close to one another, though each emphasizes a different aspect of mental development. (p. 268)

Extremely interesting discussions follow concerning the two authors—discussions that require lengthy study and warrant the conduction of comparisons between the studies of Luria and Ferreiro in regard to the construction of writing by the preschool-age child.

The new works on the development of writing, originating with the studies by Ferreiro, are quite revolutionary. According to these, the construction of writing by the child is tied to neither the development of motor abilities nor the possession of a graphic code, but rather, it is the result of a process of representation of the language, a historical and individual process of structuring an entire system of symbolic representation. Nevertheless, we become even more astonished upon discovering that these "revolutionary" ideas already guided all of Luria's research on the development of writing among preschool children in the decade of the twenties.

How can we explain trajectories that are, at one and the same time, so close and yet so distant? We believe that the impact of the revolution in which they were involved, as well as the impact of the very special group of scientists who systematically studied and questioned topics that would be of interest to us decades later, allowed the Russian scholars to reach, half a century earlier, the point which would only be attained by Ferreiro in the 1970s. Despite the differences in historical, social, and political circumstances, as well as in place, some scholars such as Ferreiro and her group arrived at almost the same conclusions reached by the Soviets 50 years earlier. However, as a consequence of the political situation in the Soviet Union in the 1930s through 1960s, most of the world was unfamiliar with the work that Luria's group had performed under the intellectual leadership of Vygotsky. Vygotsky invented experimental models to develop such research. It was Luria's task to carry out a study whose objective was to investigate the forms by which the development of what was defined as prewriting was processed among preschoolers.

As Luria himself relates, at the time some of these tasks could be better characterized as student projects—very ambitious and broad—but little by little they took shape and were refined, with the majority ultimately becoming effective, fundamental achievements. When, in response to Vygotsky's proposal, Luria (1988a) offered to direct the study on the construction and development of writing, his theoretical conviction was that the history of writing among quite small, preschool children begins long before they are able to write their first words and sentences. Vygotsky had claimed that

> Children are taught to draw letters and construct words with them but the written language is not taught.... The only way for us to reach a correct solution for the psychology of writing is through an understanding of the entire history of the development of signs in the child. (1984, pp. 119–120)

Luria was also profoundly interested in the epistemological bases that enable us to comprehend the development of writing among small children. Thus, he did not work with the child at the moment when learning begins. He is basically interested in "excavating the prehistory of writing," since, in his view, this history "begins long before a teacher first puts a pencil in the child's hand and shows him how to form letters" (1988a, p. 143).

The work of Luria and Ferreiro starts from the same initial concern, which is that of investigating the manner in which this type of knowledge develops in young children before they enter school. While Luria attempted and was able to "excavate the prehistory of writing," Ferreiro's central objective in her research carried out between 1974 and 1976 was

> to demonstrate that learning to read, conceived of as the questioning of the nature, function and value of this cultural object called writing, begins much earlier than the school imagines, moving along unforeseen paths which go beyond the methods, the manuals, the didactic resources. (Ferreiro & Teberosky, 1984, p. 11)

According to Luria, the fundamental condition for the child to be able to "write down" some notion or phrase resides in the fact that he already has a type of "private hypothesis" for "recalling" something.

And in order for this to occur, it is necessary that the child is already able to establish "differentiated relations" with the things which interest him. Thus, through his lengthy work with children, Luria attempts to "trace the development of the first signs" which already indicate "the emergence of a functional relation," however primitive, of the children's lines and scribbles to some object of reference. The Russian scholar attempts to discover at what moment these lines and scrawls are utilized by the child as the means of expressing a relationship, of producing meaning.

## LURIA AND FERREIRO: DIFFERENCES AND SIMILARITIES

While some of Luria's and Ferreiro's concerns are similar, the differences between them must also be pointed out. If for the former the prehistory of writing originates at the moment when the child becomes capable of relating scribbles and a variety of graphic marks to a specific reference, for Emilia Ferreiro the very imitation of the act of writing (which does not necessarily have a corresponding interpretation linked to a specific reference) already corresponds to the first level in the actual construction of writing.

How did Luria and Ferreiro conduct their experiments? Luria mentioned,

> we took a child who did not know how to write and gave him the task of remembering a certain number of sentences presented to him. Usually this number exceeded the child's mechanical capacity to remember. Once the child realized that he was unable to remember the number of words given him in the task, we gave him a sheet of paper and told him to jot down or "write" the words we presented. Of course, in most cases the child was bewildered by our suggestion. He would tell us *that he did not know how to write,* that he could not do it. We would point out to him that adults wrote things down when they had to remember something and then, exploiting the child's natural tendency toward *purely external imitation,* we suggested that he try to contrive something himself and write down what we would tell him. (1988a, p. 147)

According to Luria, it was possible to verify that children 3, 4, and up to 5 years of age almost *never carried out the instructions,* to the extent that they didn't perceive writing as a tool, as a means, as a form of symbolic mediation.

The experiment would begin by the child's being presented with some series of six or eight simple, short, unrelated sentences, from day-to-day speech. Thus, what Luria and his group did was to furnish the child with a device already *outwardly* familiar to him, but with an unfamiliar *internal* function. In addition, they made use of the child's ability to imitate adults. As the child had a notion of only the external aspects of the technique, it was possible to observe throughout the entire process some "strategies," "inventions," and "discoveries" that this child attained to enable himself to use the device.

Luria then asked the children to write down the sentences he was dictating to them. Here also some similarities with the procedures followed by Ferreiro appear; while she explores the problem differently and proposes different questions, some of her proposals parallel those of Luria. Both use an experimental situation for their research.

Ferreiro lists six procedures, of which two stand out and are expressed in the following manner: a) "The children were asked to write the words which are normally used to initiate learning at school (mommy, daddy, boy);" and b) "It was suggested that they attempt to write some phrases such as, for example, 'my girl sunbathes'" (Ferreiro & Teberosky, 1984, p. 182).

As in Luria's experiment, these tasks were proposed without any close link being established between them. As the author relates, in the beginning, the children tried to avoid the assignment by saying that "they didn't know how to write" (Ferreiro & Teberosky, 1984, p. 182).

Luria's proposal consisted of studying the prehistory of writing by attempting to discover "the various tendencies and factors involved," in order to be able to use these "to describe the stages we observe as a child develops his ability to write," as well as "the factors that enable him to pass from one stage to another, higher stage" (1988a, p. 144).

Luria still intended to describe his own efforts "to trace the development of the first signs of the emergence of a functional relation to lines and scribbles in the child and his first use of such lines, etc., to express meanings" and thus, by this development, "shed some light on the prehistory of human writing" (1988a, p. 146).

In turn, Ferreiro's work was modeled on a dialogue between "subject and interviewer," by which the author sought to *show evidence of the mechanisms of infantile thought* which enabled her to discover the defining characteristics of the research carried out.

In this manner, the research conducted by Ferreiro and her group was oriented in the following fundamental directions: identification of the cognitive processes which underlie the acquisition of writing, comprehension of the nature of the hypotheses created by the children, and discovery of the type of specific knowledge that the child possesses when he initiates his school learning. Therefore, just as Luria had done earlier, the researchers created a very flexible experimental situation that permitted them to discover the type and nature of the hypotheses which arose and of the operations carried out by the interviewees.

Ferreiro and her group define five differentiated levels which underlie the child's construction of writing. Here, too, we stress the relationship to Luria's work which, in turn, defined five different levels to be attained by the child in the development of his writing. If, on the one hand, there are similarities between them in the themes chosen, the research method, and the concern shown with the type of knowledge possessed by the child before total command of the written form can be mastered at this age, on the other hand, there are *considerable differences in the manner of conceptualizing the operations carried out* by the children and also in the interpretation of certain data obtained during these investigations.

For Ferreiro at the first level, "to write is to reproduce the typical features of writing which the child identifies as the basic form of writing" (Ferreiro & Teberosky, 1984, p. 183); however, for Luria, writing can be considered to exist only when, in addition to the reproduction of strokes, the child grasps the possible concept ("primary hypothesis") of writing as a process that serves *to help remember, to register,* something. Perhaps Luria demanded too much of such young children, who, as he himself claims, had a difficult time understanding the researchers' proposal. Ferreiro certainly reached a more profound understanding of the existence of some basic properties of writing in those initial manifestations.

Even if we consider this aspect and continue a bit longer at this Level 1 of writing proposed by Ferreiro, we see that the author states a second time that even at this so-called primitive level, "attempts at figurative correspondence between writing and the object being referred to can appear (Ferreiro & Teberosky, 1984, p. 183).

In comparing Luria's study on writing (1988a, p. 151), Ferreiro and Teberosky's descriptions (1984, p. 197), and the respective graphic representations found in both texts, we can make the following observations: In his experiment conducted with 4-year-old Lena, Luria tells us that he had dictated some sentences to her, asking her to "write them down." According to the author's statement, little Lena heard only the first three sentences, and after each, "began to write down her scribbles, which were the same in each case, i.e., they were indistinguishable from one another" (1988a, p. 150). According to Luria, these undifferentiated scribbles, shown in Figure 2.1, characterize this first phase of written production, in which writing emerges dissociated from a defined reference, since the lines are used in an undifferentiated manner, thus remaining *external* to any function that would have truly associated the scribbles with a specific objective.

Attributed explanations:
1. There are five pencils on the table
2. There are two plates
3. There are many trees in the forest
4. There is a column in the yard
5. There is a large cupboard (written prematurely)'
6. The little doll (written prematurely)

*Source:* Luria (1988a, p. 151).

**FIGURE 2.1. An example of prehistory of writing (from Luria, 1988a, p. 151).**

For Luria, what is depicted in this figure (scribbles drawn and explained by Lena) does not constitute writing, but rather, a complex set of mere scrawls. It would be a typical example of this first stage which Luria considered to be *prehistory* of writing.

To this first stage proposed by Luria, we have the corresponding *Level 1 of writing* designated by Ferreiro, who believes that at this level "to write is to reproduce the typical strokes of writing which the child identifies as the basic form of writing" (Ferreiro & Teberosky, 1984, p. 183), even though attempts to link writing and the object referred to can occasionally appear. Ferreiro, like Luria, agrees that "the strokes are very similar to one another," even though the child can view them as being different.

Figure 2.2, reproduced from Ferreiro's research with children whose production is registered as Level 1, shows some similarity between the observations by the two authors, despite their conceptual differences.

In this case, the scribbles and strokes resulted from dictation tasks that the author gave to Alejandra and Ximena, 5 and 4 years old, respectively. By the proposed tasks and by the scribbles presented, we can verify that both Lena, on the one hand, and Alejandra and Ximena, on the other, are performing very similar experiments, though the interpretation and categorization of their products present differences, in light of the criteria adopted by the authors.

Even though he considers this "undifferentiation" demonstrated by the children an indication of the lack of comprehension of the function of writing, given the predominance of zigzag forms, Luria agrees that these young children already hold a clear idea that adults write in this manner and that what they are attempting to do in obeying the suggestion to "write down" the sentence is, in reality, to reproduce adult writing.

In his classification of the stages of writing, Luria speaks of a "second moment," when, "upon reading" a specific scribble, the child gives the sentence that he regards as corresponding to it. Here Luria sees writing as a "memory aid," although the mnemonic function is not yet fully developed. Thus, we find the origin of a process of differentiation of the resource utilized, the differentiation of writing in relation to the object of reference, the memory's auxiliary sign. In this way, upon always attributing the same sentences to the same scribbles, the young children were, without a doubt, enabling the process that leads to the system of writing unfolding.

In turn, at what she considers Level 2 of writing, Ferreiro observes that "in order to be able to read different things (that is, attribute different meanings), the child should create an objective difference between the writings" (Ferreiro & Teberosky, 1984, p. 189). Graphic progress becomes clearly evident since the graphic shapes are better defined. In our opinion, the third and fourth stages proposed by Luria (1988a) correspond to Ferreiro's Level 2.

Luria and the other researchers with whom he worked noticed that instead of arranging the scribbles in straight lines, some children began to make a stroke or mark in one corner of the paper, and another on another side of the paper, and in that way, they associated the sentences with those notations. Indeed, here we find the graphic progress referred to by Ferreiro, which is made greater by the fact that it assumes a mne-

Alejandra (5a CM)

Ximena (4a CM)

*Source:* Ferreiro and Teberosky (1984, p. 197).

**FIGURE 2.2**

monic function for the children who end up remembering the *place* where they made the marks and scribbles better than the scribbles themselves. And they associate the sentences with these *topoi*.

Continuing this line of research, in proposing the fourth stage characterizing the development of writing, Luria observes the presence of two factors that are decisive in this development. These factors help graphic activity move from one of undifferentiated activity to the following, which consists of differentiated and well-defined graphic productions. They are the *number* or quantity of objects of reference and the *nature* of this object, its form.

Lena, the same 5-year-old girl, and other children of the same age produced only totally undifferentiated scribbles during the first work sessions. Upon continuing the sessions, when sentences containing ideas of quantity, such as "Lilya has two hands and two legs," were proposed, they began to make a specific scribble for the segment "two hands" and another for "two legs." For Luria, it is at this moment that the child really begins "to write," and "to read" what he writes.

With respect to form, during the course of the sessions Luria began to perceive that when the dictated sentences referred to an object that was conspicuous, due to size, color, or shape, the writing almost always became differentiated, presenting pictographic characteristics. It is at this moment that the fifth stage of the development of writing proposed by the Russian author is achieved. According to Luria, at this stage the child begins to use drawing (which has already been in use for a long time) as a means of remembering something. And this now differentiated drawing is the form taken by an intellectual activity which for Luria is much more complex and is located at the threshold of phonetic writing, which is to follow.

If for Ferreiro and Teberosky writing Levels 3 and 4 are characterized "by the child's attempt to give a phonetic value to each of the letters that compose a written product," (1984, p. 193), where each letter is worth a syllable, thus giving rise to the "syllabic hypothesis" (which in the sequence will be followed by the "alphabetic hypothesis"); nonetheless, the authors do not ignore the value of the quantity, shape, and size of the object of reference for the child, which to a certain extent corresponds to the fourth stage proposed by Luria.

Thus, referring to work with proper names, Ferreiro emphasizes the importance of the length of these names for small children. The author demonstrates that the child expects the written names of people, and even of animals, to be proportional to the size or age of these people or animals with which they are acquainted. For her, based on this experience with the names and other data she was able to obtain during the course of various research projects, there is a tendency for the child to reflect certain characteristics of the object in his writing. And, regarding this, Ferreiro points out the importance of the notion of quantity, also discussed by Luria.

According to Ferreiro, a relationship is established between certain quantifiable aspects of the object and quantifiable aspects of writing, even though little occurs regarding the figurative aspect itself. It is true that, if we observe one of the other illustrations from Luria's work, we will find some of Ferreiro's reflections present there. When jotting down some sentences that were dictated to him, 5-year-old Vova at times behaved in a quite differentiated manner (see Figure 2.3).

If in sentence numbers 1, 2, 3, and 5 he "scribbled" without establishing any closer connections between "writing" and the object of reference, in numbers 4 and 6 he surprised the researchers. Given Sentence 4: "Very black smoke is coming out of the chimney," Vova immediately reacted, saying, "Black. Like this!" Immediately afterwards, he grabbed the pencil and began producing very dark scribbles, by pressing hard and passing over the same place several times.

In relation to Sentence 6: "Very black coal," Vova acted similarly, drawing heavy lines over which he passed several times with the pencil so as to make them darker and thicker, thus making the quantitative and qualitative aspects of the object represented predominate.

If, for Luria, this fifth stage in the development of writing is characterized by the predominance of the pictograph (*a topic requiring discussion and urgent reexamination*), for Ferreiro that which is designated as the fifth level is considered *"alphabetic writing"* already totally developed and understood by the child.

The stages proposed by Luria and Ferreiro, which are compared here, clearly do not constitute the core of both bodies of research. Rather, they constitute unequivocal evidence of the same. Recently, Ferreiro (1994, p. 3) elegantly responded to the reflections I presented on the occasion of an early study (Rocco, 1990) in which, as here, I compared her work to that of Luria. She commented on the fact that the text emphasized the stages of development of writing, which are "obvious and of little relevance" for the establishment of a comparison process. However, the comparison between Luria and Ferreiro was not based exclusively on the general characteristics defining these stages. Throughout the work, an outline of the pertinent theoretical concerns of each researcher was elaborated, similar to what, among other things, is being proposed in the current work.

If earlier I covered the study of the stages, I have done so once again by considering them illustrative to the extent that they are able to serve as useful indications which can contribute to a better understanding of the theoretical positions and the objectives of these researchers.

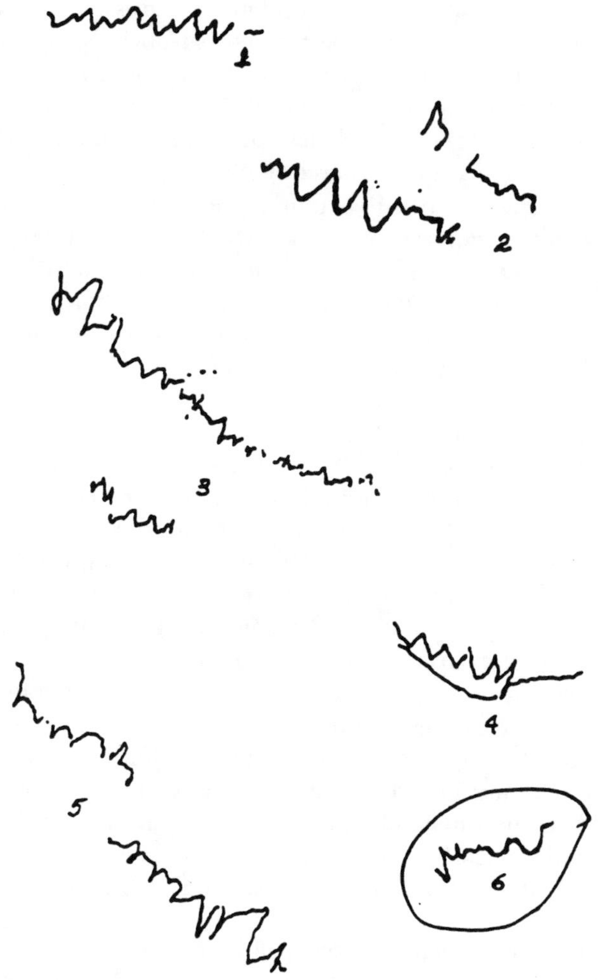


*Source:* Luria (1988, p. 167).

**FIGURE 2.3**

The starting points of the two scholars were a variety of inquiries and hypotheses which allowed each to discover something new in the written products of preschoolers. However, Emilia Ferreiro stresses that the inquiries they conducted were not the same. And it is on this point that the greatest differences between the two exist.

Ferreiro is correct. Fifty years separate them—50 years which gave rise to cultural and social changes of great magnitude, and moreover, the advancement of science. These brought progress unimaginable half a century ago and are among the factors that obviously exercise an influence over not only the nature of the theoretical options of each researcher, but also the definition of the very objectives, which could not be exactly the same, due to their separation by decades, although they reveal some similarities of different types.

This is so true that before beginning her discussion of the dissimilarities between the inquiries of the two works, Ferreiro (1994, p. 73) states with a great deal of relevance: "Some of Luria's claims are so close to those which I myself made (without having read him) that they are surprising." The author then proceeds to discuss the essential differences that she believes to exist between the arguments that orient her research and that of the Russian scholar.

Initially, in referring to Luria's concepts of writing, Ferreiro (1994, p. 73) comments that for him, "writing has two functions: the mnemonic and the communicative," and adds that since the communicative function is still not within the grasp of small children, it is only possible for the author to analyze the mnemonic function. From this, she concludes that "regarding writing as a technique," Luria "does not attempt to determine which functions could accomplish this writing from the point of view of a subject in process of development."

Ferreiro's assertion appears correct, if we concentrate our attention on certain initial sentences written by Luria (1988a) on the topic, in the article "The Development of Writing in the Child." However, in light of this same text and his other writings, as well as some work by Vygotsky published in the same collection, we can verify that Luria's concept of the role and scope of preschool writing is not so narrow.

Thus, in a study also cited by Ferreiro, Luria claimed:

> Psychologically, a child is not an adult in miniature. He fashions his own primitive culture; *though he does not possess the art of writing, he still writes;* and though he cannot count, he nevertheless does so. Empirical study of these primitive forms of acculturation *will not only help us attain a better understanding of the child, but will also enable us to trace the genesis of the most important forms of culturally acquired skills,* which are such important tools in the life of the civilized, adult, human being. (1988b, p. 102)

As can be observed in the passage transcribed above, the hypothesis that writing can and should be thought of, as so well expressed by Ferreiro (1994, p. 73), as an "object in and of itself, suitable for epistemological examination," and appropriate for assisting in the comprehension of the development of the young child, was also present in Luria's work.

Reflections by Vygotsky reiterate the assertions. Referring initially to orality and immediately afterwards to written production, Vygotsky claimed:

> Language originates in the first place as a means of communication between the child and the persons surrounding him.... Research by Baldwin, Rignano and Piaget demonstrated that the need to verify thought first appears when there is a discussion among children and only afterwards does thought appear in the child as an internal activity, whose characteristic is the fact that the child begins to acquaint himself with and to verify the foundations of his own thought. We have confidence in the power of the word—says Piaget—but only during the process of communication does the possibility of verifying and confirming thought arise. (1988, p. 114)

Moving on to discuss writing, Vygotsky made a provocative comparison between *learning to type*—which merely forms a certain number of habits, which "in and of themselves, absolutely do not change the psychointellectual characteristics of man," and the internal process of *learning to write*—an operation that is different in origin, since this learning activates a phase of development of the psychointellectual processes that is entirely new and very complex, promoting "a radical change in the general psycho-intellectual characteristics of the child."

An aspect that is crucial to Ferreiro and is considered "the most important point of discrepancy" between her and Luria, is the manner in which the Russian psychologist perceives the historical evolution of writing. Ferreiro (1994, p. 74) expresses it well when she says that Luria was "strongly influenced by a view—a view predominant in his period and until recently"—of a history of writing which, we believe, very deterministicly pointed to an evolutionary process in which the pictographic stage would necessarily precede phonographic-alphabetic writing.

Moreover, in broaching the topic of the evolution of writing, Ferreiro (1994, p. 74) is justified in claiming that in his studies, Luria "fails to provide us with any psychological evidence of the steps necessary for studying the topic." And, in regards to the specific question of the pictograms, she emphatically states that in relation to the point which should address the transition from pictographic to alphabetic, "Luria leaves us in total darkness."

In total agreement with Ferreiro, I believe that in view of the fact that Luria did not question the traditional history of writing—considered correct and accepted by the majority of researchers—he too hastily jumped to some conclusions and, as Ferreiro clearly demonstrates, even had to resort to new and external cultural agents in order to explain them.

However, it is necessary to consider the period in which Luria produced his work on writing. In other words, it was towards the end of the decade of the twenties, when no one even dreamed of questioning the already classic history of the evolution of writing—which subsequently became even more crystalized in light of the success of the work of Ignace Gelb (1982).

Regarding this, Ferreiro (1994, pp. 74–75) accepted that she herself is also very much influenced by references to the history of writing. She demonstrates having taken special care in her work so as not to make hasty generalizations. And, even while acknowledging the fascination that Gelb's theory (1982) of the history of writing exercised over both her and Ana Teberosky, Ferreiro concludes that "some aspects of the evolution—as presented by Gelb—openly contradicted data on the development of the child, in particular, the issue of pictography" (1994, p. 75).

Further, Ferreiro makes a very important observation regarding this same topic, when she claims that "in psychological development *there is no data which allows us to assume that pictography precedes phonographic writing*" (1994, p. 75).

If we are unwilling to condemn Luria (1988a) for not having questioned the history of writing 50 years ago, we must applaud Ferreiro (1994) for her forceful intervention. Without a doubt, she corrects a grave epistemological bias which has for years permeated the serious work of respected scholars, including her own, in regards to the history of the evolution of writing, which contains concepts until recently accepted as uncontestable. In reality, the current concepts used to analyze the function of pictography in the evolution of writing are eventually shown to be unquestioning repetitions, nearly always based on common sense.

In a revision of her own ideas, Ferreiro (1994) reveals a solid set of arguments and, further, refers us to the texts of Léroi-Gourhan and Denise Shmandt-Besserat which, simultaneously, form the basis of and reaffirm the current convictions of Ferreiro on the theme under discussion. However, another remark made by Ferreiro (1994), this time regarding the concept that Luria has of the child's writing activity after he starts school, appears to be incomplete. In mentioning another one of the differences verified between her own work and the research by the Russian scholar, Ferreiro (1994, p. 74) observes that "for Luria, admission to the school institution would, in and of itself, create a rupture with previously attained knowledge," while in the author's opinion, "admission to the school institution interacts with the child's previous notions and, thus, does not automatically bring about alterations on a conceptual level." Ferreiro claims that she was capable of demonstrating this, while Luria didn't even attempt to question in what manner previously acquired concepts would interact with the school education (Ferreiro, 1994, p. 74).

Her claim appears limited, however. Considering only the beginning of a statement by Luria: "This primitive period of infantile literacy ... comes to an end when the teacher gives a child a pencil" (1988a, p. 180), Ferreiro does not examine the passage immediately following, which complements Luria's (1988a, p. 180) thinking on the topic under discussion:

> ... But we should not be completely correct in saying such a thing. From the time a child first begins to learn to write until he has finally mastered this skill is a very long period, which is of particular interest for psychological research. It is right at the borderline between the primitive forms of inscription we have seen above, which have a prehistoric, spontaneous character, and the new cultural forms introduced in an organized fashion from outside the individual. It is during this transitional period, when the child has not completely mastered the new skills but also has not completely outgrown the old, that a number of psychological patterns of particular interest emerge.

Turning again to the question of the history of writing, we believe that Ferreiro (1994, p. 75) took a decisive step in the discussion of this theme when she stressed that "one must not confuse the history of graphic marks with the history of the systems of linguistically interpreted marks." The author goes even further with her reflections, clearing up common misunderstandings. She addresses epistemological biases and conceptualizes in an irreproachable manner the relations involved in the history of writing when, for example, she points out that "the appearance of writing does not eliminate pictorial marks because they continue to serve other purposes."

Ferreiro further questions:

> What about the accounts repeated in all of the published books addressing the evolution of writing which present, for example, the evolution of the drawing of an ox's head, its stylization and finally the Greek letter alpha, thereafter transformed into our letter "A"? The answer is simple: the history of individual writing marks is one thing and that of systems of writing is another. (1994, p. 75)

## GENERAL CONCLUSIONS

As a final observation, I would like to add some data on Luria which, in some way, respond to Ferreiro's final reflection. After declaring her great admiration for the pioneering work of the Russian scholar, she laments "profoundly that, rather than following this course, Luria abandoned it to such an extent that in later work on the topic—which was certainly much more focused on pathology—no mention can be found of this work on 'youth'" (1994, p. 76).

That the scientific and social restrictions placed on Luria beginning in the forties and continuing until the end of the fifties were severe is a well-known fact. According to an account by Cole (1979), in the former Soviet Union, the order was to carry on the work of Pavlov, considered exemplary. Therefore, Luria was required to stray from the course he himself, Vygotsky, and their collaborators had initiated and to even praise unacceptable psychological topics, as in the case of the *combined motor method* proposed by Ivanov-Somolensky.

However, while he could not openly pursue the proposal of Vygotskyan research, Luria cleverly managed to resolve certain dilemmas. For example, even when adopting the combined motor method, a conditioning experiment, he utilized it solely for the study of the elementary psychological functions, since he knew that the Pavlovian positions were not suitable for evaluating the higher psychological functions. Thus, he concentrated on the study and role of language in order to analyze the transition from these lower functions to the higher ones.

Without a doubt, a void exists. In Luria, a sense of continuity is lacking, as Ferreiro (1994) observes in regards to the specific studies on the construction of language—both oral and written. However, on the one hand, we must understand the social and political limitations placed on him and, on the other, identify the numerous passages in which Luria alludes to oral language and, particularly, to writing, in his descriptions of his patients. Luria declared that during that period he set aside psychological testing—so commonly used at that time—to evaluate the intellectual level of his patients. He dedicated himself to the study of various forms of aphasia, analyzing them, above all, by means of concepts related to the development of oral and written language in persons without problems.

In this way, a good number of Luria's descriptions of treatments used with clients are based on concepts that attempt to explain the nature and the role of speech and writing, above all among children. In concluding, I return to the question of teaching and would like to cite one more observation made by Ferreiro, with which I am in total agreement. She says:

> It is not possible to imagine, to presume, to take for granted or to explicitly determine that the current pedagogical option (with respect to the development of writing in the child) corresponds to Luria (1929-1930) *or* Fer-

reiro (exclusive disjunction). In any event, what is important is to conduct the experiments necessary to bring the debate up to date. (1994, p. 76)

Achievements by yesterday's scholars should be *read* in view of their periods and then *reread* within the context of today. In this way, they can be incorporated in the progress made by contemporary researchers whose proposals can be expanded by those who came before, as long as the former can be placed within the theoretical scope of their specific work.

As we have already observed, any tendency to opt exclusively for one theory, to the detriment of another, will be transformed into a process which is biased and reductionist by nature, and which will only serve to impede the scientific research that investigates human development in its many facets.

## REFERENCES


Cole, M. (1979). Epilogue: A portrait of Luria. In A. R. Luria, *The making of mind* (pp. 189-225). Cambridge, MA: Harvard University Press.

Ferreiro, E. (1994). Luria e o desenvolvimento da escrita na criança [Luria and the development of child's writing]. *Cadernos de Pesquisa, 88*, 72–77.

Ferreiro, E., & Palacio, M.G. (1987). Resumo da discussão [Abstract of the discussion]. In *Os processos de lei-tura e escrita [In processes of reading and writing]* (pp. 268-273). Porto Alegre, Brazil: Artes Médicas.

Ferreiro, E., & Teberosky, A. (1982). *Literacy before schooling*. Exeter, NH: Heinemann.

Gelb, I. (1982). *História de la escritura [History of writing]* (2nd ed.). Madrid, Spain: Alianza Editorial, S.A.

Lemos, C.T.G. (1986). Interacionismo e aquisição de linguagem [Interactionism and language acquisition]. Unpublished paper, State University of Campinas.

Luria, A.R. (1988a). O desenvolvimento da escrita na criança [The development of child's writing]. In L.S. Vygotsky et al., *Linguagem, desenvolvimento e aprendizagem [Language, development and learning]* (2nd ed.) (pp. 143-189). São Paulo, Brazil: Icóne-EDUSP.

Luria A.R. (1988b). A psicologia esperimental e o desenvolvimento infantil [Experimental psychology and child development]. In L.S. Vygotsky, et al., *Linguagem, desenvolvimento e aprendizagem [Language, development and learning]* (2nd ed.) (pp. 85-102). São Paulo, Brazil: Icóne-EDUSP.

Luria, A.R. (1979). *The making of mind*. Cambridge, MA: Harvard University Press.

Oliveira, M.K. (1993). *Vygotsky: Learning and development, a sociohistorical process*. São Paulo, Brazil: Scipione.

Piaget, J. (1981). Comentários sobre las observaciones críticas de Vygotsky [Comments about Vygotsky's critical observations. In L. S. Vygotsky, *Pensamiento y lenguaje* (pp. 199-215). Buenos Aires: La Pleyade.

Rocco, M.T.F. (1990). Acesso ao mundo da escrita [Access to the world of writing: The parallel roads of Luria and Ferreiro]. *Cadernos de Pesquisa, 75*, 25–33.

Vygotsky, L.S. (1984). *A formação social da mente [Mind in society]*. São Paulo, Brazil: Martins Fontes.

Vygotsky, L.S. (1988). Aprendizagem e desenvolvimento intelectual na idade escolar [Learning and development in school age]. In L.S. Vygotsky et al., *Linguagem, desenvolvimento e aprendizagem [Language, development and learning]* (2nd ed.) (pp. 103-117). São Paulo, Brazil: Icone-EDUSP.

chapter 3

# Educational Tendencies in the Beginning of Reading and Writing Instruction*

Berta P. de Braslavsky
Buenos Aires, Argentina

"Children should be taught the written language, not the writing of letters." (L.S. Vygotsky, 1979, p. 170)

## INTRODUCTION: A PANORAMIC VIEW OF BEGINNING READING AND WRITING INSTRUCTION IN THE LATIN AMERICAN REALITY

Literacy policy was closely related to the independence of the Latin American countries at the beginning of the nineteenth century and later to their internal organization and development. Particularly in the Río de la Plata region (today Uruguay and Argentina), the independence leaders adopted the ideas of the democratic revolutions in Europe, combated the ignorance of the colonial period and attempted to establish schools to teach the people to read and write. Following a long period of anarchy, the most influential statesmen created, from the last decades of the century onwards, the triology "schools, libraries, teacher training schools." Some, such as Sarmiento in Argentina and José Pedro Varela in Uruguay, became personally involved in

*This essay was written in 1992.

the teaching of reading and its methods. From their innovations "the great debate" evolved (Braslavsky, 1962).

The present reality contradicts nineteenth century optimism. Sociologists of education (Rama, 1980) demonstrate the existence of external variables associated with the degree of insertion in international markets, which enable us to explain the substantial differences in rate of literacy among the different Latin American countries. The situation is becoming progressively worse since countries which were in the vanguard in the middle of this century, in particular Argentina, show a notable decline in the statistics.

## QUALITATIVE ASPECTS

Few studies of the qualitative aspects of beginning reading and writing instruction are known; among them is that carried out in the Proyecto Desarrollo y Educación de América Latina y el Caribe (Development and Education Project for Latin America and the Caribbean) (Braslavsky, 1981) and that by the International Reading Association (I.R.A.) in 1982 (unpublished).

The view of Argentina that follows can be considered representative of what is occurring in other Latin American countries where the indicators analyzed could present even more negative characteristics. The Ministry of Education recently carried out a comparative study of curricular designs—on the basis of documentation, rather than the "true curriculum"—of the 24 districts of the country (Ministerio de Educación, DEIP, 1992). Concerning the realm of presented objectives of the curriculae, in 40% of the districts the goal of teaching reading and writing appears as part of the documentation for the area of language; in 32% these objectives can be inferred from the general objectives for the first grade; in one district specific guiding principles are presented; and two lack any reference to beginning reading and writing.

As far as approach to the reaching of objectives was concerned, in most cases general guidelines of a methodological type are given. In three districts, the global method is favored, and in seven, the generative theme (synthetic-analytic) is favored. In 52% the choice is left up to the teacher "to avoid coercion" and "favor the interests and needs of the children." In the provinces of Buenos Aires and San Luis the designs "consider process rather than methodology," in accordance with psychogenesis. In the municipality of the city of Buenos Aires (MCBA) and in the province of Córdoba teachers are offered support through self-action units for reflection and update.

It should be clarified that in *at least* the 52% of the cases where teachers are free to choose, debates are carried out in great confusion. The older teachers, who are in the minority, received their training in the teaching of reading and writing in high-school-level teacher training schools. The others received their degrees in the university-level teacher education courses which replaced the training schools several decades ago. In the latter, only one unit, offered during one month by the program "Didactics of Language," is dedicated to beginning reading and writing, and practice teaching is rarely performed.

We can observe the appearance of two tendencies which are the exception. One is based on research by Emilia Ferreiro, in conformity with psychogenesis. The other calls attention to the autodidactic units elaborated for the correspondence courses conducted between 1985 and 1989, the contents of which were the responsibility of the present author.

Some information on the application of Whole Language, based on the work of K. Goodman, was presented in the Third Latin American Congress on Reading and Writing held by the I.R.A. in Buenos Aires in 1991, but it was limited to specific cases in some cities. We shall concern ourselves with the pedagogical origins of Emilia Ferreiro's research and, subsequently, with the didactic alternative implemented in schools of the city of Buenos Aires.

## PEDAGOGICAL ORIGINS OF EMILIA FERREIRO'S RESEARCH

Because Piaget's genetic epistemology serves as the framework of Emilia Ferreiro's research, her basic concepts obviously coincide with those of her illustrious teacher. Many pedagogical experiences have owed their inspiration to these same concepts, have been widely disseminated, and have also been analyzed and debated by researchers of world renown. For our purposes, we will attempt to analyze some of the concepts utilized by the author in relation to the topic with which we are concerned.

### Endogenous Nature of the Construction of Writing and the Cultural Object

From the beginning, Emilia Ferreiro's research tends to demonstrate that the child's first written products are endogenous. No adult could have taught him the first hypotheses (of name, quality, quantity), and those relative to the parts of the word (presyllabic, syllabic-alphabetic, alphabetic) which follow owe their existence to cognitive conflict, according to what is known as the principle of equilibration (Ferreiro & Teberosky, 1979).

Nevertheless, while writing is the result of an "internal construction" "originating with the child" which is produced in a psychogenetically ordered sequence, at the starting point the presence of the cultural object "writing" is needed. The authors of the book cited said that "knowledge is constructed from the cognizant subject and the object of knowledge, where the object serves as an opportunity for the development of knowledge" (p. 45).

This relationship of subject to object appears throughout the entire work of Emilia Ferreiro as a difficult contradiction to resolve. She postulates the difference between "conceptualization" and "perception" and arrives at the conclusion that, although the conceptualizations were not learned through environmental influences, without the material existence of writing the children could not reflect on it (Ferreiro & Teberosky, 1981). The epistemological problem, which arises between a subject who actively constructs knowledge and his passive object, discovers a solution in "the informant," who offers the subject information on the conventions of writing—the names of the letters, direction, capitalization—, but does not interfere with the structuring of the system. In this way, individual variability can be explained when we consider differences in the students' social origins.

## The School and Writing as Passive Object

The first consequence of this solution is the influence of the "environment or surroundings of reading and writing instruction" which permits some children to receive information that is not received by "those who grow up in illiterate families or in homes with low levels of literacy" (Ferreiro, 1989, p. 4). Emilia Ferreiro claims that the school does not recognize these differences; within the much-criticized "formal egalitarianism," this has been and continues to be the case.

Furthermore, she accuses the school because "during the course of the centuries," writing has been undergoing change and "from social object it has been transformed into a purely school-related object" (p. 4). While it is true, as many studies show, that "school culture" is unaware of the social aims and functions of the written language, this matter can be analyzed from other perspectives. Cultural anthropology demonstrates that, when in the far-distant past the written sign (cuneiform) began to be utilized in social transactions, it was so closely associated with power that it was necessary to create schools to train "scribes" (Cole, 1990) which, we know, were elitist and hermetic. Beginning with its creation as an institution of popular education at the end of the eighteenth century, the public school produced a socialization of writing by encouraging written expression which replaced the oral and visual codes used earlier in theater, the circus, or pantomime as more or less informal agents of popular education. The public school created a public reader who, in turn, stimulated the printing industry and gave rise to a radical change in the circulation of culture (Zilberman, 1985). The historical perspective permits us to comprehend the social and political conditioning factors in the changes in the school, just as the social and, above all, political perspective explains the lack of homogeneity in reading and writing instruction. The "school" is not a metaphysical entity that always remains the same.

She also criticizes the school because, by not permitting the child to interact with writing—which is treated as a passive object in an attitude of blind respect for form and orthography—less privileged children will become reproducers of strange signs. Those at a higher level had already begun to learn to read and write earlier, because they had had the opportunity to come into contact with, to interact with, the written language.

To simply interact, to come into contact? In this case, all children could spontaneously learn how to read and write: in the lettered environment of the large cities, or if this environment were extended to the school as proposed by "Whole Language." The most current research on emergency literacy, while recognizing the active role of children who precociously learn to read, also reveals the role played by the parents through their demonstrations of the purposes and pleasure of reading and the practice of writing (Teale & Sulzby, 1989).

## Teaching and the Role of the Teacher

In a study conducted in the schools of Mexico (Ferreiro, 1983), it was proposed to find out whether or not children who start school with preliterate types of conceptualization will continue through primary school "with the same progression followed by children before entering school ... in spite of the methods and procedures which attempt to lead them directly to the alphabetic system of writing." In addition to other interesting evidence on the 38% which skip the syllabic and presyllabic levels, it demonstrates that half of the population that enters at presyllabic levels does not reach the alphabetic level.

Without questioning the universality of the levels of conceptualization, she asks, under the *current circumstances* (author's italics), "what would occur if we managed to change the teachers', as well as the educational psychologists' conceptual schematizations?" (Ferriero, 1983).

More recently she says that, according to her research, "children are easily taught to read and write; it is the adults who have rendered the literacy process difficult" (1989, p. 3). We know that this is a position typical of the doctrine upon which such studies are based: Instruction only introduces adult forms of thinking, which enter into conflict with those of the children and interfere with or supplant them.

Although speaking of preschool, Emilia Ferreiro passes the following judgment: "It is not necessary to teach but it is necessary to allow the child to learn" (1989, p. 7) and she insists that the "only way" to allow someone to learn—whether child or adult—is "to permit him to enter into contact, to interact with (that) the object."

Since her earliest work, the author has manifested an interest in establishing the necessary distance between that which is taught and that which is learned. This dissociation, characteristic of the psychological models (Gimeno Sacristán, 1985), not only ignores the theory of teaching but also subordinates teaching to the theories of learning.

Paradoxically, in the psychological models subordinated to the paradigm focused on the child, "the most didactic formulations focus on the teacher herself" (Gimeno Sacristán, 1985, p. 107), implicitly limiting teaching "to the manner in which teachers have utilized the theory of learning... and say explicitly what teachers need to do, because that is what they do" While in her earliest work, the author saw the teacher as merely an informant, in the most recent she makes it clear that "knowledge of the psychogenesis of literacy certainly does not involve remaining static until the following level appears" (Ferreiro, 1990a). In the "literacy environment" (for a long time now, the environment of reading) the teacher can provide information in diverse direct or indirect manners, stimulate or avoid conflicts, and stimulate exchanges among the children in order to comprehend how they are thinking and evolving. It is not the "pedagogy of waiting."

"In my opinion," she says, "it is necessary to think about school situations in terms of literacy environments and not of teaching methods (as has traditionally been the case)" (Ferreiro, 1990a, p. 24). She does not recognize differences among the methods elaborated throughout the history of teaching (Braslavsky, 1985), nor does she bear in mind experiences such as those of Olga Cossetini, Jesualdo, Luis Iglesias, and many other teachers in Latin America, according to whom not all the so-called methods have been simply "accumulative information processes" (Ferreiro, 1989, p. 5).

Educational research demonstrates the relativity of "method" in the covariance of factors which intervene in the highly complex realm of education. But method cannot be identified with "teaching." It is legitimate to criticize the "new materials" or the "new tests" which commercialize beginning reading and writing instruction. But it is an exaggeration to label all of the "pedagogical gadgets" as behavioristic, thereby implicitly disqualifying all of teaching.

The theories of teaching, elaborated within the framework of the theory of education, do not respond precisely to behaviorism. (See, among many others: Stenhouse, 1984; Gimeno Sacristán & Perez Gomez, 1982; Gimeno Sacristán, 1985; Gallimore & Tharp, 1990; and Coll Salvador, 1990.) The culpability of the adult in the difficulties of reading and writing instruction, the distinction between teaching and learning, and learning as a process of interacting with the object are among the reasons for limiting the teacher's duties.

## School Practice and the "Emilia Ferreiro Method"

Although the negation of method in benefit of "internal constructive progression" is a leitmotiv in the work of Emilia Ferreiro, the so-called "Emilia Ferreiro method" became popular just as the labeling of children as "presyllabic," "syllabic," and "alphabetic" spread. A wide variety of interpretations appeared, from confusion between the successive levels of conceptualization and the old syllabic and alphabetic methods—applied knowledgeably or naïvely to promote progression from one level to another—to interaction with written material which relied on the spontaneous evolution of conceptual levels. Many teachers have acclaimed the application of psychogenesis or the "Emilia Ferreiro method" after taking a brief course, sometimes limited to only 2 day courses.

In order to avoid passing judgment on random data, it is advisable to turn to the papers of the Latin American meeting which took place in Mexico in October of 1987. Emilia Ferreiro, the coordinator, considers its primary characteristic to be the unanimity of all the participants "upon attempting to use the recent discoveries regarding the genesis of the written language in the educational context" (1990b, p. 10). On bearing witness to the discussions, she considers "that there is still much to discuss in order to construct an alternative pedagogy which is coherent with psychological knowledge, with the ideological commitment assumed, and which takes into consideration the educational traditions of each country or region" (p. 14).

Although it is acknowledged in the introduction that "the participants may exhibit notable indicators of success in their actions" (Ferreiro, 1990b, p. 14), a reading of the debate demonstrates many doubts and questions. We can observe that answers are lacking for educational topics as important as planning, evaluation, and the very definition of literacy (as set forth by Clotilde Pontecorvo). Nor can we find answers for aspects of the process when, for instance, we ask why they are alphabetic in writing but not in reading (Grossi, in Ferreiro, 1990b, p. 69). In some cases we recognize that "psychological research is possibly always behind with respect to the requirements of the school" and "that it is not a question of copying what psychology is doing, but rather, of requesting more information from psychology in order to know how and at what moment *to intervene to promote development*" (Teberosky, in Ferreiro, 1990b, p. 14, author's italics). "We must continue researching the pedagogical aspects supported by this knowledge.... which are not *the* pedagogy" (Gomez Palacio, in Ferreiro, 1990b, p. 74). The questioning of pedagogical intervention (Kaufman, in Ferreiro, 1990b, p. 14), dictation to children as "language experiences" (L.E.A.) (Abaurre, in Ferreiro, 1990b, p. 116), and metalinguistic activities (Proyecto Recife, p. 168) continues.

In the previously cited publication (1990a), Emilia Ferreiro herself finally says, "Knowledge of the evolution of the system of writing does not solve any of the problems which teachers have with their class activities. Some practices become ridiculous..."

In the Third Latin American Congress on Reading and Writing of the I.R.A. (International Reading Association), she publicly discredited the so-called "methods" applied in her name. The responsibility is very great; according to information, in some countries tens of thousands of teachers and hundreds of thousands of children have been involved (Ferreiro, 1989, Appendix).

## The Curricular Orientations

In spite of the fact that the conceptual framework summarized in the previous section does not solve the teacher's problems in the class, it does acquire singular importance in the author's curricular proposal. She formulates the following objectives for the first 2 years of schooling: "Comprehension of the mode of representation of the language which corresponds to the alphabetic system of writing (thus differentiating it from mathematical writing, which corresponds to the ideographic system)"; comprehension of the social functions of writing that determine organizational differences in the written language and; generate different expectations ... in the multiple social objects bearing the written word (books, newspapers, packaging, letters, signs); comprehensive reading of texts that correspond to a variety of written records (narrative, informative, and journalistic texts; instructions; letters; messages; lists) emphasizing silent reading... ; the production of texts which recognize and utilize these diverse types of written records; and an attitude of curiosity and a lack of apprehension in relation to the written language (Ferreiro, 1989, p. 4).

The first objective has been textually quoted because I feel obliged to make some observations regarding the author's basic research. This research is concerned with the construction of the system of writing, by carrying out an analysis of the parts of the word within the classic phonemic description of alphabetic writing. But, on the one hand, it ignores the procedural aspects of reading and writing, known as the comprehension and production of texts. And, on the other, it ignores the lexical and syntactic characteristics of the written language and the discursive organization peculiar to it.

Without entering into an epistemological and methodological discussion of how the hypothesis was developed (see Smolka, 1988), one might point out that access to the alphabetic hypothesis might lead one to believe that learning to read and write consists only of discovering the correspondence between graphemes and phonemes. In the much criticized "traditional school," decodification or deciphered codification was very frequently the first step in reading and writing instruction. Classic phonemic analysis has been the basis of the phonetic methods, later surpassed by the "global" methods which take as the starting point the unit of meaning.

The author repeatedly refers to the relationship between sounds and graphic marks (Ferreiro, 1983, and others). During the entire process, the child's relationship to the object, his own construction, and the cognitive conflicts serve as the starting point for the child as he seeks correspondence until he "systematically carries out a phonetic analysis of the words he is going to write" and begins to construct writing on alphabetic foundations. According to the internal construction of the hypotheses, it would be a "conceptual" process, but one that does not address the meaning of the text.

In this manner, the first curricular objective is limited to aspects referring to the system of writing at the phonological level. How is this objective related to those that follow? How are they established from the levels of conceptualization of the psychogenetic framework? This analysis does not mean to deny the importance of the relationship between the spoken and written language in the literacy process which, moreover, responds to other requirements beyond the link between the flow of speech and that of writing.

Understandably, "phonics" has concerned many researchers (Vernon, 1971; Downing, 1979, chapters 5 and 6) and present discussions of the topic are relevant (Adams et al., 1991), in terms of the relationship that shows "the phonetic" with "the semantic" as the primary objective of the educational process, even before preschool or the first grade.

## DIDACTIC ALTERNATIVE IN THE CITY OF BUENOS AIRES

We present here the basis of a current exploratory study by the Department of Education of the Municipalidad de la ciridad de Buenos Aires

(MCBA). Then we shall analyze some of its earliest results (1990-1991). It was (and continues to be) based on a political strategy that creates a school hierarchy, and a didactic paradigm that reestablishes the status of teaching and the teacher. The sociohistorical cultural theory, with its implications for formal education, supports this strategy and this didactic paradigm. When this latter focuses on initial reading and writing instruction, this theory offers the experiences of Vygotsky and his disciples, Luria and Elkonin, and their reflections on the written language. It also incorporates empirical and theoretical antecedents by other distinguished researchers (see, for instance, Moll, 1990).

## Political Strategy and the Reestablishment of the Status of the School

The decline in the school's reputation can be explained by a quantitative and qualitative deterioration of the school system which, in Latin America and in Argentina in particular, could be observed as early as the third decade of this century. But it has received strong support from the theories of "reproduction" and "deschooling," originating in sociology and pedagogy, respectively.

Some sociologists and educators argue these theories, even while recognizing many of the criticisms of them. There are politicians in education who sound an alert with regard to the "black legend," which they consider as exaggerated as the "rose legend" of the traditional school (Filmus, 1990), and above all, as objectively and subjectively risky for its continuity and efficacy as an institution of popular education. They defend the school as the unit of an educational system that possesses programmatic contents in accordance with aims that propose to transmit socially accumulated cultural goods, not only to be assimilated, but to be shared and transformed as well.

## Didactic Model That Reestablishes the Status of Teaching and the Teacher

The psychological models, which at least in theory began to dominate didactics at the primary level, starting from the "nondirectivism" of "new education," disassociated teaching from learning with the predominance of the latter, in a movement that culminated in the theory of "constructivism."

For some time now, this asymmetric concept is being surpassed by a "new dimension of constructivism" which values the respective roles of student and teacher "in the progressive construction of meanings" shared in learning and teaching (Coll Salvador, 1990, p. 203). In this interaction, the child, the student, is the undisputed agent of the construction, but it is the teacher who, in principle, knows the meanings that she (the teacher) hopes to share (p. 204). The teacher plans her projects and classes, oriented by aims and objectives and always bearing in mind the child's mental constructions which, in turn, prompt her to make decisions in class that were not necessarily foreseen in the planning.

This relationship requires that the teacher consider the student as a whole and not as a purely cognitive subject, as a subject who constructs his knowledge not only through his socially acquired experiences and knowledge, but also and above all, by motivation—by the meaning that he attributes to the content and by his attitudes towards the school, the teacher and his schoolmates, which, in turn, are all related to the cultural and social environment.

### Vygotsky's Hypotheses and the Reestablishment of the Status of Formal Education

Vygotsky's fundamental hypotheses offer clear support for the reestablishment of the status of the school and the teacher. Contrary to Piaget's law of equilibration, which explains the endogenous development of mental operations starting with relationship to the object, Vygotsky's "law of internalization" demonstrates in what manner an interpersonal, interpsychic, external operation is transformed into an intrapersonal, intrapsychic one (Vygotsky, 1979, p. 92–94).

Interaction with the object of the construction of knowledge is replaced by the relationship between persons, between the child and the adult, who, at first, provides him with help in elaborating knowledge of the object. The active intervention of the social environment, beginning at the child's birth, explains that early childhood "is the center of the prehistory of cultural development" (Vygotsky, 1979, p. 79). The difference between spontaneous and scientific learning (Vygotsky, 1964, chap. VI), both socially acquired, the former in the home and the latter in the school with the first reflections on symbols, indicates that the school is the choice place for the acquisition of the specifically human, superior psychological processes.

The role of the teacher is scientifically interpreted in the famous concept of the Zone of Proximal Development (ZPD). Upon explaining the differences that exist between learning without assistance (at the Level of Real Development) and learning with assistance (at the Level of Potential Development), he shows the importance of the teacher's intervention. When he constructs the scaffolding (Bruner, 1988) to enable the student to progress towards the solution of more difficult problems, the teacher is participating in the maturation process until the child can carry out, consciously and on his own, tasks which earlier he could only accomplish with help. Vygotsky said that "learning awakens a series of internal developmental processes which are capable of occurring only when the child is interacting with the persons in his surroundings and in cooperation with his peer.... Once these processes have been internalized, they become part of the child's independent achievements" (Vygotsky, 1979, pp. 138–139).

In this manner, "the school years as a whole are the optimal period for the instruction of operations which require awareness and deliberate control" (Vygotsky, 1964, p. 119). Intervention by the teacher makes it easier for the child to construct his consciousness and achieve his autonomy (Bruner, 1988).

## Concepts Essential to the Acquisition of Written Language

The model used in the autodidactic materials destined for teacher training (MCBA, SICaDIS, 1985), was based on the one elaborated by John Downing as a result of his comparative research (1973). The model cited (Model 3 of the SICaDIS) acknowledges the influence on the cognitive process during initial literacy instruction of the child's experiences with the spoken and written language and his need to learn to read and write. At the same time, it acknowledges the influence of the school and its internal variables when these are coherent with the expectations held by society for this same purpose.

This model appears to be compatible with Vygotsky's concepts of the prehistory of written language and, at the same time, the scientific changes for which he strove in school teaching. It appears equally coherent with Luria's observations on the relationship between the knowledge of writing constructed before entering school and the teaching that the school offers.

## Oral and Written Language as Praxis

Wertsch considers that in today's terminology, Vygotsky's works "might be termed discourse analysis or pragmatics" (Wertsch, 1990, p. 115) and he finds connections and compatibilities with Vygotsky's contemporary, Bakhtin. Thus, the action research that we are discussing rests on theories that recognize the process of social elaboration and sociohistorical transformation of language as praxis between people and it adopts an interactive, circular (between transmitter and receiver) conception, in accordance with the characteristics of speech in each particular situation. It bears in mind the differences between out-of-school discourse and school discourse—conventional, unidirectional, restrictive, with the standard language predominating. For this reason, it emphasizes the need to promote real situations of communication in the spoken and written language. It respects and, furthermore, stimulates the dialectical variations of the students and, at the same time—by promoting interpersonal, interpsychic relations with the teacher and among peers—it facilitates the natural internalization of the standard language by all.

## Linguistic Awareness

We must bear in mind the linguistic awareness research, according to which the child very early achieves an empirical, spontaneous "knowledge of action" of the grammar of the language and the importance of this knowledge in anticipating the acquisition of the written language. Among the many known studies, the already classic ones by Liberman et al. (1974) on syllabic and phonemic analysis in early childhood stand out. Those that demonstrate the ease with which the small child recognizes syllables, but not phonemes, are very significant. Elkonin had already noticed that between 2 and 3 years of age, a child can distinguish between two words that differ by only one phoneme, but his analysis is incomplete and confusing. That is why he prepared games to facilitate research with the "phonematic ear" and to perfect the child's knowledge of the structure of the spoken word (Elkonin, 1973). Following their own research, Liberman and his collaborators declared that, "like Elkonin, we should think that it is possible and desirable to develop this ability by methods of adequate training" (1974). Other researchers demonstrated the effects that some programs to stimulate phonologic awareness in preschoolers have on their subsequent learning of reading and writing (Lundberg, Frost, & Petersen, 1988).

## Differences Between "External" and "Internal" Language

Vygotsky considers that "the relationship between thought and word is a process" (Vygotsky, 1964, p. 139), "a continuous coming and going," an inner flow that takes place on various levels, and he reports that his studies reveal "the need to distinguish two levels of language: its internal, meaningful and semantic aspect and the external or phonetic one, which, while forming a true unity, have their own laws of movement." He considers this unity to be complex and that "specific events in the child's linguistic development indicate independent movement in the semantic and phonetic spheres." These differences have been important to more clearly define the process of acquisition of the written language and to produce the pedagogical reconsiderations that Vygotsky himself initiated.

## The Written Language as a Symbolic Function of the Complex Sign System of Writing

Vygotsky's most significant contribution is considered to be his work on sign mediation (Wertsch, 1990). Included in the role that instruments played in the development of mankind, the sign's distinguishing characteristic is an orientation towards the subject (rather than the object, as with instruments), who, upon internalizing it, can carry out indirect, complex, transferable operations. At his remote origin, man utilized signs to recall, to communicate, and to register facts that served as mediators in his mental activity.

Vygotsky considers that "only by understanding the history of the evolution of signs, can we gain access to a correct solution for the psychology of writing" (1979, p. 89). He considered two forms of symbolism (or representation): one of first order, a sign system that directly represents the meaning of things or their relationships; and one of second order that represents things or their relationships indirectly with the mediation of an intermediate symbol. In games and drawing an evolution of symbolisms is produced which is initiated at the first order, moves to the second order, and returns to the first when the mediator disappears (pp. 162–171). They are the precursors of writing because in writing the same evolution of symbolisms is produced.

The first marks or signs, letters or words, acquire meaning as first-order symbols when they directly designate things or actions. In alphabetic writing, the child moves to second-order symbolism when he begins to create or utilize sign systems to represent the spoken language. Finally, he manages to do without the mediation of speech and returns to first-order symbolism because, by means of the written language, he discovers meaning directly, without the need for the intermediation of the spoken language. Thus, in the beginning, comprehension of the written language is accomplished through the spoken language but this route is abbreviated until the written language itself becomes significant.

## Pedagogical Reconsiderations

The conception of written language as a symbolic function with a social origin, the differentiation between the external and internal levels of language, and the evolution of symbolisms have given rise to pedagogical reconsiderations important for curricular development and the activities in the class.

In its first manifestation, writing appears as a motor discharge, but it cannot be considered within the line of biological development like a psychomotor function. Rather, it must be understood within the qualitatively different line of cultural development, as the result of a process of interaction with the adult. (Vygotsky, 1979, p. 78) Thus, corporal, muscular, visuo-motor readiness exercises and "requirements" or prior "skills" are not meaningful.

With regard to the differentiation and the relationship between "external" and "internal" planes, we can debate the sequence between the process of codification and decodification with which it is initiated and that of comprehension which follows. This sequence has predominated throughout the history of teaching, with the commendable exceptions of those renovators who sought comprehension and were the precursors of the discursive dimension. It is present in the great majority of curricular orientations and is now a motive of continual debate.

Vygotsky himself was concerned with the second moment in the evolution of symbolisms, "when the child moves from the drawing of objects to the drawing of language" (1979, pp. 173–174). But it concerned him as a mediative part of the process, to "lead the child to an internal comprehension of the written language," in other words, to the depth of semantics, of meaning. For that reason, he said that drawing and games should be preliminary but "the secret of teaching is the preparation and adequate organization of the complex process of transition from one symbolism to another, following this process through its most critical symbolisms" (p. 178).

## Teacher Strategies in the Classroom

Other considerations are important for the teacher's strategies, planning, and decisions in the classroom. They concern those characteristics peculiar to the acquisition of written language, which are different from those of the acquisition of oral language.

According to Vygotsky, when the child begins to speak, he does so to request, to ask, or to respond to someone physically present. On the other hand, in order to produce meaningful writing, whether destined for an interlocutor who is not present or for no one in particular, a new and unusual situation is created. He has little motivation to learn. "He does not feel the need to do so and he has only a vague idea of its usefulness" (1964, p. 114).

Essentially, the child has to be acquainted with what he is going to learn, just as the teacher needs to know what she is going to teach. In order to develop the intention to write, everything seems to indicate that he must be motivated externally, above all by making him understand in practice the meaning of the written language, its aims and its functions.

However, our experience shows that the motivation roused by the teacher should be based on the child's internal motives. In schools with scarce resources, certain external stimuli show different values for each student, depending on his specific living conditions: whether the origin of his family is urban or rural, his uprooting by migrations, or the insecurity resulting from his marginal existence. Differences also exist between the acquisition of oral language and the acquisition of writing in relation to the reflective activity that should occur in the latter.

When the child begins to speak, he is conscious of neither the sounds he is pronouncing nor the mental operations that he is carrying out. Shortly thereafter, as already stated, he becomes conscious of the grammar and phonology of the language of his environment. While he can produce writing prematurely as an expression of the external knowledge acquired of the same, in order for it to be significant, on one hand, he needs to imagine the interlocutor not present and, on the other, it requires "the symbolization of the auditory image of the written signs" (Vygotsky, 1964, p. 113). "The abstract quality of the written language, rather than the defective development of the small muscles and other mechanical impediments, constitutes the principal obstacle." But the difficulties also originate in the syntactic differences that exist between the oral language, the internalized language, and the written language. To summarize, the abstract nature of alphabetic writing and the structural characteristics peculiar to the written language require that the child carry out a reflective, conscious activity. According to his studies, the differences between the "linguistic age of speech" and the "linguistic age of writing" are due to the fact that "the psychological functions upon which the written language is based still have not begun their development in the true sense" (p. 115).

For Vygotsky, the "linguistic age of writing" does not mean that learning begins in the school. On the contrary, he clearly said that "every type of learning the child encounters in the school always has a previous history... which only near-sighted psychologists could ignore" (1979, p. 130). Pursuing this idea upon Vygotsky's suggestion, Luria carries out his introductory research, which is published in this volume. In it, the psychological importance of the change in sign stands out in the translation of the primary sign which "signals the '*presence*' of a new form, into a sign which uncovers a specific *content* in the step from *sign-stimulus to sign-symbol*" (Luria, 1987, p. 52). In other words, the importance of the content, which corresponds to the profound, "internal" plane of writing, is present in the "roots of the process of writing."

## The Discursive Dimension

An internal comprehension of the written language necessarily leads to an approach to the same in its discursive dimension. Vygotsky said that "children have been taught to draw letters and form words, but they haven't been taught the written language" (1979, p. 159). It's obvious that the "written language" is not the grapheme, or the syllable, or the word. It is the language as a whole and in this particular aspect I personally agree with Whole Language; but, I do not agree with K. Goodman's concepts of a formal education, stripped of its objectives and contents, where the child learns by immersion with a limited participation by the teacher, upon which it is based. I believe that he has interpreted Vygotsky out of context when he says that "it is necessary that letters become elements of the children's lives in the same way that language is. In the same way that children learn to speak, they should learn to read and write" (Vygotsky, 1979, p. 177). To assume that these lines justify learning by immersion (the immersion view—Goodman and Goodman, 1990) is to ignore the law of internalization and Vygotsky's research and reflections on reflective, conscious learning, as well as his advice on teaching. (Vygotsky, 1979, pp. 175–178)

Although it is true that the child can achieve meaning only through discourse, research subsequent to Vygotsky's has called attention to the obstacles that hinder the child in his access to comprehension of the text. Among these, some from the field of learning difficulties, have called attention to the impossibility of establishing an association between symbols and sounds by means of memory (Vernon, 1971), or to the disturbances or deficiencies in one or more aspects of linguistic functioning (Vellutino, 1982). Others have stressed an ignorance of the meaning of the written language resulting from an ignorance of its purposes and functions (Reid, 1966), and we could cite many others.

The environment for reading and writing instruction is a condition that is absolutely necessary, but not sufficient. The child should have access to a library and materials that permit him to use newspapers, magazines, pamphlets, and guidebooks. But he needs more than this. Luria said that the teacher should rely on the knowledge that the child brings with him to school and that the "primitive period of children's writing is especially interesting" but that "nevertheless ... between the early stages in the learning of writing and its full mastery lies an important zone which is very significant" and "it is found at the intersection of the forms of primitive recording of a prehistoric nature ... and the new, cultural, organically-introduced forms" (Luria, 1987, p. 55).

The action research that we conducted in the city of Buenos Aires is concerned precisely with this zone, in its early stages during the first 2 years. The data obtained between 1991 and 1992 suggest some hypotheses to be proved by subsequent, more rigorous research. And they suggest objectives that relate to the comprehension of the symbolism of the sign system of writing. In the first year, the majority approach the threshold of mastery of the written language, "the most elevated form of language," which follows oral language and internalized language. Some need several months or a year longer. With some luck, they will be literate upon completing primary school, in accordance with the cultural requirements of reading and writing instruction of this era in which we are now living.

## IN THE SCHOOL: AN ORGANIZED AND FLEXIBLE PLAN

### Background

The project, which takes place under the Department of Education of the city of Buenos Aires, goes back to a debate that developed in 1982 around the 1981 Curricular Design imposed by the military dictatorship (Braslavsky, 1983). When constitutional government was reestablished in 1984, the Department of Education of the municipality of the city of Buenos Aires gave priority to beginning reading and writing, put into practice a research project (MCBA, 1984), and implemented a massive teacher information and refresher program through the Extension Service for Educational Innovations (Servicio de Innovaciones Educativas a Distancia, SICaDIS), with the elaboration of seven autodidactic units (MCBA, 1985-1989). At the same time, training was observed through the mediation of 30 tutors (coordinators) who were at the service of the teachers and who met with them monthly.

In 1989, a new administration in the Department of Education of the MCBA intended to bring the formal curriculum closer to the real curriculum by proposing to follow a cohort that would enter the first grade in 1990 and would remain with the same teacher in 1991. For this reason, action research on "the effects of teaching on beginning reading and writing instruction" was carried out under the authority of the person in charge of contents in the SICaDIS. Some of the teachers who acted as coordinators, together with others who were their students, were voluntarily incorporated as teachers in 18 first grades of the 14 districts involved in the research. In this manner, an incidental sample took shape in which three social levels (middle, middle low, and low) can be distinguished, according to the criterion of unsatisfied basic needs.

As put in practice, two fundamental aspects of the project stand out:

1. the socialization and interaction of the teachers (whose training is based on common principles), who function as teachers and researchers, by coordinating their activity weekly without affecting their personal initiatives; and

2. the continual analysis of the students' production in writing and reading, which is chosen as the unit of analysis.

**Observations on Contents and Activities**

Once the objective of achieving comprehension of the symbolism of the signs of writing is clearly established, a combination of "motivational," "cognitive," and "linguistic" actions is developed, including the metalinguistic ones that are generally superimposed and applied to a variety of curricular and chance contents. They are not curricular guidelines; they are not carried out as readiness exercises; they are not developed in chronological order. The teacher bears them in mind and implements them through her strategies which are dialectically combined with the student's strategies.

In an environment rich in written language—with reading for listening pleasure; consultation of the library, newspapers, and magazines for information; multiple experiences for the purpose of communication; maintaining written records for future recall; and experimentation with all the functions of written language—the teachers utilize the "language experiences" conceived in Freinet's Free Text Method and the Language Experiences Approach (L.E.A.). As we know, in both cases children are encouraged to think about individual and group experiences. To encourage them to express verbally what they are thinking, the teacher or a more advanced child writes what the child said (this same child may or may not dictate) and then the child reads with the other children what was written. He may then copy it, if he chooses.

In these experiences, thought is related to oral language, and oral language to written language. It is one of the means of traversing the second moment in the evolution of symbolisms. Numerous other occasions for experiencing this relationship are incorporated, either intentionally or unintentionally, when the teacher relies on her own creativity and uses to her advantage the creativity of the children.

There is some interesting, but not yet completely evaluated, written evidence on the children's strategies in this second moment, when the spoken language acts as the mediator of comprehension. As has been observed more frequently among children of humble origins, when they want to write, many children cannot verbally structure what they want to say by themselves; they appeal to the teacher to formulate it for them and when she does so, the children write it. Another stage follows in which the children whisper, "they dictate to themselves," until finally they write in a "readable" manner, directly for the reader, without the mediation of oral language. Many questions remain about the relationship between oral language, inner language, and written language in this process.

## Construction of an Access to Meaning Scale

For the purpose of realizing a continual analysis of access to meaning, it was decided that a writing test should be given twice monthly. These were to be included in individual files, along with data on the child such as his place of birth, his schooling, as well as that of his father and mother, and the sociocultural level of the family.

Bearing in mind the discursive dimension of the teaching, it was decided to induce the children to write a text by using instructions that reflected the children's familial and social experiences, reading stories, and other possibilities. Only one was the same for all the first grades: "Write to the principal, inviting her to visit you." Other examples are: "What do you imagine your grandfather's pipe can draw in the air?" and "Write a short letter to the World Cup players."

These instructions must have seemed strange to the small children (whose average age was 6), but the great majority produced graphic, although disconcertingly different, responses. After three tests, it was decided that the production should be codified and the 41 items that were obtained were ranked in four categories of increasing difficulty:

A. Absence of graphic gestures; drawings; undifferentiated lines; a mixture of unconventional signs; numbers; letters.
B. Printed or sometimes cursive letters in either continuous or discontinuous lines, or in a discursive format; unreadable.
C. Printed or cursive letters, either continuous or discontinuous, with incomplete readability, although indicating progress.
D. Continuous or lexically differentiated text; increasing richness of meaning; more extensive and with greater readability.

When the scale and its graphs were empirically constructed, they were found to correspond to Vygotsky's evidence on operations with signs as "a series of qualitative transformations" (1979, p. 78), where each of these transformations receives the necessary conditions from the previous state and prepares for the following. In no case did the most primitive lines such as the motor discharge or spiral scribble appear. In category A, we find indications of sociocultural expressions such as linearity, and letters mixed with other signs and lines appear. In B, letters become independent and are presented in diverse formal manifestations of the system of writing. In C, printed and cursive letters appear in the same format as in the preceding category, but with increasing attempts to produce meaning. These attempts rely on the phoneme-grapheme relationship and provide access to category D, where "readable" texts of varying length and complexity are grouped.

We can clearly distinguish the difference between categories A and B, on the one hand, and categories C and D, on the other. Pursuing Luria's thinking, the transition would express the step from external and preinstrumental knowledge of the system of writing to its use for the expression of meaningful contents. In the last two categories, the students move progressively from sign-stimulus to sign-symbol (Luria, 1987, p. 52). In D, they would clearly be found in the symbolic phase which, according to Luria, is the culminating point in the prehistory of children's writing.

Thus, the empirically constructed categories could be classified in the following manner:

A. No writing or sketches independent of the biological origin of graphomotor production. The first indications of access to external knowledge of writing and its signs.
B. External, noninstrumental knowledge of the system of writing.
C. Access to instrumental use which makes possible the symbolism of writing.
D. Symbolic, meaningful writing, as a complex form of cultural behavior.

These categories have been illustrated in various publications (Braslavsky, 1991a and b; Braslavsky, Natali, & Rosen, 1991; Braslavsky, 1992).

**Analysis of the Process of Movement From One Category to Another**

By means of this scale, the process is analyzed with the tests taken on March 23, 2 weeks after the beginning of classes; July 7; and November 8, the end of the school year. Those students who repeat the school year are omitted and followed separately.

Considering the overall results for the 323 students, on the first test the preinstrumental categories (A+B) (95+144) total 74.22%, and the symbolic categories (C+D) (52+23) total 23.29%. So, it is acknowledged that, in the schools participating in the research, the children start school with knowledge of the written language but show considerable heterogeneity, which also appears in the comparison of the schools: In less than half of the first grades, children are classified in Category D and in four of them only Categories A and B are recorded.

The results obtained on July 7, 3 months later, show surprising changes. The instrumental categories (7+54) add up to 20.7%, and the symbolic ones (101+108) total 70.4%. A quantitative inversion has been produced at the level of access to meaning. Finally, in the data recorded for November 7 no student is registered in Category A; the (C+D) symbolic categories add up to 88%. A case-by-case study of the 6.7% that remain in Category B (21 students) proves that all of them suffer from some severe individual problem or from extreme marginality (Braslavsky, 1991b, p. 48; 1992, p. 76). However, they were passed to the second grade with the same teacher. (For an illustration of the categories, please refer to the tables and the graphs in the bibliography cited previously.)

### Probable Associations Between Categories and Parents' Socioeducational Levels

Taking the precautions required by the incidental nature of the sample, a statistical study was carried out to analyze the probable association between the level of schooling of the parents and the distribution of categories. After analyzing the data from the beginning and the end of the year, we are unable to reach any generalizable conclusions, but can make the following observations: (a) the level of formal education of the father and, to a greater extent, that of the mother, was more influential in cases where literacy had already been attained before the child entered school; and (b) at the end of the year, the significant association diminishes in relation to the mother's schooling, and the father's schooling is no longer significant.

### Hypothesis on the Effects of Teaching

We do not intend to reach any conclusions from the data obtained. However, this exploratory research permits us to formulate a hypothesis about the effects of teaching, at least in the short run, based on two types of evidence: (a) the movement from one category to another, from the observed heterogeneity at the beginning of 1990 to the tendency towards uniformity at the highest level at the end of the year; and (b) the students' accomplishments indicate that they had overcome the educational inequalities of their parents, their family backgrounds, and their social environment.

## THE FUTURE OUTLOOK

Having achieved a symbolic, instrumental knowledge of the different aims of the written language, the children show an interest in reading; they enjoy it, they utilize it appropriately for obtaining information, and they use their ability to communicate and to express, without restrictions, their thoughts and emotions. Their written product attracts our attention, above all for its breadth and quality, although its content is unorganized, like chattering. This product is "readable" but is generally not expressed in well-defined, related sentences, although as a whole, its content is coherent with the proposed theme. In the majority of the cases, we still observe expressions from oral language and problems with spelling. They still have not mastered the syntax of the written language. This mastery creates new challenges for the relationship between teaching and learning.

In 1991, in the second grade, the teachers exchanged, compared, and debated numerous resources that favored student reflection on his own product and about different discourses regarding literary, disciplinary, and other contents. Group and individual criticism was frequently offered, based on the errors made by each one.

While continuing to pursue reading instruction, in accordance with the techniques applied during the previous year (Braslavsky, 1991a, p. 58; 1992, p. 86), a bimonthly collection of writing samples was conducted as well. A considerable body of material was gathered which will be processed with the assistance of linguistic professionals, with the prospect of didactically elaborating the observations.

In 1991, three documents were produced for internal circulation that are made available to whomever wants to voluntarily and creatively extend the procedures tested. We have begun to publish teacher accounts of the original initiatives that explain the "how to" in the classroom (Braslavsky, 1992). The project is currently being reformulated as a means of initiating its progressive expansion in the system of primary education of the city of Buenos Aires.

## REFERENCES

Adams, M. J. et al. (1991). Begining to read: A critique by literacy professionals and response by Marilyn Jagger Adams. *Reading Teacher, 44* (6), 370–395.

Braslavsky, B. P. (1962). *La querella de los métodos en la enseñanza de la lectura [The methodological struggle in the teaching of reading]*. Buenos Aires, Argentina: Editorial Kapelusz.

Braslavsky, B. P. (1981). La lectura en la escuela de América Latina [Reading in Latin American school]. In *Proyecto Desarrollo y Educación en América Latina y el Caribe*. UNESCO-ECLA-UNDP (File 17).

Braslavsky, B. P. (1983). La lectoescritura en el ciclo básico de un diseño curricular [Reading and writing in the elementary levels of a curricular design]. *Lectura y Vida, 4* (2), 29–33; *4* (3), 31–36; *4* (4), 25–32. Buenos Aires, Argentina: International Reading Association.

Braslavsky, B. P. (1985). El método: Panacea, negación o pedagogía? [Method: Panacea, negation or pedagogy?] *Lectura y Vida, 6* (4), 4–9. Buenos Aires, Argentina: International Reading Association.

Braslavsky, B. P. (1991a). Entorno, escuela, maestro, alumno [Environment, school, teacher, pupil]. Paper presented at the 3rd Congreso Latinoamericano de Lectura. *Lectura y Vida*. Buenos Aires, Argentina: I.R.A

Braslavsky, B. P. (1991b). *La escuela puede [School can do it]*. Buenos Aires, Argentina: Aique Grupo Editor.

Braslavsky, B. P. (1991c). La lectoescritura inicial: Ensayo de un paradigma didáctico [First reading and writing steps: Practice of a teaching paradigm]. *Revista Latinoamericana de Innovaciones Educativas, 3* (4), 89–150. Buenos Aires, Argentina: Organización de los Estados Americanos and Ministerio de Educación y Justicia.

Braslavsky, B. P. (1992). *La escuela puede [School can do it]* (rev. ed.). Buenos Aires, Argentina: Aique Grupo Editor.

Braslavsky, B. P., Natali, N., & Rosen, N. (1991). Alfabetización emergente y escuela [Emerging literacy and school]. *Lectura y Vida, 12* (1), 10–19.

Bruner, J. (1988). *Realidad mental y mundos posibles [Actual minds, possible worlds]*. Barcelona, Spain: Ed. Gedisa.

Cole, M. (1990). Cognitive development and formal schooling: The evidence from cross cultural research. In L. C. Moll (Ed.), *Vygotsky and education. Instructional implications of sociohistorical psychology*. Cambridge, MA: Cambridge University Press.

Coll Salvador, C. (1990). *Aprendizaje escolar y construcción del conocimiento [School learning and the building of knowledge]*. Buenos Aires, Argentina: Paidós editor.

Downing, J. (1973). *Comparative reading*. New York: MacMillan.

Downing, J. (1979). *Reading and reasoning*. Great Britain: W. R. Chambers.

Elkonin, D. B. (1973). USSR. In J. Downing, *Comparative reading*. Chapter 24.

Ferreiro, E. (1983). Procesos de adquisición de la lengua escrita dentro del contexto escolar [Processes for the acquisition of the written language in the school environment]. *Lectura y Vida, 4* (2), 11–18, Buenos Aires, Argentina: I.R.A.

Ferreiro, E. (1989). *El proyecto principal de educación y alfabetización de niños: Un análisis cualitativo [The main project for children's education and literacy: A qualitative analysis]* (Informational bulletin). Buenos Aires, Argentina: Aique Grupo Editor, 17.

Ferreiro, E. (1990a). Literacy development: Psychogenesis. In Y. M. Goodman (Ed.), *How children construct literacy. Piagetian perspectives*. U.S.A.: International Reading Association.

Ferreiro, E. (1990b). *Los hijos del analfabetismo [Children of illiteracy]*. Mexico: Ed. Siglo XXI.

Ferreiro, E., & Teberovsky, A. (1979). *Los sistemas de escritura en el desarrollo del niño [Writing systems in child development]*. Mexico: Ed. Siglo XXI.

Ferreiro, E., & Teberovsky, A. (1981). La comprensión del sistema de escritura. Construcciones originales del niño e información específica de los adultos [The understanding of the writing system. Children's original construction and adults' specific information]. *Lectura y Vida, 2* (1), 6–14. Buenos Aires, Argentina: I.R.A.

Filmus, D. (1990, August 3). No desvalorizar la escuela pública [Let's not underrate public school]. Buenos Aires, Argentina: *Diario Clarín.*

Gallimore, R., & Tharp, R. (1990). Teaching mind in society: Teaching, schooling and literate discourse. In L. C. Moll (Ed.), *Vygotsky and education. Instructional implications of sociohistorical psychology.* Cambridge, MA: Cambridge University Press.

Gimeno Sacristan, J. (1985). *Teoría de la enseñanza y desarrollo del currículo [Theory of teaching and curriculum development].* Madrid, Spain: Ediciones Anaya.

Gimeno Sacristan, J., & Perez Gomez, A. (1982). *La enseñanza, su teoría y su práctica [Teaching, theory and practice].* Madrid, Spain: AKAL.

Goodman, Y. M., & Goodman, K. S. (1990). Vygotsky in a whole language perspective. In L. C. Moll (Ed.), *Vygotsky and education. Instructional implications of sociohistorical psychology.* Cambridge, MA: Cambridge University Press.

Liberman, I. Y., Shankweiler, D., Fisher, F. W., & Carter, B. (1974). Explicit Syllable and Phoneme Segmentation in the young child. *Journal of Experimental Child Psychology, 18*, 201–212.

Lundberg, I., Frost, J., & Petersen, Ole-P. (1988). Effects of an extensive program for stimulating phonological awareness in preschool children. *Reading Research Quarterly,* Vol. XXIII (3), 263–284, I.R.A.

Luria, A. (1987). Materiales para la génesis de la escritura en el niño [Materials for the genesis of writing in the child]. In *Biblioteca de psicología soviética.* Moscow, USSR: Progresso.

Moll, L. C. (Ed.) (1990). *Vygotsky and education. Instructional implications of sociohistorical psychology.* Cambridge, MA: Cambridge University Press.

MCBA [Municipalidad de la Ciudad de Buenos Aires] (1984). *El diagnóstico del aprendizaje inicial de la lectoescritura [Diagnosis of elementary learning of reading and writing].* Proyecto 1.

MCBA [Municipalidad de la Ciudad de Buenos Aires] (1985–9). Servicio de Innovaciones Educativas a Distancia (SICaDIS), Units 1,2,3,4,5,6,7.

Rama, G. W. (1980). Introducción [Introduction]. In UNICEF (Ed.), *Educación y sociedad en América Latina.* Santiago de Chile.

Smolka, A. L. (1988). *A criança na fase inicial da escrita: Alfabetização como processo discursivo [The child in the fist stages of writing: Literacy as a speech process]* (2nd ed.). Campinas, Brazil: Cortes & Editoria da Unicamp.

Steinhouse, L. (1984). *Investigación y desarrollo del curriculum [Curriculum research and development].* Madrid, Spain: Ed. Morata.

Reid, J. F. (1966). Learn to think about reading. *Educational Research, 9*, 56–62.

Teale, M. H., & Sulzby, E. (1989). Emergency literacy: New perspectives. In D. Strickland & L. M. Morrow (Eds.), *Emergency literacy.* U.S.A.: International Reading Association.

Vellutino, F. R. (1982). Teorías e investigaciones en el estudio de la dislexia en la niñez [Theories and research works in the studies on child dyslexia]. In M. Condemarín (Ed.), *Teorías y técnicas para la comprensión del lenguaje escrito [Theories and techniques for the understanding of the written language]* (pp. 77-90). Chile: UNICEF y Universidad Católica de Chile.

Vernon, M. D. (1971). *Reading and its difficulties.* Cambridge, MA: Cambridge University Press.

Vygotsky, L. S. (1964). *Lenguaje y pensamiento [Language and thinking].* Buenos Aires, Argentina: Editorial Lautaro.

Vygotsky, L. S. (1979). *El desarrollo de los procesos psíquicos superiores [The development of higher mental processes].* Barcelona Spain: Ed. Grijalbo.

Wertsch, J. V. (1990). The voice of rationality in a sociocultural approach to mind. In L. C. Moll (Ed.), *Vygotsky and education. Instructional implications of sociohistorical psychology.* Cambridge, MA: Cambridge University Press.

Zilberman, R. (1985). La lectura en la escuela [Reading in school]. *Lectura y Vida, 6* (1), 5–13. Buenos Aires, Argentina: I.R.A.

# part II

# Learning and Meaning in Childhood

chapter 4

# Approaching Knowledge and Meaning Elaboration in the Classroom: Some Theoretical and Methodological Issues

Ana Luiza B. Smolka
Universidade Estadual de Campinas, Brazil

The purpose of the present text is to address the issue of knowledge construction and sense production in school settings (a) by discussing some conceptions of language that have been supporting psychological research as well as educational practices; (b) by thematizing and focusing on the discursive dynamics in the classroom, taking the empirical material as locus of inquiry; and (c) by proposing a way of looking and analytically approaching interlocutory movements in everyday teaching situations that do not correspond to ideal dialogical and instructional models. With this we hope to be contributing to the present-day discussions on the relevance of discourse in psychological research and to the understanding of discourse—some aspects of its functioning—in educational institutions.

## INQUIRING INTO LANGUAGE AND MEANING: SOME PROBLEMS AND SOME ASSUMPTIONS

Psychology has conceptualized cognition as something of individual nature, thus highlighting the study of processes at the individual level, which would result in the social, collective functioning. From this perspective, psychology does not consider, or it underestimates, the question of signification and meaning as it neglects the interpersonal feature of sense production. Vygotsky's theses, formulated in the scope of developmental psychology and centered on the "sign" and on the "other," affirm the social and semiotic nature of consciousness, hence transferring from the individual to the sociocultural the origin of the mental functioning.

Studies that consider the role of sign/word in psychological processes, from the historico-cultural perspective, usually derive from Vygotsky's formulations the conception of language as instrument. One of Vygotsky's greatest contributions to contemporary psychological studies consists in the explanatory status of the sign and the privilege he attributes to sign/language in the social constitution of mental functioning (Wertsch, 1985; Smolka, Goes, & Pino, 1997).

Inspired by the Marxist idea of work as the main form of relationship that man establishes with the environment, Vygotsky expands its psychological implications, proposing to investigate possible relations between the use of tools and language development. Basing his work on Hegel and Marx, Vygotsky elaborates on the mediating function, stating and exploring some possible relationships and analogies between sign and instrument, and highlighting the essential distinctions that consist of their different forms of orienting human activity: Instruments are oriented towards the object, with the purpose of changing, controlling, and mastering nature; signs are means of internal activity, orienting and controlling (the behavior of) the individual.

Expansions of such formulations by different authors do not always explore the Marxist idea of the uses of tools by men, and have included a diversity of interpretations, which raises the need to discuss and conceptually deepen the nucleus of the Vygotskian statements about language. In fact, on what concerns the notion of instrument, specialists on Vygotsky like Van der Veer and Valsiner (1991), Wertsch (1985), and Kozulin (1990) have traced, or argued for, distinct origins: Marx as well as Spinoza, Pavlov as well as Köhler seem to have contributed to the Vygotskian formulation.

The reference to the instrumental character of language might be related to the making and using of instruments, in their utilitarian and functional aspects. Seen through this perspective, language is a medium to reach an end and it does not distinguish this notion from the (classic) conception of language as a way and vehicle of expression, communication, representation.

Another distinct way of conceiving language implies language as an instrument that is part of an action, belongs to a certain action, and yet is not the very action. The subtlety in this conception is that the instrument does not only serve "for some end" but it is what enables or makes an action possible. This way of conceiving language—as instrument, not as action—leads us to raise some questions concerning its very nature: What is the nature of language conceived as instrument? What is instrument, and for what, after all: language or the sign? Is language instrument for thought? Is sign instrument for language? If we take the sign as instrument isn't it pertinent to conceive language as action, not just "vehicle" but *mode* of action? Should we speak of sign as instrument and language as instrumental action for thinking and communicating?

And yet, if we take language as action, it does not necessarily bring any specificity to the Vygotskian conception, since this way of conceiving also applies to other tendencies of pragmatic character (for example, Austin, 1975) as well as of cognitive character (for example, Piaget, 1976). In both, the instrumental action of language is highlighted, be it for interaction/communication or for operation/representation.

In the studies I have been conducting with my colleagues and students we have been discussing that the "language-as-instrument" conception runs the risk of misplacing the crucial, unique, and constitutive aspect of the sign/word in the social formation of mind, highlighted by Vygotsky especially when he relates social interaction, generalization, and meaning development, inquiring: "What distinguishes the word from other things? How does the word represent the thing in consciousness? What makes a word a word?" (Vygotsky, 1987, p. 247).

Following along this line of reasoning, we could still ask: What distinguishes a sign/word from other instruments? What distinguishes language from other actions? More broadly speaking, given the symbolic materiality of the sign, how can we conceive its instrumentality, its "incorporation" to the many different forms of human action? What does the sign do to human actions? Can we speak of human action without the sign?

From our point of view, we find it important to recoup at this point some basic Marxist assumptions that sustain the proposition of language as instrument, highlighting, nonetheless, the signifying processes, or in other words, giving special relevance to the process of sign and sense production, in/from the very dialectic movement of production/product. It seems to us that it is this dialectic movement of meaning/sense production that, including the instrumental aspect, allows for its surpassing. In this sense, we could say that if the notion of instrument appears as fundamental, this notion is not at all sufficient to account for language complexity, dynamicity, and peculiarities.

Language does not always communicate what it is meant to. Language is not transparent. It signifies through the "non-spoken" and it doesn't necessarily mean through what is said. It admits a plurality of senses and meanings, it is polysemic. In this sense, we can say that it "works" or "functions" sometimes "by itself," producing multiple effects, independently of the speakers' intentions. It changes and/as it escapes man's knowledge, power and control. Language is a source of misunderstanding, illusions, mistakes. In this sense, language is not an instrument for information and communication since it does not simply express or transmit contents.

As Vygotsky explores the multiple and intricate relationships between word, sound, meaning, and sense, he is suspicious of the linear explanations and stable relations, mentioning the complexity and announcing the incompleteness of language: Concepts change; grammatical subject and psychological subject do not coincide (1987, p. 281); the word does not coincide with the thing, does not coincide with thinking; sense is independent of the word; we need to study how meanings transform the words, how concepts relate to words (p. 276). So, how are meanings and senses produced? How can we conceive and understand communication and knowledge? If we assume this dynamicity of signifying processes and we conceive language functioning in such a complex way, what could be taken as points of anchorage for sustaining knowledge construction and sense production? And, more specifically, how to conceive of teaching and learning practices from this perspective?

These secular epistemological issues have come almost inescapable for educators and psychologists. After the provocative and unfinished work of Vygotsky, together with many other echoing voices of semioticians, linguists, and anthropologists, authors like Wertsch (1991); Bruner (1990); Edwards & Potter (1992); and Smolka, Goes, & Pino (1997), among others, have approached and tried to (re)frame the question of meaning and sense production within the scope of psychology. What does it mean, then, or what are the implications of taking into account semiotic aspects in the study of psychological processes? And how to conceive discourse related to psychological functioning?

In our attempts to deepen the theoretical discussion, we chose to empirically approach interactive instances in one first-grade classroom, focusing on the discursive dynamics and questioning knowledge and meaning elaboration in an institutional context of formal education. Assuming the social, interactive, and constitutive nature of language, we propose to investigate modes of knowledge elaboration and sense production in daily classroom activities. One of our attempts is to understand how subjects and objects of knowledge emerge and become configured as such in and through discourse.

When we speak of discourse, we refer to language as (inter)action, and we highlight its peculiar feature of reflexivity, that is, the property and the possibility of verbal material to refer to itself. We speak of language with and through language. Indeed, man speaks of himself, (re)cognizes himself, and reflects over/about himself through language, which may speak of its own event.

Thus, object and means of approaching the issue get (con)fused: We use language to configure, to study, to know, and to analyze the very phenomenon in which we are immersed, from which we cannot get detached, and which we circumscribe as the object of investigation. Even if a certain distancing is possible, even if reflexivity is possible, man can never be "outside" of language. Hence, more than a simple means or mode of approaching the issue, language is constitutive of knowledge and of the cognitive processes themselves.

When we speak of discourse—a term that carries multiple interpretations (Maingueneau, 1991)—we do not strictly refer to the grammatical structuring of sentences; nor to the propositional aspects or to the logical structures; nor to individual speech acts. We refer to the enunciative event in certain conditions of production (borrowing from Foucault, 1987; Pecheux, 1988, 1990; Orlandi, 1987). Discourse has, thus, the feature of language in functioning, that is, language not only as human activity, but as social practice, historically produced and contextualized.

These multiple aspects require an attentive and careful study about the social phenomenon of verbal interaction, about the specific materiality of language and its conditions of production.

Indeed, when studies of psychological processes take as point of departure, or even as "data," the verbal interactions, they do not specifically inquire about the verbal material, and work basically from a conception of language as means of expression, information, and communication, which often implies an idea of speech transparency. Especially when it comes to matters of classroom discourse, this notion of language becomes particularly emphasized, as clarity and coherence are considered fundamental aspects in teaching practices.

In the present work, we inquire about language, both as "event" and as object of knowledge in an institutional context of formal instruction. When we refer to event we mean that language does not exist by itself, but only in the concrete (individual) enunciation. It is only in uttering that language acquires vital power and becomes reality (Bakhtin, 1981). In this sense, we highlight not only the pragmatic aspects and the importance of agency, but also the uniqueness and the "unrepeatedness" of utterings. At the same time, as we take language as object of knowledge, we look for relationships and regularities in discursive practices, attempting to understand its modes of functioning and of constituting knowledge.

In this sense, we take discourse as object and locus of theoretical and empirical investigation, and we ask about the implications of such theoretical and methodological options in research procedures. We believe that the way we epistemologically conceive language and thinking sets a framework for investigating, and actually working, knowledge and teaching in school settings.

## THE EMPIRICAL WORK AS A LOCUS OF INQUIRY

The empirical work, based on ethnographic principles, was carried out in a low-income first-grade classroom of a public elementary school in Campinas, SP, Brazil, during the school year of 1992. Thirty 6–7-year-old children were enrolled in this classroom, one third of which had attained preschool or daycare centers. The infrastructure of this school was fairly decent: new desks and chairs, lights, blackboard, chalk. Material resources like books, papers, pencils, paint, and so on were scarce. In the context of this classroom, if the majority of children were exposed to writing due to the fact that they live in a literate society, they did not necessarily have specific knowledge about it.

The observations happened twice a week, for a period of 2 hours a day, when the activities in the classroom were videotaped and notes were taken in a diary.

While in the classroom, the researcher walked with the camera through the room, as a participant observer, getting involved in activities and problem solving if and when demanded to by the children. Different moments of the classroom dynamics were registered: proposals and explanations made by the teacher to the whole classroom; work in small groups of children; direct interaction of children with the researcher, and so on.

The teacher who was participating in the project graduated with a degree in teaching at the secondary level, and had about 10 years of experience in first-grade classrooms.

Concerning literacy and teaching practices, the teacher attempted to use diversified materials to introduce the pupils to formal reading and writing instruction. She often changed the desks' dispositions, grouping children in many different ways.

The following episode was taken from the observations in the third week of classes (first week of systematic observations for the research project). In the process of recording, transcribing, and analysing it, our first impressions were of discontinuity, rupture, lack of syntony, and chaos in the interlocutory movement and teaching procedures. Indeed, our strangeness in relation to episodes like this one led us to choose it as an exemplar.

March 17, 1992

The children were sitting at individual desks, facing the board. The teacher was in front of the class.

1. Teacher: So. I asked you to cut away things that start alike.
   (Children talking)
2. Teacher: You know that newspaper of Casas Bahia...(the advertising newsletter of a local department store)
   (Children talking)
3. Teacher: Good Lord! You know that newspaper of...
   Bruno! Evelyn!
4. Children: Mappin
   Vovo Luzitana
   C&A
   Carrefour
   (all names of department stores and supermarkets)
5. Child: Teacher, my dad works at Ceasa...
6. Teacher: So, that little newspaper...Rose!
7. Child: Look, It's raining!
8. Child: It's raining!
9. Child: Yeah, It's raining!

(Children go to the window)...

10. Teacher: Look! (getting a reading book from her desk)
    *Ca*sa (house)
    *Ca*deira (chair)
    *Ca*chorro (dog)
11. Child: Gato! (cat)
12. Teacher: Another combination:
    *ga*to (cat)
    *ga*linha (hen)
13. Evelyn: *ga*lo (cock)
    *ga*to (cat)
14. Andre: The hen puts the egg, the little chick is born. The cock goes on top of the hen...
15. Teacher: Andre!
16. Child: Pato (duck)
17. Child: Gato (cat)
18. Child: Cavalo (horse)
19. Child: Peixe (fish)
20. Teacher: *Pa*to (duck)
    *Pa*pagalo (parrot)
    *Pa*tinho (little duck)
21. Child: Arara! (macaw)
22. Teacher: Do you think that papagaio goes with arara? Are you listening to the sound?

## APPROACHING KNOWLEDGE AND MEANING: ONE POSSIBLE ANALYSIS

There are certainly many different ways of analysing this episode. Our main point, as stated above, concerns the understanding of knowledge and meaning elaboration in the classroom, related to teaching practices, and in this specific case, to the teaching of literacy. We won't be making here a linguistic analysis of empirical material, nor an analysis of talk-in-interaction; also, we won't be strictly focusing on the pragmatic aspect of language use or situated speech, as featured in ethnomethodology or symbolic interactionism. Neither do we pretend to realize a discourse analysis in the theoretical and methodological terms suggested by the French specialists in the field. But we'll be taking into account these different perspectives and inquiries which, in fact, not just contributed to, but constituted, our positioning within the boundaries of education, psychology, and the philosophy of language.

Our effort, at this moment, is not to theorize about discourse itself, nor to propose an explanatory or analytical model, but to understand the functioning of language in a specific teaching situation. Our effort concerning research in psychology and education has been to incorporate in a microgenetic analysis some constitutive interactive/discursive aspects. We think that through an analysis of the discursive dynamics we might trace emerging functioning processes and merging intersubjective knowledge.

From the point of view of social psychology, Potter and Wetherell mention that "there is no method to discourse analysis in the way we traditionally think of an experimental method or content analysis method. What we have is a broad theoretical framework concerning the nature of discourse and its role in social life...discourse analysis is heavily dependent on craft skills and tacit knowledge" (1987, p. 175). From a different—linguistic—perspective, and commenting on the heterogeneity of scientific and intellectual traditions, Maingueneau states that "discourse analysis does not have as object the textual organization taken in and by itself, neither the situation of communication, but the intricacies of a given mode of uttering and a determined social place" (1957, p. 7, our translation).

In the midst of the many theoretical positions, our initial questions for methodological procedures were: What are the participants saying? What are they talking about? How are they talking? How (and what) knowledge is being constructed? How is meaning being produced? Broadly speaking: How do the discursive dynamics happen? And what happens in and through such a dynamics?

As we analytically approach discourse in this particular episode, we may see that the teacher's and children's speech concerns, at first, something quite unspecified that might become highlighted or configured as a possible object of knowledge. In our attempts to circumscribe the very focus of research, we tried to identify modes and strategies of approaching and delineating such objects in and through the teacher's and children's utterings.

The teacher's way of speaking and initiating the morning work—"So, I asked you to cut away things that start alike" (Turn 1)—carries the history of the group as it refers to a shared past experience. Also, in this typical school situation, characterized by an explicit teaching relationship, the teacher, as privileged interlocutor, makes efforts to highlight for the pupils some aspects of the written form of speech (as a possible object of knowledge).

But how does she do this? In Turns 1 through 6, the teacher refers to the activity of clipping out "things that start alike," mentions an advertising "newspaper" from which the children could possibly have cut away such things, and calls the attention of some talking children. In this movement—from "the things that start alike," to the advertising newspaper, to the chatting children in the classroom—the teacher interrupts her speech three times for disciplinary measures. The interrupted speech of the teacher and the simultaneous talk of the children seem to produce a confusion as the focus of attention occilates between possible *objects* (things, newspaper) and *subjects* (speaking subjects and those spoken to—Bruno, Evelyn, Rose) *of knowledge*.

It is interesting to note that this succession of nonconclusive references by the teacher leaves open some "intervals" for the children. In fact, the teacher does not ask any questions, but the pupils "fill in" the blanks in her speech, as they establish and work on a paradigmatic axis related to and initiated by the teacher's reference to the local department store. "Casas Bahia" (Turn 2) and "that newspaper of..." (Turn 3) set a framework in which the children may operate (Turn 4), naming department stores and supermarkets.

In Turn 5, one child breaks this paradigmatic axis by introducing a narrative. From the analytical point of view, it is also interesting to note that this movement to a syntagmatic frame corresponds to a subtle change in the category of the commercial establishment, since Ceasa is not a department store or supermarket, but a center of direct wholesale by producers—of fruits, vegetables, and so on. One could point out that, if the category of this commercial establishment does not strictly fit the paradigmatic axis, the work of the child's father seems nonetheless compatible with the activity carried out in the other types of establishments.

In the midst of the classroom dynamics, the world seems to, literally, knock at the window: "It's raining!" (Turns 7 through 9). The rain sounds stronger, and more interesting, than the talking in the classroom and the children get agglomerated close to the window.

After this break (forced by the children), the teacher re-orients the activity. She does not refer to the newspaper anymore and chooses to work with the introductory reading book. She picks it up from her table and, pointing out the pictures to the children, she names three objects (Turn 10)—casa (house), cadeira (chair), and cachorro (dog)—which, in Portuguese, "start alike," with the "ca" syllable. One cannot notice any specific emphasis in her voice, or cue, that may indicate or make explicit for the children the criterion for choosing such words (for teacher and researcher the sound of the first syllable appears as evident).

We could identify many instances of noncoincidence between the teacher's and the children's criteria in Turns 10 through 22. Turn 11, for example, indicates one of the possible modes of apprehension of the teacher's speech in Turn 10 by one child: She seems to organize the words in two pairs, according to a semantic categorization: "casa/cadeira (house/chair), cachorro (dog)..." and she says "cat" as a complement to the second pair.

The last word uttered by the teacher in Turn 10 (cachorro) provokes again paradigmatic relationships (animals) within which the children start to operate (Turns 11 through 21). In this interlocutory movement, the teacher tries to organize the children's speeches, re-wording and transforming the students' suggestions, making them match her criteria (Turns 12 and 20).

In our attempts to describe and understand the logic of the interactive dynamic that articulates the teacher's criterion in selecting and presenting the words to the students, with the paradigmatic axis on which the children operate, we went back to the teacher's first uttering in the episode.

A more attentive analysis of this uttering shows that it establishes two basic paradigms, which sustain and support, in a certain way, the event (and the very analysis of the event): When the teacher says "cut away things," she refers to the *world*; when she says "which start alike" she refers to *language*.

So, that's how the discursive dynamics evolves: teacher and children working in different paradigms and perspectives—the teacher referring to the instance of language, the children referring to things in the world.

The teacher's speech in Turn 10 generates two types of reply, simultaneously uttered by two children: In Turn 13, the child echoes the teacher's speech, transforming it. She inverts the order, using the masculine: gato/galinha (cat and hen), and galo/gato (cock and cat), producing at this moment a coincidence between the language and the world criteria.

In Turn 14, the child also echoes the teacher's speech, saying the "same word" (galinha, hen), but with different referent and reference (thing in the world). His narrative, which explicitly carries his knowledge and experience, breaks once more the paradigmatic axis.

The teacher's intervention in Turn 15—"Andre!"—interrupts the child's narrative in a scolding tone. In her uttering, however, there are many "non-spoken" things: In this way, what cannot be said, or is not convenient to be said by the child becomes implicit in the teacher's voice as she reproachably utters the child's name. In this way of speaking, multiple meanings, deeply rooted in social practices, get condensed.

In the web of sounds and meanings interwoven in the words spoken by children and teacher (Turns 12 through 21)—pato, gato, cavalo, peixe, papagaio, patinho—one word ends up by producing a difference at the level of the significant: among the distinguishing features of occlusive sounds (p/t/g/k) followed by "as" and "os," the word "arara" (Turn 21), initiated by a vowel and intertwined with soft "r's," sounds different, interrupts a certain pattern.

This word, by its difference, seems to capture the teacher's attention. She tries, by her turn, to call the attention of the children to her (up to now) nonexplicit criterion of analysis. "Do you think that papagaio goes with arara? Are you listening to the sound?" (Turn 22).

If the teacher disregards at this moment the child's categorization (parrot and macaw might "go together" as birds), she explicitly refers here to the "sound," although her way of putting the question opens, once more, many different possibilities of meaning construction and sense production: sound of words? sound of things/animals in the world?

## TAKING SOME DISTANCING FROM THE ANALYSIS: OTHER LOCI OF INQUIRY

Throughout our analysis of this classroom discursive dynamics we have been trying to relate knowledge, language, and meaning, giving priority to certain aspects that deserve some further expansion at this moment.

First of all, we should make explicit that as we developed the analytical procedures to account for knowledge and meaning in a school setting, we became each time more aware of the transient feature of meaning, that is, as we wove the analysis and traced possible meanings, we knew, at the same time, that meaning could always be an other/different one. From our point of view, our analysis and interpretation find theoretical and methodological points of anchorage on Bakhtin's notion of speech genres (1984) and Foucault's discursive formations (1987). Although holding important conceptual distinctions, both notions point to the historically and implicitly established rules and regularities which support, allow for and constrain social/discursive practices and the interpretation of such practices (in our case, school or teaching practices).

We also should point out that, concerning the investigative work, assumptions and findings become deeply interrelated because the theoretical perspective shapes and sustains the raising of issues and the very modes of circumscribing, approaching, and analysing objects of investigation.

As we proposed to look at the discursive dynamics in daily classroom situations, we could identify the functioning of discourse in (at least) two levels (or two focuses and perspectives): (a) teacher and students approaching objects of knowledge (words/things); and (b) researcher approaching objects of investigation (discourse/knowledge). Expanding on this idea a little further, we could say that it seems to be in the interplay of these levels, which involve many different modes of actions and elaborations by subjects in interactions, as well as different social positions (teacher, students, researcher), that institutionalized knowledge construction (scholarly, academic, scientific) takes place (the knowing about language, the knowing of how to teach, the knowing about teaching and learning practices, the knowing about language functioning, etc.). However, we cannot "observe" knowledge construction processes, signifying processes, or sense production. We may only "make visible" through analytical procedures some aspects of the processes we want to understand.

We assume that cognitive elaborations at an individual level (intramental) do not happen "outside of" the discursive web of meanings (intermental), which necessarily involves the (concrete) "other," and the voices (words, perspectives, knowledges) of others. In the analysis of the intricate web of voices, referents, and references, we were faced with the complexity of multifaceted objects of knowledge, and we could identify some aspects of their becoming configured in the very interactive, interlocutory dynamics.

The focus on the interlocutory movement indeed allowed for some understanding of the modes of approaching objects of knowledge and making sense in the context of teaching relationships. These modes of approaching did not necessarily imply clear, linear, or transparent sequences of speech. Teacher and pupils referred to things, including language, in the world. And in and through the discursive dynamics, language itself appeared as a possible object of knowledge. However, we could also identify many non-coincidences in the participants' utterings: not just among the subjects' experiences, knowledge, and perspectives; but between words and referents; between words and meanings; between things in the world and the word that crafts such things; within the very utterings. Teacher and children were (apparently) (not) talking about the "same" things.

A certain analysis of the teacher's way of speaking and conducting this classroom activity could lead to the questioning of the instructional strategies she used in order to work the children's awareness of specific features of written language and to make herself understood. Her speech might appear as lacunar and unspecified. However, we could also identify in her way of speaking, in her particular way of referring to written language as an object of knowledge, a mode of teaching that becomes embodied in her speech. On focusing again on the teacher's opening sentence, "So, I asked you to cut away things that start alike" (Turn 1), as well as on her asking the children in the last turn, "Are you listening to the sound?", we could identify a pedagogical intentionality in her way of speaking that seemed to frame, although rather loosely, the configuring of words as an object of knowledge. Nonetheless, the children's positioning as interlocutors constituted a crucial intrinsic condition in this framing.

The teacher's mode of teaching, her way of speaking, may not strictly correspond to a proposed logic of formal instruction (which presupposes clarity, fluency, explanation, etc.), and yet it echoes a common, broadly disseminated way of formally introducing children to literacy. The teacher's way of conducting the activity results in an effective outcome as children become engaged in the interlocutory movement. In fact, we could observe how teacher and children sustain themselves as interlocutors, and could also trace some threads in the weaving (and the logic) of discourse as the interactive dynamics happened. This is not to say that the interlocutory movement "in itself" accounts for knowledge construction and sense production, but that knowledge and sense, as historical cultural production, are necessarily built up within discursive practices.

## SOME FINAL REMARKS

In the present paper we have discussed some issues concerning conceptions of language that pervade, in some way or another, psychological research and educational practices. We have commented on the implications of assuming a conception of language (just) as instrument or (just) as action to account for knowledge construction and sense production, pointing to the complexity and peculiarities of language in functioning that require the reframing of many assumptions and questions. To substantiate the problematization of language, we drew upon the empirical material constructed along the course of a research project carried out in a public school first-grade classroom, where the formal teaching of literacy had just begun. Assuming language as interaction and constitutive of knowledge, we focused on the discursive dynamics as object and locus of investigation.

We attempted to analyze the chosen episode, highlighting the positioning of subjects as well as the configuring of objects of knowledge in the interlocutory movement, exploring possibilities of empirical analysis. The analysis of such a dynamic placed in evidence the complex question of word/world relationships.

Indeed, if we assume that the relationships between *word* and *world* are not given *a priori*, if they are historically and culturally constructed (see especially Foucault, 1981), we could also see that these relationships were taken for granted in the teaching of literacy—they were not easily perceived, or at least were not thematized. These relationships, and the distancing between word and world, could also (in pedagogical terms, should?) become objects of knowledge and investigation in many different levels.

Our analytical procedure highlighted the interlocutory movement, pointing to the fact that the possibility of understanding and sense production are not to be found in the "clarity" or "quality" of utterings (since reference does not guarantee meaning), or in the correctness of language itself, but within the multiple relationships that become established among the interlocutors trying to understand each other. What emerged in the analysis was a "constitutive interincomprehension" (Maingueneau, 1989) which allowed for the building up of knowledges, meanings, and senses. In this sense, utterings are not vehicles through which messages are transmitted, but must be considered as "events" that happen, and yet constitute the dynamics of interactions.

Hence, if we assume that *interactions are constitutive of knowledge*, we must assume that it is in this very interactive/interlocutory movement, as it gets established, that knowledges are built and senses and meanings are produced. The question then is how do we conceive, and theoretically and methodologically work, the opacity of relationships, the nontransparency of everyday interactions, "the essential precariousness of the consolidation of meaning in the course of dialogue" (Petit, 1985, p. 432), especially when teaching and formal education are at issue. This continues to be one of our most intriguing points of inquiry.

(This ongoing research work has been sponsored by Grants of CNPq—Conselho Nacional de Desenvolvimento Cientifico e Tecnológico, Brasil.)

## REFERENCES

Austin, J.L. (1975). *How to do things with words.* Boston: Harvard University Press.

Bakhtin, M. (1981). *Marxismo e filosofia da linguagem [Voloshinov, Marxism and the philosophy of language].* São Paulo, Brazil: Hucitec.

Bakhtin, M. (1984). *Esthetique de la creation verbale [Aesthetics of verbal creation].* Paris: Gallimard.

Bruner, J. (1990). *Acts of meaning.* Cambridge: Harvard University Press.

Edwards, D. & Potter, J. (1992). *Discoursive psychology.* London: Sage Publications.

Foucault, M. (1981). *As palavras e as coisas [Words and things].* São Paulo, Brazil: Martins Fontes.

Foucault, M. (1987). *Arqueologia do saber [Archeology of knowledge].* Rio de Janeiro, Brazil: Forense.

Kozulin, A. (1990). *La psicologia de Vygotsky [Vygotsky's psychology].* Madrid, Spain: Alianza Editorial.

Maingueneau, D. (1989). *Novas tendências em análise do discurso [New tendencies in discourse analysis].* Campinas, Brazil: Pontes/Unicamp.

Maingueneau, D. (1991). *Analyse du discours: Introduction aux lectures de l'archive [Discourse analysis: Introduction to archive's lectures].* Paris: Hachette.

Maingueneau, D. (1995). Les analyses du discours en France: Presentation. *Languages, 117,* 7.

Orlandi, E. (1987). *A linguagem e seu funcionamento [Language and its functioning].* Campinas, Brazil: Pontes.

Pecheux, M. (1988). *Semântica e discurso: Uma critica à afirmação do óbvio [Semantics and discourse: A criticism to the obvious].* Campinas, Brazil: Unicamp.

Pecheux, M. (1990). *O discurso, estrutura ou acontecimento? [Discourse: Structure or event?]* Campinas, Brazil: Pontes.

Petit, J.C. (1985). The making and breaking of dialogue. In M. Dascal (Ed.), *Dialogue: An interdisciplinary approach* (pp. 427–440). Amsterdam: John Benjamin Publishing.

Piaget, J. (1976). *Le langage et la pensee chez l'enfant [Language and thinking in the child].* Paris: Delachaux et Niestle.

Potter, J. & Wetherell, M. (1987). *Discourse and Social Psychology.* London: Sage Publications.

Smolka, A.L.B., Góes, M.C.R., & Pino, A. (1997). Dynamics and indeterminism in developmental and social processes. In A. Fogel, M. Lyra, & J. Valsiner (Eds.), *Dynamics and indeterminism in developmental and social processes* (pp. 153–164). Hillsdale, NJ: Lawrence Erlbaum.

Van der Veer, R. & Valsiner, J. (1991). *Understanding Vygotsky: A quest for synthesis.* Oxford: Blackwell.

Vygotsky, S. (1987). Thinking and speech. R. Rieber & A. Carton (Eds.), *The collected works of L.S. Vygotsky. Vol. 1.* New York: Plenum Press.

Wertsch, J.V. (1985). *Vygotsky and the social formation of mind.* Cambridge: Harvard University Press.

Wertsch, J.V. (1991). *Voices of the mind.* Cambridge: Harvard University Press.

chapter 5

# Why There Might Be Several Ways to Read Storybooks to Preschoolers in Aotearoa/New Zealand: Models of Tutoring and Sociocultural Diversity in How Families Read Books to Preschoolers

Stuart McNaughton
University of Auckland, New Zealand

> Alice was beginning to get very tired of sitting by her sister on the bank, and of having nothing to do; once or twice she had peeped into the book her sister was reading, but it had no pictures or conversations in it, "and what is the use of a book," thought Alice, "without pictures or conversations?" (*Alice's Adventures in Wonderland* by Lewis Carroll, 1982, p. 17)

> I am good at prayers because, since I was a tiny boy, my father he get me and my brothers and my sisters and my cousins for to learn how to make the prayers. He also get us for to read from the Holy Book until now I am sixteen years old and am an expert in the reading of the Book. ("Exam Failure Praying" by Albert Wendt, 1986, p. 54)

In the stories from which these passages come a Samoan adolescent and an English girl reflect on different forms of expertise with books. The characters' interests have been shared by developmental and educational researchers, because the family activity of book reading is a significant site for studying developmental processes that have important educational meanings. This chapter is concerned with our understanding of the development of expertise in reading storybooks during story-reading episodes. It examines the application of a contemporary psychological model of tutoring to the family literacy activity of reading books to preschoolers. The central issue is how adequately this model accounts for the activity as practiced by different sociocultural groups.

This chapter argues that some families in Aotearoa/New Zealand read storybooks with their preschoolers in ways that are at odds with normative assumptions about effective tutorials. This stems from other conceptualizations of the uses of text than Alice's purposes of picturing and conversing (about narratives). It includes the expertise reflected on by the 16-year-old Samoan boy in Albert Wendt's story.

## STORYBOOK READING AND SCAFFOLDS

Studies of the developmental properties of storybook-reading episodes have yielded two summary characteristics. The first is the identification of a standard tutorial pattern. The second is the presence of some diversity in the use of that tutorial pattern across different sociocultural groups (Sulzby & Teale, 1991).

The standard description of interactions between readers and preschoolers employs a generic social interactionist model, often sourced to Wood, Bruner, and Ross's (1976) study of maternal tutoring of problem solving. The original description used a scaffolding metaphor to model the functions of the tutor's behaviour. Since then that model has been extensively applied and elaborated in further studies of family tutorial processes in problem solving and complex skill development, particularly in the development of language and literacy (Cazden, 1988; Rogoff, 1990; Wood, 1989).

A variety of behavioural indices for the tutorial functions have been employed in different studies. This poses problems for generalizing about the effectiveness of the model, and several writers have commented on an imprecision and ambiguity in applications (Cazden, 1988; McNaughton, 1991). This raises questions about the model's usefulness in setting boundaries between different types of tutorials.

However, under pressure to set researchable criteria, general agreement has emerged about its core features. In general, scaffolds are described as providing tutorial support that is adjustable and temporary. In the reading of storybooks with children at home, the selection and use of storybooks themselves is a form of support. In addition, dynamic support typically has been identified in conversations that are interspersed during the reading of the text. The reader structures the interactions using, and responding to, questions and comments. The function of this structuring is to yield conversational exchanges that are shared ways of constructing meanings from written narratives. The tutor's language functions to model, direct, and prompt these exchanges.

The tutor adjusts the interlocutor role contingently on the child's developing contribution to gaining meanings. Within repeated readings of books and across different books the matrix of conversational support for the child's actions with the text shift. Over time responsibility for learning how to interact with text without mediation by the reader in interspersed exchanges transfers from expert to novice (through personal constructive processes labelled "internalization" or "appropriation;" see Rogoff, 1990). It is argued that increasingly reflective and self-regulated performance develops through the interactional processes. This arises through particular functions of the tutor's language, for example, in highlighting effective performance and in the negotiation of meanings.

Scaffolds enable participants to share a representation of the task which is linked to jointly held goals. Partly this is captured in the concept of developing intersubjectivity, in the sense of knowing about each other's focus or intentions. It has been identified as developing in the negotiations during conversations and the success of conversational exchanges.

Tutorials that scaffold expertise in family language and literacy are described as engaging the learner in activities that are recognizably forms of mature social and cultural uses of narrative texts. This means that children are engaged in something that in itself is not isolated, fragmented, and disembedded from everyday uses. The reading of storybooks rather than, for example, a fixed focus on letter-sound associations in texts, is more like adult uses of written language. An important feature then is the notion that scaffolds are socialization processes analyzable at several levels, including the focus of the tutorials and the tutorial structure. Tutorials that have these features are predicted to be effective for acquiring expertise in general, and particularly effective for the development of early literacy skills (see Cazden, 1988; Rogoff, 1990; Sulzby & Teale, 1991; Wood, 1989).

Similar features are present in more recent analyses of tutorial processes in everyday child-rearing settings. For example, Rogoff's (1990) description of cognitive development as "guided participation in social activity" incorporates scaffolding features such as engagement in social and cultural activities, and structured and dynamic support that is goal-directed. Similarly, Lave and Wenger's (1991) analysis of everyday tutorials as "legitimate peripheral participation in communities of practice" shares the core features of intersubjectivity, cultural relevance, and structured pedagogy.

In the case of storybook reading the detailed application of the model is based on intensive case studies and group studies, mostly of white-middle class families. When the core features have been applied to this activity, the structuring and shared goals are described in terms of a collaborative enterprise in which narrative meanings are negotiated through dyadic exchanges. A recent review notes that

> In the situations and cultures studied, children almost never encounter an oral rendering of the text of the book in a storybook-reading situation. Instead, the words of the author are surrounded by the language of the adult reader and the child(ren) and the social interaction among them. During this interaction the participants cooperatively seek to negotiate meaning through verbal and nonverbal means. (Sulzby & Teale, 1991, p. 733)

Where differences have been found in interaction patterns across sociocultural groups they have been described as variations from the canonical form, which is consistent with Sulzby and Teale's (1991) review. However, the research is somewhat difficult to interpret because comparisons often have not controlled for differences between families in book-reading experience and types of texts used (Pellegrini, Perlmutter, Galda, & Brody, 1990).

Studies of low socioeconomic status (SES) families in which storybook reading has been a regular family activity are described as interacting in restricted ways, with a more limited focus on extended narrative meanings and reduced cooperative participatory dialogue compared with middle-class families (Heath, 1982; Sulzby & Teale, 1991). However, accounts by researchers who have deliberately introduced narrative texts into the literacy practices of black, low-SES families have noted the similarity between subsequent interactions and those in mainstream families (Heath & Branscombe, 1986), although in one report these cooperative exchanges were infrequent (Pellegrini et al., 1990).

There is one major implication of this view: There is a right way to read storybooks to children. Scaffolded storybook reading, described in terms of both a focus on narrative meanings and in terms of a collaborative style, is the appropriate and most effective way to socialize children into expertise with written language. What follows is the conclusion that those families who do not read with their children in this manner are socializing their children inadequately. The available evidence suggests that more frequent storybook reading that uses the standard pattern is related to higher achievement levels in learning to read at school (Sulzby & Teale, 1991).

## THREE STUDIES OF STORYBOOK READING

At the end of the chapter I will return to discuss the theoretical and empirical practices that have underpinned a normative view of scaffolding in storybook reading. Before this, I will discuss data from three studies of storybook reading in different families in Aotearoa/New Zealand. These studies show the presence of substantially different patterns from those described in the aforementioned literature. The extent and nature of those differences has led to the questioning of the usefulness of the standard model as it has been generally applied to the activity of storybook reading. These studies are briefly described and a modified model of tutorial processes is proposed that helps to account for differences.

### Study One (Phillips & McNaughton, 1990)

In the first study 10 families responded to advertisements in suburban libraries and bookshops for families interested in books and book reading. These families were Pakeha. (Pakeha is a term used in Aotearoa/New Zealand to refer to those of European descent and, given the colonial history, this particularly applies to British descent.) The incomes and occupations of family members placed them in the top two SES groups in Aotearoa/New Zealand. In each family there were two adults and one or two children, and the mother was the major caregiver. The children (6 boys and 4 girls) were between 3 years and 4 years, 6 months of age.

Through diary records and indirect observation it was established that the families read frequently (a mean of 87 books read over a 28-day period) and selectively (95% of the books read were books with a narrative structure). The families' deployment of resources, including the selection of reading materials and time commitment, created what Valsiner (1987) has called a Zone of Promoted Actions, in this case of book-reading sessions. Both readers (predominantly the mothers) and children initiated these sessions, but it was primarily the child who chose the book to be read.

After this initial period new texts were introduced. Texts that were unfamiliar but rated as similar in type and value to those typically read were given to the families for 2 to 3 weeks. This meant that tutorial processes could be examined on texts that controlled for familiarity across the group of families. The first, second, and last readings were audiotaped and subsequently analyzed. Families were asked to read these texts as they typically read books.

A book-reading episode typically entailed reading of the text punctuated by verbal exchanges. Infrequently other behaviours occurred, including parental verbal and nonverbal invitations to read and child attempts at reading. These occurred so infrequently that they were not included in the resulting analysis.

The goals of the reader and the child in storybook reading were established through an analysis of insertions, defined as verbalizations by reader or child, that were not part of the actual text. Insertions lasted in exchanges between reader and child until text reading resumed. The first utterance of the insertion was categorized into one of four types of focus.

Narrative insertions were focused on information relevant to, or consistent with, the events and goals of the narrative. In Dialogue 1, the reader's comment in reference to an illustration, "Goodness! He's a big frog," and the child's question in a subsequent reading of the same text "I wonder what those frogs are looking at him for?" were utterances beginning an insertion that was focused on the narrative.

Dialogue 1: Example of insertions with narrative focus

*Text*: "In the dream time there lived a giant frog called Tiddalik. One morning when he awoke, he said to himself, 'I am so thirsty, I could drink a lake!' And that is what he did."

(Initial reading)
Reader: Goodness! He's a big frog.
Child: And look at those little frogs.
Reader: Yes (laughing). They're all looking at him. Probably going huuu what an enormous one!

(Subsequent reading)
Child: I wonder what those frogs are looking at him for?
Reader: Why do you think?
Child: I don't know.
Reader: What! Do you think they're a bit surprised at how large he is and what he's doing?
Child: I think...well, he's eating all their water.
Reader: Yes, I do too.

Print insertions were focused on concepts about print, including references to letters, words, and pages as well as attributes of books and print. The reader's directive in the exchange shown in Dialogue 2, "First you can show Mummy where the front of the book is," begins an insertion focused on concepts about print

Dialogue 2: Example of insertion with print focus

| | |
|---|---|
| Reader: | First you can show Mummy where the front of the book is. Show me where the front of the book is. |
| Child: | Yeah. |
| Reader: | The front, where's the front? |
| Child: | Here. |
| Reader: | Okay. You turn the page. Where's the back of the book? |
| Child: | Here. |
| Reader: | Where do you start reading? Which side? Which side do you start reading? |
| Child: | This side. |
| Reader: | Which one? |
| Child: | This side. |
| Reader: | That's right. Oh! (page turned). This is where the story begins. "No more cakes." That's the ... that's the name of the story. |

Other book insertions included questions and comments that were book-related but not focused on the narrative or on concepts about print. An example with the text shown in Dialogue 1 was a question about an illustration unrelated to the narrative: "Mum. I run over to those trees?" Other insertions were those unrelated to book reading, typically to do with child management and interruptions to reading.

Counts of insertions revealed that the focus for both the readers and the children overwhelmingly was on the narrative structure of the texts they read (see Table 5.1). Of the 647 insertions analysed, 86% of them were focused on the narrative.

The interaction pattern was well-captured by the standard scaffolding model as it has been applied to this activity. Reader and child collaborated in exchanges to construct meanings for the text. The preschooler participated as a full conversational partner in setting the topic. (The readers and children initiated insertions at mean rates of 3.8 and 3.7 per book reading, respectively, and the mean rates of narrative insertions were 3.4 and 2.9 for the readers and children, respectively.)

Core features of the scaffolding model are illustrated in Dialogue 1. The child was engaged in a form of a mature task (reading for meanings) that was valued and functional in the family setting. Among other resources these families had over 450 adults' and children's books, and the parents estimated that they spent over 2 hours in reading and writing activities per day. The tutorial support was adjustable and temporary. Dialogue 1 shows that the mother on a first reading focused the

**TABLE 5.1. Focus of Exchanges in Storybook Reading: Mean Percentages of Insertions (647) for 10 Families**

| Focus | Mean Percent |
|---|---|
| Narrative | 86% |
| Print | 3% |
| Book—Other | 7% |
| Other | 3% |

From: Phillips & McNaughton (1990)

child's attention on the central narrative problem in the story (the giant frog has drunk all the water and the other animals have to find a way to get it back). By the last reading the child took responsibility for inserting dialogue at this point, also focusing on the problem. In the ensuing conversation the mother's part in the dialogue supports, through prompts, the child's articulation of the problem. ("I think...well...he's eating all their water.")

Quantitative analyses showed that the readers concentrated on clarifying the narrative on the first readings and over time reduced their emphasis as children more often initiated clarificatory dialogue. The reader then shifted the focus towards making links with anticipated text segments. It was argued that self-initiated questioning and checking by the children provided evidence for the development of self regulation.

### Study Two (McNaughton & Ka'ai, 1990)

A second study, involving families from different sociocultural groups, illustrated the conditions under which the model might be applicable and some limitations to generalizability.

The study was concerned with markers of literacy at home for children from nonmainstream homes who achieved well in beginning reading. Preschoolers were identified who were predicted to be high-progress readers and writers at school. The prediction was made through the identification of older siblings already at school. A group of 12 families is described here for whom there were audiotaped samples of books currently being read when the children were aged between 3 and 4 years. The families self-identified as Maori (3), Pakeha (6), and Samoan (3). The incomes and occupations placed them in the 4th and 5th levels of the New Zealand SES index of 6 levels. The families had two parents (and sometimes more adults from extended family) and three or more children. The Samoan families were fully bilingual.

Maori, Samoan, and Pakeha researchers worked with the sample of 12 families. It had been predicted from the body of evidence available that

**TABLE 5.2. Focus of Exchanges in Storybook Reading: Mean Percentages of Insertions and Routines (248) for 11 Families**

| Focus | Mean Percent |
|---|---|
| Narrative | 59% |
| Print | 12% |
| Book—Other | 9% |
| Performance | 16% |

From: McNaughton & Ka'ai (1990)

book reading in general and storybook reading in particular would be occurring in the standard format of the model that is associated with progress at school.

Similarities and differences were found with the families in the previous study. For example, a common feature was that reading and writing for a range of purposes were highly valued adult activities creating salient, ambient literacy activities. Self reports and diaries indicated that book reading was a daily occurrence. But unlike the previous families, in the majority of the Maori and Samoan households triadic or multiparty settings for book reading were typical, and other members of the family such as an older sibling or an aunt still at school often took the role of reader. Eleven of the 12 families read storybooks. But in 7 families other books, including church texts, were selected more often for reading.

Samples of storybook reading revealed the presence of the standard tutorial pattern. The majority of insertions (60% of total insertions; see Table 5.2) and subsequent exchanges showed readers and children collaborated in constructing text meanings. But on some occasions a different form of interaction took place. These are included in Table 2 as insertions but the exchanges are better described as a type of language routine (Peters & Boag, 1986), which we termed performance routines.

Performance routines occurred when part of the text was repeated by the child. Imitations often were signaled by the reader through verbal and paralinguistic means such as pausing and a rising intonation. On these occasions (a mean of 16% of the insertions and routines) the reader indicated through intonation patterns and pauses that a model had been provided and the child's task was to imitate. These performance routines were even more noticeable on texts that were not storybooks. Examples of both types of interactions are shown in Dialogues 3 and 4. They come from one book-reading session in a Maori family (Child age 4;11). A storybook was read collaboratively (all 13 insertions had a narrative focus). However, a beginning reading text brought home from school by a cousin was read using performance routines (performance routines occurred on every line of text).

Dialogue 3: A narrative routine

*Text 1*: Patch had been given the job of painting white lines for the running lanes.

Reader: What are they doing there, D...?
Child: Painting...a line.
Reader: So that they can run down the track straight.

Dialogue 4: Performance routines

*Text 2*: Andrew had an engine called Red Streak.

Reader: Andrew.
Child: Andrew.
Reader: had.
Child: had.
Reader: an engine.
Child: an engine.
Reader: called.
Child: called.

The tutorials within which performance routines occurred did not appear to share the characteristics of the standard scaffolding model. Among other things, the focus was different, it was on accurate rendering of the text, and it was not overtly collaborative. The presence and characteristics of this tutorial involving performance routines are discussed further in a third study.

Comparisons between families in the two studies showed that the Maori and Samoan families read with a textual (or perhaps pedagogical) dexterity. That is, they selected a wider range of books than their mainstream counterparts from the previous study and they could shift the elements of the tutorial within and across texts.

**Study Three (Wolfgramm, 1991)**

The performance style of reading was examined further in a more homogeneous group of families. Eight Tongan families, permanent residents in New Zealand who were part of one church group, were contacted through personal networks. They identified their families as Tongan (Mo'ui Fakatonga). Their occupations placed them at levels 4 and 5 on the New Zealand SES index of 6 levels. Adults other than parents as well as nieces and nephews lived in five of the eight households.

**TABLE 5.3. Focus of Exchanges in Storybook Reading: Mean Percentages of Routines for 5 Families**

| Focus | Mean Percent |
|---|---|
| Narrative | 0% |
| Print | 0% |
| Book—Other | 0% |
| Performance | 100% |

From: Wolfgramm (1991)

There were two to five children in the families, one of whom, a 3 or 4 year old, was the focus of our attention.

Interview and diary records showed that four families read daily with the 3 or 4 year old. The other four families read three times a week. In four of the families one person consistently read, in the other families young aunts and older siblings also assumed the role. The book-reading settings were all multiparty but often with an adult caregiver present.

All families read storybooks and in five families, other books too. Five families supplied audiotapes in which at least two storybook readings occurred over a week. In one family there were no insertions or performance routines; the reader read without interruptions. For the remaining four families, three "stages" of tutorials that only employed performance routines were observed in different readings (see Table 5.3). These are shown in Dialogue 5. In the initial stage, the reader demonstrated a part of the text and the child imitated. In the second stage, children read much of the text by themselves and hesitations or misreadings were repaired by the reader. In the third stage, the whole text was performed alone (there were examples from three families of preschoolers reading texts entirely by themselves).

Dialogue 5: The development of routines with a performance focus

(Early reading)
Reader: Why hares have long ears.
Child: Why hares have long ears.
Reader: Once upon a time.
Child: Once upon a time.

(Intermediate reading)
Child: She is up on the tree.
She is up on the...(pause)
Reader: Stool.
Child: Stool.
She is up on the horse.

(Later reading)
Child: One day mouse, rabbit, and elephant went to the fair. Mouse went up, rabbit went up, elephant went up.

## PERFORMANCE TUTORIALS AND SCAFFOLDING

A tutorial pattern that does not fit the standard application of the scaffolding model is utilized by some families in Aotearoa/New Zealand. Some families practice this relatively exclusively. Others are pedagogically dexterous, shifting between two major forms, each of which appears to have distinct goals. If the mainstream children in Study One could be described as apprenticed to comprehension, then children engaged in storybook reading within the performance tutorial were apprenticed to verisimilitude.

It can be argued that this nonstandard tutorial form shares most if not all of the core features of effective tutorials noted earlier. The more obvious features are easy to identify. For example, clearly a very effective tutorial structure could be created that was both adjustable and temporary. The support afforded by a complete demonstration of the text could be systematically reduced, and reapplied contingently on the child's growing control over the text. As a consequence, responsibility for accurate performance shifts to the child. A shared focus is suggested by the lack of confusion over what was expected, by the participation of siblings and other family members, and by the finding that some families (in the second study) could shift, seemingly with ease, between the two forms of tutorials.

The development of self-regulation through this tutorial form is more problematic. The behavioral indicators of self-regulation in the mainstream book reading—checking, reflection, and inquiry—do not appear to be appropriate indicators for the performance activity. Greenfield (1984) also noted that overt self-correction, inventive exercise, and play with patterns was not a priority for Zinacanteco apprentices learning to weave. Errorless learning of fixed patterns was linked to functions of weaving within the society. Yet she, too, described the tutorial patterns as instances of scaffolding because of the presence of the features of dynamic flexibility and shifting support.

This question has to do with the focus and constraints on self-reflection and regulation. In the case of becoming an expert performer, monitoring to prevent inaccuracy and, at least during acquisition, to limit creative generalization are important responsibilities. This is an argument for variation in the status and forms self-regulation might take across different tutorial forms.

## PERFORMANCE TUTORIALS, PEDAGOGY, AND CULTURE

The last feature to consider is that the children were engaged in a form of a mature task that expressed and constructed social and cultural meanings. Connections can be sketched between two types of messages and the tutorial form as used by Maori, Samoan, and Tongan families. The performance pedagogy carries messages about the authority of texts and experts, and the role of the individual in teaching and learning.

However, Kessen's (1991) caveat, that we are likely to underestimate the extensiveness and subtlety of cultural diversity in products and processes, is apposite. Cultural messages are multifaceted, and only limited observations can be made here. Similarly, there are important differences both within and between groups of families that can not be treated in depth.

### Authority

The performance tutorial form is a core part of Maori preferred pedagogy (Metge, 1984). In traditional contexts of formal teaching, rote learning and memorization were key instructional devices, especially for the essential shared knowledge of the tribe contained in genealogies, songs, and narratives.

> Maori puukenga (knowledgeable experts) set unfashionable store by memorisation and rote learning. Nowadays the memorisation process itself has become a matter of "teaching" in the form of group practice led by an expert. The puukenga leading these learning sessions follow a similar procedure, with variations, repeating each name or phrase a couple of times, adding the next, repeating again from the beginning, adding the next, repeating again, and so on to the end. Some "teachers" using this method give little or no explanation of the content until the words have been mastered; others discuss meaning at intervals during the memorising arguing that it is easier to remember what is understood.... it is clear that rote learning is not an end in itself but the first step towards the goal of meaningful performance...knowing which to use and when, and that depends on knowing the background, being able to size up the situation, and to make the right choice. (Metge, 1984, p. 8)

Among other things this pedagogy can be linked to beliefs about the authority of oral texts and the nature of knowledge. In an oral culture traditional needs for the accuracy of oral texts and a stress on the preservation of knowledge are central concerns. It is also linked to a principle that knowledge is precious and to be treasured. This sense of guardianship and protection reinforces the value of representing knowledge accurately and without embellishment. (Although Metge [1984] points out that both in traditional and contemporary contexts form and content are continually adapted to serve current needs.)

For Samoan families written texts reflect a set of values associated with the authority of church teachings and a strong respect for the church and for schooling. Early literacy experiences and resources are promoted and channelled by the pastor school (in Samoa) or church and Sunday-school-sponsored activities in Aotearoa/New Zealand. Because of the relationship between the church, schooling, and literacy the reading of texts also represents the authority of elders, and supports adherence to significant religious beliefs (Duranti & Ochs, 1986).

These and other associated values can be seen in daily reading from the Bible and family devotions (lotu) which are common in Samoan families (McNaughton & Ka'ai, 1990). Several purposes are entailed in this activity. There are the purposes associated with religious beliefs. But there are also others, including the cohesion of the family and its commitment to shared beliefs, roles, and responsibilities in the Fa'asamoa (the Samoan way). For example, Tagoilelagi (cited in McNaughton, 1995), describing a family's lotu, identified grandparents, parents, children, and grandchildren being present. The performance tutorial was used when younger members were taught biblical passages. During lotu the leader (who reads first) has a position of prestige. Asking the young 7- and 8-year-old grandchildren to take over the role of leading the devotion marked the later stages of shifting of responsibility. But this was seen also as fulfilling the older members' responsibility for nurturing the younger ones (including aiding their reading development) and as a way of telling them that they were cared for.

This illustrates the close interweaving and multiplicity of cultural meanings in activities. The net result is to produce an essential high redundancy of messages in the socialization process (Valsiner, 1994). In the present case of lotu the Bible-reading activity carried mutually reinforcing meanings about authority and also group cohesion.

The authority of texts and the presence of performance tutorials is associated with religious values in Tongan families, too. For example, the performance tutorial is a standard form used in Sunday schools to learn hymns and church texts. The Tongan children in Study Three also were observed learning hymns, Bible verses, and articles of faith at their Sunday school. Performance tutorials were used in these activities. A segment of one such tutorial, part way through the learning of a new hymn, is shown in Dialogue 6 (Wolfgramm, 1991). For these families, similar cultural messages were being transmitted across activity settings in the use of written texts, again creating redundant messages for socialization.

Dialogue 6: A segment from a performance tutorial for learning a hymn in a Tongan Sunday school.

| | |
|---|---|
| Teacher: | ... Taha ... Hiva!<br>(... One ... Sing!) (pointing at the board) |
| Class: | (They sing the first line of the hymn.) |
| Teacher: | Toe ai ... Ua ... Hiva!<br>(Again ... Two ... Sing!) |
| Class: | (They repeat the first line of the hymn.) |
| Teacher: | Sai ...<br>(Good ...)<br>(Teacher sings second line of the hymn.) |
| Teacher: | A'i pe ia ...<br>(Sing just that line) |
| Class: | (They sing the second line of the hymn.) |

## The Role of the Individual

Important views of family roles and the nature of literacy are carried in the participation structures of book-reading sessions. All of the sessions of book reading taped with the Tongan families were multiparty (involving more than one other person) rather than dyadic. All of these families had two or more children, so this finding may not be surprising. But the list of participants included more than siblings who were present; it included aunts and female cousins. By contrast, even though 7 of the 10 Pakeha families in the first study had two or more children, only a third of the sessions recorded over a 28-day period involved more than one reader and the preschooler. In all of the Maori and Samoan families involved in the second study there were examples of multiparty sessions, whereas in only two of the Pakeha families was this the case. This was despite the fact that in all of the families there was an older sibling.

Group learning is a preferred pedagogical mode for Maori (Metge, 1984). This preference does not exclude personalized learning interactions, which can be seen occurring in group settings and shared activities. But the development of individual expertise carries responsibilities for the group. For Maori, knowledge is a group possession, not belonging to the individual, and to be used in the service of the group. The pedagogical preference is derived also from significant cultural values associated with the concept of whanaungatanga (literally, "familiness"). One expression of this principle in the socialization of Maori families is the relationship referred to as Tuakana-Teina (Hohepa, Smith, Smith, &

McNaughton, 1992). This describes the role of an older sibling or more expert member of the group in taking responsibility for the needs of a younger or less expert member of the group.

Similarly, descriptions of Samoan socialization patterns identify older siblings and extended family as often being expected to take immediate responsibility for looking after the needs of the younger siblings. The responsiveness of older siblings and extended family to young children, at times instead of a parent, carries meanings about differential status of child-rearers. Child-rearing patterns reflect values associated with the priority of familiness, including loyalty to the extended family unit (Ochs, 1982).

In Tongan families similar principles are at work in who reads to the preschooler. In traditional society, as soon as a child is weaned and becomes less reliant on his or her mother, older children in the family take charge. The values of this responsibility within the group is derived from the principle of Fatongia (the Tongan way). Older extended family members have a role to care for the younger members (Wolfgramm, 1991).

## TUTORIAL CONFIGURATIONS

These three studies suggest the presence of two major configurations of tutorials for the activity of storybook reading in different families in Aotearoa/New Zealand. Recently, writers have discussed core features of effective scaffolding that may be universal to socialization tutorials (Rogoff, 1990; Lave & Wenger, 1991). A similar general position has been adopted in this chapter. But the analysis here has stressed the presence of different configurations for tutorials expressing these core features in activities across sociocultural groups. The first configuration might be described as collaborative participation (in the construction of narrative meanings). The second configuration can be described as directed performance (of accurate renditions of text). But each configuration operationalizes the core features.

The concept of different configurations may be a useful device to study variations in tutorial patterns. Other examples of tutorials in literacy activities can be described using the concept of configuration. For example, the activity of reading picture books typically is configured differently, with repeated display questions occurring during sequences of reader questions, child responses, and reader evaluations (Sulzby & Teale, 1991).

The concept of configurations holds implications for further research. For example, different configurations in book reading are likely to have different developmental outcomes. Research evidence supports the argument that schema for narrative structures and comprehension strategies develop from collaborative participation (Sulzby & Teale, 1991).

Extensive and generalized experience with performance tutorials for text is likely to produce other forms of expertise, particularly in the development of recitation memory. We are currently pursuing this question in our research, following the limited support for this prediction in Wagner and Spratt's (1987) Moroccan study. They compared cognitive outcomes for children in Quranic preschools with several groups of other Moroccan children. The pedagogy in the Quranic preschools consisted of large amounts of recitation and memorization of verses from the Quran in Arabic. Compared with children in other preschools not emphasising this pedagogy, and children not going to preschools, the Quranic preschool children had superior performances on specific cognitive tasks to do with serial memory. The patterning of results suggests that the specificity of the profiles was due to the pedagogy, not Arabic literacy per se (Wagner & Spratt, 1987, p. 1217).

Another implication bears on a concern raised by Van der Veer and Valsiner (1994). They describe a "blind spot" in the understanding of Vygotsky's writings and the use of sociocultural concepts that underlie the scaffolding model. It is the uncritical assumption that an "educational utopia" is achievable with collaborative encounters. Clearly, good and poor tutorials are possible within multiple socialization goals. The task is to plot how variations in configurations enable effective learning and which ecological conditions facilitate or impede families from functioning with effective tutorials.

Different configurations will have their own internal criteria for effectiveness. Tutorials can be well or poorly implemented to achieve the purposes of the family's literacy practices and more general socialization goals. For example, the degree of overt collaboration and the coherence of the questions and comments in collaborative participation might determine the development of comprehension strategies for narrative texts. In directed performance tutorials, the clarity and chunking of the model may determine the speed of acquisition of accurate performance. Different configurations and their developmental outcomes may have different relationships with school forms of literacy.

A final comment concerns the growth of what has become a normative model. Tutorials take place in family activities. Activities reflect, express, and construct social and cultural practices (Rogoff, 1990). One reason why some configurations may have been judged as inadequate is because researchers have not understood the relationships between what is being observed and their social and cultural meanings in activities (McNaughton, 1994). Recent evidence suggests that published research involving

African Americans has substantially decreased in Journals of the American Psychological Association over the last 20 years (Graham, 1992). In Aotearoa/New Zealand similar marginalization and ethnocentricity in research has occurred. There are few researchers who are Maori or members of Pacific Islands groups, and barriers to increased participation are present in such things as editorial policies and definitions of appropriate research practice.

Another reason for the normative view stems from assumptions about the nature of development. Literacy development often has been assumed to follow a fixed unitary sequence dictated by universal stages (e.g., Goodman, 1990) or constructed through a core set of concepts (e.g. Mason & Allen, 1986). In either case development is seen as moving inexorably towards a final state defined by schooled forms of literacy. Differences from the standard scaffolding model have been linked to the further development of literacy at school. Limited storybook reading, as well as infrequent experience of storybook reading, has been associated with problems in the development of literacy at school (Sulzby & Teale, 1991).

This position means that diversity in book-reading experiences comes to be seen explicitly or implicitly as nonfunctional or inadequate. However, an alternative view, from which the concept of configurations is derived, sees literacy in terms of increasing participation in social and cultural practices, within which multiple forms of expertise may develop (e.g. Lave & Wenger, 1991; Rogoff, 1990).

However, there are problems in uncritical analyses of pedagogical diversity. Developmental trajectories associated with different pedagogies intersect with developmental sites other than the family. Some forms of literacy carry more cultural capital in an educational system than others. For example, the early teaching of reading in schools in Aotearoa/New Zealand recognizes expertise in reading texts for narrative meanings, rather than expertise in recitation.

The challenge here is to employ explanations that clearly locate expertise in terms of the cultural identities of families and the immediate and more distant sites for their children's development. The analysis is limited if multiple trajectories and multiple settings are not considered (see also Damon, 1991). Consideration of multiple trajectories is especially important at the transition point between home and school. It is at this point that the complementarity of literacy practices across socialization settings assumes significance in literacy development and the "privileging" of different cultural messages occurs (McNaughton, 1995).

The reason why the Samoan adolescent in Albert Wendt's story and Alice in Lewis Carroll's have particular understandings of what to do with texts can be linked to their socialization experiences. Similarly, socialization practices are the reason why there might be more than one way to read storybooks to children in Aotearoa/New Zealand. The concept of tutorial configurations may contribute to understanding the significance of different practices and to increasing the degree to which socialization settings may become complementary.

## ACKNOWLEDGMENTS

This chapter partly is based on a paper presented at the Biennial Conference of the Society for Research in Child Development in New Orleans, March 1993. I would like to thank the families with whom we worked and the New Zealand Ministry of Education, which funded some of the research.

## REFERENCES

Carroll, L. (1986). *The complete illustrated works of Lewis Carroll.* London: Chancellor Press.

Cazden, C. (1988). *Classroom discourse*. Portsmouth, NH: Heinemann.

Damon, W. (1991). Problems of direction in socially shared cognition. In L. B. Resnick, J. M. Levine, & S. D. Teasdale (Eds.), *Perspectives in socially shared cognition* (pp. 384–397). Washington DC: American Psychological Association.

Duranti, A., & Ochs, E. (1986). Literacy instruction in a Samoan village. In B.B. Schieffelin & P. Gilmore (Eds.), *The acquisition of literacy: Ethnographic perspectives* (pp. 213–232). Norwood, NJ: Ablex.

Graham, S. (1992). "Most of the subjects were white and middle class": Trends in published research on African Americans in selected APA Journals, 1970–1989. *American Psychologist*, *47*(5), 629–639.

Greenfield, P.M. (1984). A theory of the teacher in the learning activities of everyday life. In B. Rogoff & J. Lave (Eds.), *Everyday cognition: Its development in social context* (pp. 117–138). Cambridge, MA: Harvard University.

Goodman, Y. (1990). *How children construct literacy.* Newark: International Reading Association.

Heath, S.B. (1982). What no bedtime story means: Narrative skills at home and at school. *Language in Society, 11*, 49–76.

Heath, S.B., & Branscombe, A. (1986). The book as a narrative prop in language acquisition. In B. B. Schieffelin & P. Gilmore (Eds.), *The acquisition of literacy: Ethnographic perspectives* (pp. 16–34). Norwood, NJ: Ablex.

Hohepa, M., Smith, G.H., Smith, L.T., & McNaughton, S. (1992). Te Kohanga Reo hei tikanga ako i te Reo Maori: Te Kohanga Reo as a context for language learning. *Educational Psychology, 12*(3&4), 323–346.

Kessen, W. (1991). Commentary: Dynamics of enculturation. In M. H. Bornstein (Ed.), *Cultural approaches to parenting* (pp. 185–193). Hillsdale, NJ: Lawrence Erlbaum.

Lave, J., & Wenger, (1991). *Situated learning: Legitimate peripheral participation.* Cambridge: Cambridge University Press.

McNaughton, S. (1991). The faces of instruction: Models of how children learn from tutors. In J. Morss & T. Linzey (Eds.), *Growing up: The politics of human learning* (pp. 135–150). Auckland, New Zealand: Longman.

McNaughton, S. (1994) Human development and the reconstruction of culture: A commentary on Valsiner (1994). In P. Van Geert & L. Mos (Eds.), *Annals of theoretical psychology* (Vol. X, pp. 311–324). New York: Plenum.

McNaughton, S. (1995). *Patterns of emergent literacy: Processes of development and transition.* Auckland, New Zealand: Oxford University Press.

McNaughton, S., & Ka'ai, T. (1990). Two studies of transitions: socializations of literacy and Te hiringa take take: Mai i Te Kohanga Reo ki te kura. Report to the New Zealand Ministry of Education, Wellington, New Zealand: Ministry of Education.

Mason, J. M., & Allen, J. (1986). A review of emergent literacy with implications for research and practice in reading. In E. Z. Rothkopf (Ed.), *Review of research in education* (Vol. 13, pp. 3–47). Washington, DC: American Educational Research Association.

Metge, J. (1984). *Learning and teaching: He tikanga Maori.* Wellington, New Zealand: Ministry of Education.

Ochs, E. (1982). Talking to children in Western Samoa. *Language in Society, 11*, 77–104.

Pellegrini, A. D., Perlmutter, J. C., Galda, L., & Brody, G. H. (1990). Joint book reading between black Head Start children and their mothers. *Child Development, 61*, 443–453.

Peters, A. M., & Boag, S. T. (1987). Interactional routines as cultural influences upon language acquisition. In B. B. Schieffelin & E. Ochs (Eds.), *Language socialization across cultures* (pp. 80–96). New York: Cambridge University Press.

Phillips, G., & McNaughton, S. (1990). The practice of storybook reading to preschool children in mainstream New Zealand families. *Reading Research Quarterly, 25*(3), 196–212.

Rogoff, B. (1990). *Apprenticeship in thinking: Cognitive development in social context.* New York: Oxford University Press.

Sulzby, E., & Teale, W. (1991). Emergent literacy. In R. Barr, M. Kamil, P. Rosenthal, & D. Pearson (Eds.), *Handbook of reading research* (Vol. 2, pp. 727–757). New York: Longman.

Wagner, D.A., & Spratt, J.E. (1987) Cognitive consequences of contrasting pedagogies: The effects of Quranic pre-schooling in Morocco. *Child Development, 58*, 1207–1219.

Valsiner, J. (1987). *Culture and the development of children's action.* Chichester, England: John Wiley & Sons. (2nd ed., 1997).

Valsiner, J. (1994). Culture and human development: A co-constructivist perspective. In P. Van Geert & L. Mos (Eds.), *Annals of theoretical psycholgy* (Vol. X, pp. 247–298). New York: Plenum.

Van der Veer, R., & Valsiner, J. (Eds.). (1994). *The Vygotsky reader.* Oxford: Basil Blackwell.

Wendt, A. (1986). Exam failure praying. In *The Birth and death of the miracle man: A collection of short stories*. New York: Viking.

Wolfgramm, E. (1991). Becoming literate: The activity of book reading to Tongan preschoolers in Auckland. Unpublished Master's thesis, University of Auckland, Auckland, New Zealand.

Wood, D. (1989). *How children think and learn*. Oxford: Basil Blackwell.

Wood, D., Bruner, J., & Ross, G. (1976). The role of tutoring in problem solving. *Journal of Child Psychology and Psychiatry, 17*, 89–100.

chapter 6

# Literacy and Language Processes—Orthographic and Structural Effects

Prathibha Karanth
All India Institute of Speech & Hearing
Manasa Gangothri, Mysore, India

## INTRODUCTION

Literacy has long been considered to be closely linked to cognitive development; in fact, it is considered to be crucial for certain aspects of it. The invention of writing has been accorded the status of an important agent of both individual and societal development. It is assumed that literacy changes the basic nature of the thought processes of an individual and ultimately through mass literacy that of human societies at large. Goody and Watt (1968) suggest that the invention of writing systems was instrumental for the emergence of history as distinct from myth and the founding of formal logic. Since literacy objectifies spoken language by creating new symbolic languages for manipulation, it is thought to be associated with unique kinds of logical competency and a higher level of conceptual thought. From the viewpoint of the individual, literacy manifests itself in new modes of concept formation and in the awareness of thought itself (Dash, 1990).

Two distinct interpretations of the role of literacy in cognitive growth have been put forth—the developmental perspective and the practice perspective (Scribner & Cole, 1978). The developmental perspective suggests that literacy develops mental capacities that have widespread intellectual consequences. Greenfield (1972) argues that written speech is at a higher level of abstraction than oral speech, which is a context-dependent language. Written language requires that meaning be made clear, independent of the immediate and the concrete reference. Written language provides the means for decontextualized abstract thinking. Illiterate adults are found to confine their mental operations to the immediate, concrete, and practical with little reference to abstract and categorical associations (Luria, 1971; Cole et al., 1971). The developmental perspective on literacy and cognition therefore proposes that the effects of literacy are the emergence of abstract thinking and logical operations rather than specific skills.

The proponents of the practice perspective, on the other hand, distinguish between the intellectual effects of "schooled" and "nonschooled" literacy. On the basis of empirical evidence on schooled and non-schooled Vai's in Liberia, they concluded that there is no evidence that "reading and writing entail fundamental cognitive restructurings that control intellectual performance in all domains" (Scribner & Cole, 1978). Instead they argued that schooled literacy may be closely tied to the performance parameters of a limited set of tasks.

Researchers in traditional oral societies have also questioned the validity of the inferences on the different implications of oral and written communication for cognitive development, and charge the adherents of the developmental perspective with reintroducing the earlier discredited distinction between "logical" and "prelogical" by "literate" and "nonliterate" (Srivastava, 1990). Instead they assert that there is a need to view the orality and literacy distinction in a much wider perspective of communication theory.

Nevertheless, while the questions of whether the effects of literacy on cognition are general or limited to specific skills and whether these effects are to be found only in literates of the schooled kind or can be achieved to the same extent through alternate means by nonschooled literates, remains unresolved; it is generally conceded that literacy does contribute to cognitive development.

## METALINGUISTIC AWARENESS

An aspect of the acquisition of literacy of the schooled variety that has attracted increasing attention over the last decade or so is the language user's attitudes towards, and manipulations of, language itself. This awareness, termed metalinguistic ability, is said to be a "developmentally distinct kind of linguistic functioning that develops separately from and later than basic speaking and listening skills" (Tunmer, 1991, p. 105). Metalinguistic performance requires reflecting upon one or another aspect of language per se and is defined as "the ability to separate a word from its referent, dissociating the meaning of a sentence from its form and reflecting on the component elements of spoken words" (Tunmer, 1991, p. 105). A wide variety of metalinguistic abilities are acquired during mid-childhood and they all involve controlled processing of a sort different from the more automatic processing characteristic of speech comprehension and production. Further, the development of metalinguistic awareness is said to lead to metacognitive skills such as reflecting and monitoring one's thoughts. It is therefore seen as an important aspect of child development.

Empirical studies on metalinguistic abilities in children have elicited this information through experimental tasks involving phonemic analysis, structural ambiguity detection, grammaticality judgement, synonymy judgement, message consistency judgement, and story comprehension and narration tasks. On the basis of their empirical investigations most researchers in this area agree that metalinguistic abilities are developmental in nature and are acquired gradually around mid-childhood (Bever, 1970; De Villiers & de Villiers, 1972; Bohannon, 1976; Gleitman & Gleitman, 1979; Karmiloff-Smith, 1979; Hakes, Evan, & Tunmer, 1980; Scholl & Ryan, 1980; Van Kleek, 1982, 1984; Pratt, Tunmer, & Bowey, 1984). However, causal interpretations offered by these researchers differ. Three major viewpoints exist: (a) that metalinguistic awareness is incidental to language acquisition, (b) that it is a consequence of decentration of cognitive processes, and (c) that it is directly related to the experience of learning to read.

### Metalinguistic Awareness as a Concomitant of Language Acquisition

Psycholinguists like Clark (1978) and Karmiloff-Smith (1979), on the basis of their investigation on language development in young children, report that 5 years seems to be a frontier age representing development with a gradual passage from extralinguistic to intralinguistic references both in speech utterances and later in metalinguistic awareness. The development of metalinguistic skills around the age of 8 years is said to parallel a new phase in language development when the child seems to attain the capacity for a more abstract level of comprehension and can cope if need be without the interplay of functional, syntactic, semantic, and pragmatic clues used in normal discourse. These new skills are seen as being symptomatic of an internal reorganization of linguistic categories and a new phase in linguistic development.

### Metalinguistic Awareness as a Linguistic Manifestation of the Piagetian Cognitive Developmental Changes Occurring at the Concrete Operational Period

Researchers like Lundberg (1978); Hakes, Evan, & Tunmer (1980); and Tunmer, Herriman, and Nesdale (1988) have suggested that metalinguistic skills may be linked to the Piagetian process of decentration. Metalinguistic performance, they argue, requires the ability to decenter, to shift one's attention from message content to the properties of language used to convey content. An essential feature of both metalinguistic abilities and decentration is the ability to control the course of one's thought, that is, to invoke control processing. According to this view, poor metalinguistic skills are a reflection of a developmental lag in decentration processes. It is not suggested that high levels of metalinguistic ability emerge spontaneously in development. It is proposed that during middle childhood children develop the capacity for becoming metalinguistically aware when confronted with certain kinds of tasks, such as learning to read. However, it is also postulated that a certain threshold level of decentration ability must be attained by children before they can acquire the low-level metalinguistic operations necessary to acquire basic reading skills.

### Metalinguistic Awareness Consequent to Reading Acquisition Which Starts With Schooling in Mid-Childhood

A third viewpoint suggests that experience in reading and writing may facilitate the development of "metacommunication," because written messages "stay put" and remain accessible for critical evaluation (Olson, 1972; Donaldson, 1976). On the basis of his work relating children's performance in school with the literacy-related activities that they were exposed to in their preschool years, Wells (1982) argued that school literacy leads to better metalinguistic skills. Flavell (1985) extends this notion to include experiences associated with formal schooling that help children learn about the nature and management of communicative enterprises by making frequent and explicit demands to communicate clearly to others and to monitor the clarity and comprehensibility of the communications they receive.

Ehri (1982) proposes a more direct relationship between learning to read and write and the development of metalinguistic skills. Metalinguistic processes are said to be facilitated by the concrete picture of language provided by writing because language can be detached from its communicative function, treated as an object, and studied for its form more easily through writing, which provides the fixed visual and spatial symbols that can be seen and manipulated. Metalinguistic skills are said to benefit from print, which makes speech visible. Further, their development is said to be aided by familiarity with the terminology used to describe the structure of language, such as word, sentence, and so on, by providing children with the scheme for conceptualizing and analyzing the structure of speech. To quote Ehri,

> Written language supplies a visual-spatial model for speech and when children learn to read and spell, this model and its symbols are internalized as a representational system in memory. The process of acquiring this system works various changes on spoken language. Having a visual-spatial model for speech may facilitate performance in various metalinguistic tasks requiring speakers to detach language from its communicative form and inspect its form. (Ehri, 1982, p. 361)

### Empirical Evidence on Metalinguistic Skills in Speakers (Child and Adult) of an Agglutinative/Synthetic Language With a Nonalphabetic Script

Our interest in the metalinguistic skills of children and adults was incidental to the construction of a language test in which the grammaticality judgement task was used to elicit a quick measure of children's syntactic competence. The syntactic section of the Linguistic Profile Test (LPT; Karanth, 1980, 1984) requires the subject to judge the grammaticality of 130 sentences that systematically sample across a broad range of sentence structures covering the core syntactic features of the Kannada language—a Dravidian language spoken in Karnataka, Southern India. In one of our very first studies using this test (Karanth, 1984) a group of children ranging in age from 2 to 14 years were studied. Of these children, those below the age of 5 to 6 years seemed unable to respond to the grammaticality judgement task and either accepted or rejected all given sentences without reflecting on their grammatical acceptability. Around 70 months of age, children were seen to begin attempting the task and performing at the chance level. By around 150 months of age, about 80% proficiency in grammaticality judgement was observed, with a sharp rise in this metalinguistic ability between the ages of 6 to 9 years. These findings were in agreement with the reports of Bohannon (1976); Karmiloff-Smith (1980); Hakes, Evan, and Tunmer (1980); and Van Kleek (1982).

In order to confirm these findings and also obtain norms on a larger group of children for the LPT, a similar investigation was undertaken with 150 children ranging in age from 6 to 11 years, with 30 each from Grade I through Grade V (for more details see Karanth & Suchitra,

1993; and Suchitra & Karanth, 1990). The results confirmed our earlier findings that beginning at age 6 to 7 years and with a rapid spur at about 7 to 8 years children become increasingly proficient in the grammaticality judgement task. Even by the age of 11 years, the upper limit of the age range covered here, children's sensitivity to grammaticality of given sentences was only about 80%. Given the overall correspondence of this data with the earlier findings (Karanth, 1984), we speculated that adult-like sensitivity to grammaticality is acquired by adolescence, since two of the 13 year olds in the first study performed at a level of 90% accuracy. Confirmation of this observation is being sought in an ongoing study on 11 to 15 year olds enrolled in Grades VI to X.

These findings are in agreement with much of the earlier studies on grammaticality judgement and metalinguistic awareness. This observation that children begin to acquire metalinguistic skills around mid-childhood and gradually increase their mastery over it can be interpreted as supporting all three causal theories—as a part of increasing command over language, as being due to developmental cognitive changes of decentration, and as being due to acquisition of reading and writing skills.

Subsequently, in a study of acquired language disorders in adults (Karanth, Ahuja, Nagaraj, Pandit, & Shivashankar, 1991, 1992), 100 normal adults ranging in age from 20 to 80 years were given the same task of grammaticality judgement on the LPT. Of these 100 subjects, 67 were literate with more than 4 years of formal schooling and 33 were illiterate with no formal schooling. The 67 literate adults performed satisfactorily on the test scoring an average of 90.9% and no one performing at chance level. Among the illiterates, on the other hand, 9 of the 33 either expressed their inability to do what was required after the instructions were given, did not complete all 130 items of the test, or responded indiscriminately, performing at chance level. The average score of the 33 illiterates was 63.8%. Even when the scores of the 9 subjects who did not complete the test were omitted, the average score of the illiterates worked out to be 71.9%. The illiterates scored uniformly poorly across all subcategories. Similar results were observed on the Hindi (language spoken in North India) version of the LPT on a group 100 adult native speakers of Hindi, comprising both literates and illiterates, suggesting that literacy is in itself a variable affecting metalinguistic abilities such as grammaticality judgement.

In comparison with literate adults, the illiterate adults were also found to perform poorly on a clinical test for aphasia, particularly on tasks such as auditory verbal comprehension of complex syntactic structures and, to a lesser extent, with repetition and amount of information conveyed in expressive speech. These results are similar to that reported by

Lecours et al. (1987). Lecour et al. found statistically significant differences between the scores of their literate and illiterate sub-populations in tasks such as pointing, naming, and repetition, and emphasized the need for norms that explicitly take educational level into account for clinical tests of language.

Given our results—that the metalinguistic skill of grammaticality judgement is not present in children below the age of 6 years and gradually develops over mid-childhood, and that the same is inadequately present in illiterate adults as compared to literate adults—a more comprehensive study on 50 school-going and 50 non-school-going children in the age range of 6 to 11 years and 30 literate and 30 illiterate adults in the age range of 21 to 40 years was taken up. Because illiterate adults also seemed to have some difficulty on tasks such as auditory verbal comprehension of some verbal commands and expressive tasks such as naming and information giving (Lecours et al., 1987; Karanth et al., 1992), the 160 subjects of this study were evaluated on their ability to comprehend and produce a range of syntactic structures through picture-pointing and description tasks, in addition to the grammaticality judgement task on the LPT (for more details see Karanth, Kudva, & Vijayan, 1995). The results confirmed our earlier observation that literate and illiterate adults differ considerably in the metalinguistic task of grammaticality judgement. Differences between the two groups were also seen in the tasks on comprehension and production of some syntactic structures, confirming our earlier findings that the lack of comparable syntactic awareness among illiterates extends to tasks such as auditory verbal comprehension and expression, though not to the same extent as seen in metalinguistic tasks such as grammaticality judgement. These differences were also present among the school-going and non-school-going children. Though a developmental trend on all tasks were seen among the two groups of children, the school-going children performed significantly better than the nonschooled children, suggesting that these skills are enhanced by acquisition of literacy.

Repeatedly, in a series of investigations on grammaticality judgement, we find that children begin to acquire these skills in mid-childhood around 6 years of age and gradually master them over a period of time until adolescence. Children who receive schooling perform considerably better than nonschooled children, with this difference in performance persisting into adulthood. Further, these differences are also reflected in their language use. It is apparent that the acquisition of literacy has an important role to play in one's ability to master grammaticality judgement. Formal education enhances the ability to separate form and content, which is said to be the basis of metalinguistic skills such as grammaticality judgement. Adult illiterates, whose only exposure to form is limited to the oral speech output of other speakers, inclusive of their performance errors fail to develop this sensitivity of grammatical form to the same extent as literate adults. The process of literacy acquisition by reducing external cues increases one's ability to gather information purely through the abstractions of written language, in turn leading to a more abstract level of linguistic analysis.

That the acquisition of literacy affects linguistic awareness is not unknown. Work on phonological awareness with acquisition of literacy is documented by Ehri (1979). Ehri's observations were corroborated by Morais, Cary, Alegria, and Bertelson (1979), who demonstrated that awareness of phonetic units in speech does not develop spontaneously or as a result of cognitive maturation but requires special experiences such as learning to read.

Prakash, Rekha, Nigam, and Karanth (1993) carried out a parallel series of investigations on literacy and phonological awareness in Kannada- and Hindi-speaking adults (literate and illiterate) and children. On metaphonological measures such as rhyme-recognition, syllable-deletion, phoneme-oddity, and phoneme-deletion tasks it was observed that school-going children in the age range of 6 to 9 years (Grades I to III) performed well on rhyme-recognition and syllable-deletion but poorly on phoneme-oddity and phoneme-deletion tasks. Although syllable deletion was uniformly easy, phoneme deletion was uniformly difficult, with only a slight improvement over the grades. These results are contradictory to those obtained in similar studies on children learning alphabetic scripts, and support the notion that phoneme awareness is not a critical factor in nonalphabetic literacy, as the children in this study performed at above-average level on reading while faring poorly on phoneme tasks. Because the level of representation in Kannada is not at a phonemic level, children learning to read in Kannada may not necessarily develop phonemic awareness in their early literacy stages like their Western counterparts. However, those children who were extraordinarily good at reading were generally good on phoneme tasks as well. It is relevant that even on the grammaticality judgement tasks there were a few exceptional illiterates who performed well.

In a second study in this series, phonological awareness in adult literates and illiterates was investigated in Hindi, which shares the same orthographic features of Kannada, both being based on the Brahmi script. As expected, both illiterate and literate groups performed well on rhyme-recognition and syllable-deletion tasks but poorly on the phoneme-deletion task. Even so, there was a significant difference between the literates and illiterates on the latter task, with the results showing the influence of specific orthographic features of Hindi (for more details see Prakash et al., 1993). Thus the results clearly demonstrated that sensitivity to rhymes and development of syllable awareness are independent of literacy, though they may be enhanced further by literacy-related factors. On the other hand, literacy skills in a semi-syllabic script are inadequate for the development of phonemic awareness.

In a third study using the same procedures, the two groups of subjects consisted of adult illiterates and biliterates. Whereas the illiterates were native speakers of Kannada without any exposure to reading and writing, the biliterates were graduates proficient in both Kannada and English. The performance of the biliterates was found to be superior in all four tasks, including phoneme-deletion and phoneme-oddity tasks—a result that was attributed to their exposure to alphabetic literacy. These results clearly demonstrated that phoneme awareness does not develop spontaneously but is a consequence not only of literacy, but of alphabetic literacy in particular.

In brief, the results of these investigations on metaphonological tasks indicate that all subjects—illiterates, nonalphabetic uniliterates, and Kannada-English biliterates—performed well in rhyme-recognition and syllable-deletion tasks but only the biliterates (with exposure to alphabetic scripts) could do well in phonemic-segmentation tasks. The analysis of nonalphabetic uniliterates' responses to these tasks clearly demonstrated the influence of the spelling system they were exposed to. The performance of the Kannada-English biliterate subjects, on the other hand, show how learning the alphabetic code could influence the processing of a nonalphabetic system.

## THE SCRIPT FACTOR

These results on metalinguistic tasks at the phonological and grammatical level from a nonalphabetic milieu raise questions about the specific nature of the relationships between literacy and various metalinguistic abilities. It appears that not only is one's ability to manipulate the structural features of language facilitated by the process of literacy acquisition but, further, the level of representation of the language in the script influences specific types of metalinguistic skills. The script emerges as a variable in the study of the metalinguistic and cognitive consequences of learning to read.

The results of a few recent investigations on the cognitive and metalinguistic implications of learning to read various scripts are unequivocal. Vaid (in press), in an investigation of the effects of directionality of script (Hindu vs. Urdu) on the more general cognitive and representational processes, found that the direction of the script influenced related tasks such as drawing and scanning of pictures, suggesting that reading habits do tend to influence perceptual and cognitive activity more generally. Geva (in press) examined children who were learning to read both English and Hebrew, the scripts of which are different. She reported that reading skills were not unique to each orthography because good readers were good in both languages, and suggested that language and cognitive abilities more general than those specifically involved in decoding a specific orthography are central to reading. In contrast, Koda (in press) reported that the effects of learning to read a first language in one orthographic system influences learning to read a second language involving a different orthographic system, on the basis of her findings that readers of alphabetic scripts for L1 were disrupted by the presence of difficult, unfamiliar words in L2 much more seriously than were readers of morphological scripts in L1.

### Indian Scripts

The Indian writing systems, be they of languages of the Indo-Aryan group like Hindi, or those of Dravidian origin such as Kannada, have originated from the Brahmi script and hence have a common underlying system. This system is semi-syllabic, with the syllable and not the phoneme (except in the case of the vowels described below) being the smallest basic independent unit of writing. The substantial part of the letter (aksara) is the consonant that precedes the vowel, the vowel itself being implied or indicated by a secondary sign attached to the consonant. The primary form of the vowel is used only when it forms a morpheme by itself or as an independent syllable when it is not combined with a preceding consonant, that is, when it is in the word initial position. When more than one consonant precedes the vowel, forming with it a single syllable, their characters must be combined into a single compound character. Reading is taught syllable by syllable and it is these syllables which are sub-units of words (for more details see Karanth, 1985; Patel & Soper, 1987; Prakash & Joshi, 1989).

## LANGUAGE STRUCTURE

At the syntactic level, Kannada is a polysyllabic agglutinative language with numerous inflections. It has a basic word order of the SOV type and is richly inflected with syntactic markers that are suffixed to the noun and verb stems. Person and gender are identified by three markers each. The singular has no particular distinguishing marker; the plural is denoted by a specific marker. The seven cases are marked by adding various suffixes to the noun stem to indicate different relationships between the noun and other constituents of the sentence. Pronouns are classified in accordance with the person markers and when marked for case the pronounal stems change. Most adjectives are derivatives of nouns or verbs. The verb stem gets inflected with different suffixes and forms various verbal forms such as infinitives, imperatives, participles, modal auxiliaries, dative-stative or "defective" forms, verbal aspect markers, "causative" suffixes, "conditional" suffixes, and verbalizers, making the verb phrase forms more complex than the noun systems. Number adjective and adverb forms function in effecting changes in the noun phrase and verb phrase, respectively. Conditional clauses, relative clauses, and cleft sentences are possible by effecting changes in the verb phrase. A number of clitic constructions are also available, making Kannada a richly inflected language with fairly extensive case and complex verb systems (Schiffman, 1979).

## DISCUSSION

Prakash et al.'s results (1993) on the metaphonological tasks of phoneme oddity and phoneme deletion seem to be directly consequent to the semi-syllabic nature of the orthography. Itemwise analysis of subjects' performance on phoneme oddity revealed that children of all grades performed quite well (70% accuracy level, on average) on those items in which the target phoneme was a consonant, with further improvement over the grades being entirely due to the improved performance of higher graders on vowel items. These results can be attributed to the syllabic structure of Kannada in which the syllable is dominated by the form of the consonant, the associated vowel being attached to it in its secondary (less distinct) form. This visual/spelling strategy was also evident in phoneme deletion where, for example, if the phonemes to be deleted were "arka" or "anuswara" (the two exceptional phonemes that have independent graphemes), almost all the children found them easily. This is in contrast to the observation made by Perfetti, Beck, Bell, and Hughes (1988) that consonant blends such as /nt/ resist segmentation into phoneme constituents. This relationship between segmental awareness and alphabetic literacy was also evident in the results obtained from literate and illiterate adults on these tasks, in which the influence of specific orthographic features of Hindi was very vivid and further substantiates our observation that the orthographic features favouring segmentation skills are script-specific (for more details see Prakash et al., 1993). The results on the Kannada-English biliterates further supports this theoretical relationship between segmental awareness and alphabetic literacy, for these biliterates who had learnt an alphabetic script performed well on the phoneme-oddity and phoneme-deletion tasks in the syllabic script.

Just as the level of representation in the script affects the extent to which phonological awareness develops, the specific structural characteristics of the language could differentially affect other metalinguistic skills. Given the agglutinative, highly inflected nature of Kannada syntax, it is possible that lack of exposure to literacy affects the metalinguistic task of grammaticality judgement to a greater extent than it would in languages like English where the syntax is expressed to a comparatively larger extent through free morphemes and word order.

That script-specific features are a factor to be considered in reading, models of reading, and teaching of reading has been substantiated by evidence from the reading disorders. Several case reports of adults with acquired reading disorders exhibiting different patterns across different scripts have been documented over the last couple of decades (Sasanuma, 1974; Karanth, 1981, 1985). Two major interpretations of these dissociations have been offered. The first attributes the differential patterns to a lesion affecting neural representation of reading skills in one language while sparing the other, the two languages supposedly being organized differently in the brain. The second interpretation is based on the hypothesis that two alternate routes are used in all reading—the whole word and the phonic. Different scripts rely more upon one or the other and the severity of the dyslexia in the different languages is said to be dependent upon the extent to which the language depends upon the affected route (Obler, 1984). Our data on developmental dyslexia in biliterates (Karanth, 1992), however, is not in consonance with the above hypotheses. On the basis of our data on young developmental dyslexics who are differentially affected in English as against Kannada and Hindi, we have argued that the differential patterns and different degrees of severity seen in these scripts are dependent upon whether the strategy required by the particular script is heavily dependent upon the particular component, the neural underpinnings of which is disturbed, rather than due to selective disturbance of "routes" or "representations."

The effect of language structure on the processing of syntax, hypothesized by us with reference to the grammaticality judgement task and sensitivity to syntax, also has some support from the acquired language disorders. That agrammatism manifests itself differently in different languages depending on the structure of the language has been documented (Grodzinsky, 1984; Srividya, 1990). As in the adult alexics and developmental dyslexics, differential patterns and severity of the disorder across the two languages of the bilingual aphasic with agrammatism have also been documented (Rangamani, 1989).

Our results on a series of studies on metalinguistic skills substantiate the observation that metalinguistic abilities develop maturationally but certain kinds of language experiences, including learning to read and write, can enhance it to a significant degree. This is not to state that metalinguistic abilities and a high degree of sensitivity to language structure cannot be achieved without schooling, for the mastery of the many nonschooled literates of traditional oral societies over language and literature is well documented. The emphasis instead is on the observation that schooled literacy, by and large, automatically brings about these metalinguistic skills and a heightened sensitivity to language, possibly triggering related cognitive abilities. Along with the greater access to information, it is perhaps these abilities that make literacy such an important tool of social change. An increased interest in and sensitivity to the kinds of activities that lead to these linguistic and cognitive consequences of literacy is therefore called for.

Furthermore, the substantial effects of language structure and script-specific features on metalinguistic abilities require that the significance of these factors be acknowledged and taken into consideration, particularly in theoretical models of the acquisition and use of language and literacy.

Another important aspect of the interrelationships between script acquisition in reading and reading disorders is the method of instruction. Methods of instruction for reading have seldom been script-specific. The "whole word" and "phonic" methods developed for alphabetic scripts are being advocated for all scripts without taking into consideration the essential features of each script or script type. If different scripts are enhanced by different strategies, it follows that the teaching of reading calls for script-specific methods.

## CONCLUSION

Different scripts enhance different types of metalinguistic abilities. These need to be investigated further, along with a greater probe into their linguistic and cognitive consequences. Better understanding of the factors involved in processing different scripts will be relevant not only for theoretical models of reading and literacy but also for the teaching of reading and management of the acquired and developmental dyslexias.

## REFERENCES

Bever, T.G. (1970). The cognitive basis for linguistic structure. In J.R. Hayes (Ed.), *Cognition and development of language.* New York: Wiley.

Bohannon, J.N. (1976). Normal and scrambled grammar in discrimination and sentence imitation in children. *Child Development, 46,* 441–451.

Clark, E.V. (1978). Awareness of language: Some evidence from what children say and do. In A.J. Sinclair, R.J. Jarvella, & W.J.M. Levelt (Eds.), *The child's conception of language.* Berlin, Germany: Springer-Verlag.

Cole, M., Gay, J., Glick, J.A., & Sharp, D.W. (1971). *The cultural context of learning and thinking.* New York: Basic Books.

Dash, U.N. (1990). Literacy and the development of cognitive skills. *Indian Journal of Adult Education, 51*(4), 89–99.

De Villiers, P.A. & de Villiers, J.G. (1972). Early judgement of semantic and syntactic acceptability by children. *Journal of Psycholinguistic Research, 1*(4), 294–310.

Donaldson, M. (1976). Development of conceptualization. In V. Hamilton & M.D. Vernon (Eds.), *The development of cognitive processes.* London: Academic Press.

Ehri, L.C. (1979). Linguistic insight: Threshold of reading acquisitions. In T.G. Waller & G.E. Mackinnon (Eds.), *Reading research: Advances in theory and practice* (pp. 93–111). New York: Harcourt, Brace, Jovanovich.

Ehri, L.C. (1982). Effects of printed language acquisition on speech. In D.R. Olson, N. Torrance, & A. Hildyard (Eds.), *Literacy, language and learning.* London: Cambridge University Press.

Flavell, J.H. (1985). *Cognitive development.* Englewood Cliffs, NJ: Prentice Hall.

Geva, E. (1995). Orthographic and cognitive processing in learning to read English and Hebrew. In I. Taylor & D.R. Olson (Eds.), *Scripts and literacy: Reading and learning to read the world's scripts* (pp. 277–291). London: Kluwer Academic Publishers.

Gleitman, L.R., & Gleitman, H. (1979). Language use and language judgement. In C.J. Fillmore, D. Kempler, & W.S.Y. Wang (Eds.), *Individual differences in language ability and language behavior.* New York: Academic Press.

Goody, J.S., & Watt, I. (1968). The consequences of literacy. In J. Goody (Ed.), *Literacy in traditional societies.* Cambridge, England: Cambridge University Press.

Greenfield, P.M. (1972). Oral and written language: The consequences of cognitive development in Africa, the United States and England. *Language and Speech, 15,* 169–178.

Grodzinsky, Y. (1984). The syntactic characterization of agrammatism. *Cognition, 16,* 99-120.

Hakes, D.T., Evan, J.S., & Tunmer, W.E. (1980). *The development of metalinguistic abilities in children.* Berlin, Germany: Springer-Verlag.

Karanth, P. (1980). A comparative analysis of aphasic and schizophrenic language. Doctoral Thesis, University of Mysore, India.

Karanth, P. (1981). Pure alexia in a Kannada-English bilingual. *Cortex* 17, Milan.

Karanth, P. (1984). Inter-relationship of linguistic deviance and social deviance—ICSSR Young Social Scientist's Fellowship Report, Mysore, CIIL.

Karanth, P. (1985). Dyslexia in a Dravidian language. In M. Coltheart, K. Patterson, & J. Marshall (Eds.), *Surface dyslexia: Neuropsychological and cognitive studies of phonological reading.* London: Lawrence Erlbaum Associates.

Karanth, P. (1992). Developmental dyslexia in bilingual biliterates. *Reading and Writing 4,* 297–306.

Karanth, P., Ahuja, G.K., Nagaraj, D., Pandit, R., & Shivashankar, N. (1991). Cross cultural studies of aphasia. In J.S. Chopra, K. Jagannathan, & I.M. Sawhney (Eds.), *Modern trends in neurology.* New Delhi, India: B.I. Churchill Livingstone.

Karanth, P., Ahuja, G.K., Nagaraja, D., Pandit, R., & Shivashankar, N. (1992). Language disorders in Indian neurological patients—a study in neurolinguistics in the Indian context. (Report No. 5/8/10-1 [Oto]/84-NCO-I IRIS Cell, ICMR 8403810) An Inter-Institutional Project in collaboration with AIIMS, Delhi, and NIMHANS, Bangalore, funded by the Indian Council of Medical Research.

Karanth, P., & Suchitra, M.G. (1993). Literacy acquisition and grammaticality judgements in children. In R. Scholes & B. Willis (Eds.), *Literacy: Linguistic and cognitive perspectives.* London: Lawrence Erlbaum Associates.

Karanth, P., Kudva, A., & Vijayan, A. (1995). Literacy and linguistic awareness. In B. de Gelder & J. Morais (Eds.), *Speech and reading.* U.K.: Erlbaum (UK) Taylor & Francis.

Karmiloff-Smith, A. (1979). Language development after 5 years. In P. Fletcher & M. Garman (Eds.), *Language acquisition* (pp. 307–323). Cambridge: Cambridge University Press.

Koda, K. (1995). Cognitive consequences of L1 and L2 orthographies. In I. Taylor & D.R. Olson (Eds.), *Scripts and literacy: Reading and learning to read the world's scripts* (pp. 311–326). London: Kluwer Academic Publishers.

Lecours, A.R., Mehler, J., Parente, M.A., Caldeira, A., Cary, L., Custro, M.J., Dehant, F., Dalgado, R., Gurd, J., Karmann, D., Jokubvitz, R., Osoria, Z., Cabral, L.S., & Junqueira, M.S. (1987). Illiteracy and brain damage-1. Aphasia testing in culturally contrasted populations (control subjects). *Neuropsychologia, 25*(18), 231–245. Britain.

Lundberg, I. (1978). Aspects of linguistic awareness related to reading. In A. Sinclair, R.J. Jarvella, & W.J.M. Levelt (Eds.), *The child's conception of language.* Berlin, Germany: Springer-Verlag.

Luria, A.R. (1971). Towards the problem of historical nature of psychological processes. *International Journal of Psychology, 6*(4), 259–272.

Morais, J., Cary, L., Alegria, J., & Bertelson, P. (1979). Does awareness of speech as a sequence of phonemes arise spontaneously? *Cognition, 7,* 323–331.

Obler, L. (1984). Dyslexia in bilinguals. In R. Malatesha & H.A. Whitaker (Eds.), *Dyslexia: A global issue.* The Hague, Netherlands: Martinns Nijoff Publishers.

Olson, D.R. (1972). Language use for communicating, instructing and thinking. In R.O. Freedly & J.B. Carroll (Eds.), *Language comprehension and the acquisition of knowledge.* Washington, DC: Winston.

Patel, P.G., & Soper, H.V. (1987). Acquisition of reading and writing in a syllabo-alphabetic writing system. *Language and Speech, 30,* 69–81.

Perfetti, C.A., Beck, I., Bell, L., & Hughes, C. (1988). Phonemic knowledge and learning to read are reciprocal: A longitudinal study of first grade children. In K.E. Stanovich (Ed.), *Children's reading and the development of phonological awareness.* Detroit, MI: Wayne State University Press.

Prakash, P., & Joshi, R.M. (1989). Language representation and reading in Kannada—A South Indian language. In P.G. Aaron & R.M. Joshi (Eds.), *Reading and writing disorders in different orthographic systems.* London: Kluwer Academic Publishers.

Prakash, P., Rekha, D., Nigam, R., & Karanth, P. (1993). Phonological awareness, orthography and literacy. In R. Scholes & B. Willis (Eds.), *Literacy: Linguistic and cognitive perspectives.* London: Lawrence Erlbaum Associates.

Pratt, C., Tunmer, W.E., & Bowey, J. (1984). Children's capacity to correct grammatical violations in syntax. *Journal of Child Language, 11,* 129–141.

Rangamani, G.N. (1989). *Aphasia and multilingualism: Clinical evidences towards the cerebral organization of languages.* Doctoral thesis, University of Mysore, India.

Sasanuma, S. (1974). Kanji versus Kana processing in alexia with transient agraphia: A case report. *Cortex, 10,* 89–97.

Schiffman, H.F. (1979). *A reference grammar of spoken Kannada: A report.* Washington, DC: U.S. Department of Health, Education, and Welfare.

Scholl, D.M., & Ryan, E.B. (1980). Development of metalinguistic performance in early school years. *Language and Speech, 23,* 199–211.

Scribner, S., & Cole, M. (1978). Literacy without schooling: Testing for intellectual effects. *Harvard Educational Review, 48*(4), 448–461.

Srivastava, R.N. (1990). Orality and literacy—bipolar or continuum? *Indian Journal of Adult Education, 51*(4), 46–55.

Srividya, R. (1990). *Agrammatism in Tamil speaking Broca's aphasics.* Master's dissertation, University of Mysore, India.

Suchitra, M.G., & Karanth, P. (in press). Linguistic profile test (LPT)—Normative data for children in grades I to V. *Journal of AIISH.*

Tunmer, W.E., Herriman, M.L., & Nesdale, A.R. (1988). Metalinguistic abilities and beginning reading. *Reading Research Quarterly, 23.*

Tunmer, W.E. (1991). Cognitive and linguistic factors in learning to read. In P.B. Gough, L. Ehri, & R. Treiman (Eds.), *Reading acquisition.* Hillsdale, NJ: Erlbaum.

Vaid, J. (1995). Script directionality affect nonliguistic performance: Evidence from Hindi and Urdu. In I. Taylor & D.R. Olson (Eds.), *Scripts and literacy: Reading and learning to read the world's script* (pp. 295–310). London: Kluwer Academic Publishers.

Van Kleek, A. (1982). The emergence of linguistic awareness: A cognitive framework. *Merrill-Palmer Quarterly, 28,* 237.

Van Kleek, A. (1984). Metalinguistic skills—cutting across spoken and written languages and problem solving abilities. In G.P. Wallach & K.G. Butler (Eds.), *Language and learning disabilities in school age children* (pp. 128–153). Baltimore, MD: Williams and Wilkins.

Wells, G. (1982). Preschool literacy-related activities. In D.R. Olson, N. Torrance, & A. Hildyard (Eds.), *Literacy, language and learning.* London: Cambridge University Press.

# part III

# Literacy and Activity Contexts in Adulthood

chapter 7

# Illiterate Adults in Literate Societies: Interactions With a Social World

Ann Hagell
Policy Research Bureau, London

Jonathan Tudge
University of North Carolina at Greensboro

"Search out the school, you homeless.
Secure yourselves knowledge, you who are frozen!
You who are starving, grab hold of the book: It's a weapon.
You must take over the leadership."
—Bertolt Brecht, *In Praise of Learning*

It is inadvisable to consider issues of illiteracy without considering cultural constraints, demands, and conceptions of what is appropriate. Similarly, it is impossible to grasp illiteracy without understanding the individual's contribution and perspective. Most importantly, we will argue in this chapter that the crucial key in defining and comprehending illiteracy is the relation between the cultural and the individual factors. Illiteracy, just as much as literacy, is a co-construction formed in the course of transactions between the culture and the individual, often mediated by those (parents, teachers, the media) who help to make culture more understandable. We begin with two sections that explain what we mean by illiteracy and introduce a model for understanding its development. In the three subsequent sections, we focus first on the cultural level, second on the individual level, and third on illiteracy as an interaction between cultural and individual factors. (Considering illiteracy as encompassing three distinct components in this way is a purely heuristic device; it is our central tenet that this is, in fact, impossible to do in practice, since each level is intricately linked to the others.) The final section considers some social coping strategies of adults with reading problems who were living in one example of a literate culture—south east London in the late 1980s.

## WHAT IS ILLITERACY?

By concentrating on the "development" of illiteracy and the experiences of illiterate adults in literate societies, this chapter is largely about definitions, so this section will only aim to set out some of the main issues. When we talk about illiteracy in these discussions, we are seeking to understand both what illiteracy *is* (in individuals, in cultures, at different life stages, at different historical times), and also what illiteracy *feels like*. Thus, in this and the subsequent sections, we will be seeking to understand both the definition of illiteracy, and the experience of illiteracy.

Even at the simplest level, it is difficult to define illiteracy without considering both cultural and individual dimensions: The availability of and access to written material in a given culture interacts with cultural expectations about what constitutes age-appropriate reading. Literacy and illiteracy are relative terms. They can only be defined in relation to features of individual and cultural life that themselves vary constantly over time, country, needs, politics, and so on. What counted as literacy in medieval England would now be called the ability to speak Latin, what counted as literacy to the American armed forces during World War II is inadequate if applied to the British school system. Literacy is dynamic, composed of culturally relevant skills that change over time and between cultures, possibly between people.

The relative nature of literacy/illiteracy is seen also at the individual level, and is illustrated by the difference between literacy and reading. Two people who have the same reading level may perceive themselves quite differently: one as an illiterate, the other as a competent reader. What is "not being able to read?" Perception of oneself as a reader is likely to be based partially on culturally and personally derived expectations of what one ought to be able to read, and partially on the practical issue of what one *needs* to be able to read effectively in one's everyday life. Currently, in media treatments of the subject, the words "illiteracy" and "reading problems" are imbued with different connotations; the first tends to be considered a social issue, the second an individual issue. We would argue that definitions of illiteracy are the result of *interactions* between cultural and individual issues. We will return to this in subsequent sections.

The term "illiterate" is rarely given its most extreme meaning; most people to whom it is customarily applied are in fact capable of reading and writing a little, and the important question is "how much?" The cut-off separating literacy from illiteracy depends, in part, on the purpose to which the literacy statistics are put. These statistics are one of the main universal indices of national well-being and frequently carry political overtones. Among the first figures usually listed in national profiles are those relating to levels of illiteracy (along with infant mortality, per capita income, and life expectancy). Generally, to define a person as literate implies his or her ability to use graphic symbols to represent spoken language. Also implied is the competence needed to employ basic reading skills to respond to "real-world" reading tasks. At this point, functionality becomes important, and UNESCO, for example (1970), defined the point at which literacy becomes functional (and thus a person becomes literate) as equivalent to an American school system grade level of 5 (age 10 years). In the same decade, a national literacy campaign in Britain defined functionality as equivalent to a reading level of age 9. This connotes a very low level of reading competence given that national British newspapers require a reading age that ranges from about 14 to 17 years and government leaflets relating to issues of health and social security need a reading age of approximately 16 years (Levine, 1986). In terms of the experiences of illiterate adults in literate cultures, even those who read at 5th or 6th grade levels will suffer from feelings of inadequacy and the need to cover their tracks by employing various coping strategies. Essentially, literacy is not a black-and-white issue. In fact, those who fall into the grey area of semi-illiteracy are particularly interesting from the point of view of managing their lives in fully literate societies.

## A MODEL OF DEVELOPMENT: VYGOTSKY REVISITED

The idea of the development of illiteracy might sound like a non sequitur. However, for the purposes of this chapter, we intend to take a fairly broad notion of development in order to consider the development of the definition of illiteracy by individuals and in a culture, and also to look at the development of ways that adults with literacy problems deal with their literate cultures.

Our treatment of illiteracy in this chapter might seem to draw on a broader range of literatures than is usual. Research on literacy from the individual point of view rarely extends beyond late childhood. Development does not end with school, yet there is little systematic research on literacy development or functioning in settings beyond school. Studies do exist at the cultural level, addressing issues of adult illiteracy, but these types of studies frequently confine themselves to macro-level analyses and fail to address individual issues. Our model of illiteracy is developed within a co-constructionist, Vygotskian perspective, which allows us to consider the different levels important in the development of illiteracy and which also allows us to consider later stages of life course.

The co-construction of illiteracy is a developmental topic in two different ways. In terms of historical development, definitions of illiteracy are deeply entrenched in historical time. In addition, learning to read and becoming literate are of varying relevance at different periods of personal time, in individual development. These aspects of literacy are immediately apparent as soon as illiteracy is defined. The simplest definition is one that involves an inability to read. However, an English four year old who cannot read is not termed an illiterate, nor would that term be appropriate for the vast majority of adults in eighteenth-century England. Also, the concept of "illiteracy" would be emically inappropriate (i.e., from the perspective of the cultural group being considered) when applied to adults in cultures that do not value reading or have access to written material.

Vygotsky's model of development has been termed a "cultural-historical" theory because Vygotsky sought to explain individual development in terms of the complex interaction of individual, social, cultural, and historical factors in development (Tudge & Winterhoff, 1993; Tulviste, 1991; Wertsch, 1985; Valsiner, 1988; Vygotsky, 1978). From a Vygotskian perspective, an "individual" accomplishment, such as learning to read, is simultaneously individual, social, cultural, and historical. The materials are historical cultural products that help the beginning reader to understand the culture; the assistance and encouragement are social; the drive to make sense is individual. Such an accomplishment can most easily be understood by examining the interplay between personal factors, such as the individual's age and his or her physical and developmental status; social factors, such as the availability and willingness of more competent readers to help the individual learn to read; and cultural factors, such as the value placed by the cultural group on reading, access to written materials, and so on, as they have developed over the course of that culture's history (Tudge, Putnam, & Valsiner, 1996). Using this framework to consider illiteracy, we will discuss the contributions of the different levels to the interrelationship of individual and culture.

As well as suggesting that the determination of whether or not a person is considered illiterate is the result of many different factors, our use of the term "co-constructed" also emphasizes the point that the materials that are available to be read are cultural constructions. Those learning to read are, as individuals, actively involved in the process, while being assisted by those more competent in the culturally valued skill. As each individual becomes newly literate, his or her accomplishment is simultaneously individual and cultural. It is only by defining illiteracy as a co-constructed concept that the experience of adults with reading problems in literate societies makes sense.

## THE CULTURAL LEVEL: LITERACY AS A SOCIAL CONSTRUCTION

The development of expectations of mass literacy in Western Europe and the United States is relatively new, originating in the Victorian notion of popular education. The standard of literacy required now was once only expected of a limited elite (Goody, 1977; Heubner, 1987; Resnick & Resnick, 1977). In fact, the ruling classes in various societies have considered that literacy was inappropriate, even dangerous, in the hands of the "masses" (Turman, 1987). Similarly novel is the idea that widespread literacy should include the ability to read new material, and abstract new information from it, rather than just being the ability to do a constrained task such as reciting short (typically religious) passages aloud. The word "literacy" was not introduced into the English language until the nineteenth century (Williams, 1983). Even by the outbreak of the first World War, only a limited proportion of the British population completed elementary school. In a relatively short time, the situation has changed dramatically. By the end of the twentieth century, print has become endemic in Europe and the United States, and those who do not learn to read are considered by themselves and the rest of society as failures.

What does literacy mean for culture? Why should society be interested in educating the masses? Why have governments been so concerned with literacy statistics? These questions are important in understanding how the individual comes to think about and treat their own illiteracy, since the cultural issues interact with the person and become internalized. Literacy is "of" society, because it exists for social purposes. In literate societies, readers and nonreaders are all surrounded by and conditioned by print. By definition, literacy is shared knowledge. It is collective by necessity, and words are for communicating. However, these are not reasons why cultures have been so keen to boost literacy. These ideas do not explain what literacy does "for" society.

Many broad societal consequences have been attributed to literacy. Two main issues of contention exist in the anthropological and sociological literatures. The first concerns the relationship of literacy to industrial "take-off." Thus, at the cultural level, literacy has been considered historically as a device for inducing and accelerating economic and technical development, a necessity for progress, and illiteracy has been treated as if it were a disease to be cured: "a kind of cultural pathogen susceptible to complete eradication by the widespread administration of a standardised educational treatment" (Levine, 1986, p. 27). The decades of UNESCO surveys, initiatives, and projects, including UNESCO's Experimental World Literacy Program constitute one such example. In the United Kingdom, the UNESCO initiatives raised social sensitivity about illiteracy in the 1970s, and this culminated in a parliamentary bill and a BBC literacy campaign.

Even if it were possible to conclude that literacy had important consequences for any society or country, a second debate rages concerning the possibility of drawing global conclusions concerning the societal importance of literacy, detached from a specific cultural context. Street (1984) identifies two main models of literacy: the "autonomous" model and the "ideological" model. The former assumes a single direction in which literacy development can be traced and associates it with progress, civilization, individual liberty, and social mobility (Goody, 1977). Literacy is isolated as an independent variable and then its consequences are studied. The "ideological" model considers literacy in terms of specific social practices of reading and writing, in their culturally embedded location, and stresses the significance of the socialization process in the construction of the meaning of literacy for participants (e.g., Scribner & Cole, 1981).

There is a tension inherent in these discussions of the power of literacy at the cultural level. On one hand, individuals in literate societies are exhorted to take hold of literacy: to gain access to society and the control and development implied by literacy, to become "free" (e.g., Freire, 1972). Yet, it might be argued that the roots of the nineteenth-century imposition of literacy on civilizations in the Western Hemisphere lay in a desire to make members of various cultures "controllable" rather than free, and to eradicate the unknowable threats of pagan illiteracy by bringing people into line. The attempts of the social and religious campaigners of the last century to teach reading can be perceived as part of the general wish to "clean up" the world, to bring enlightenment, to build sewers, to eliminate cholera, to draw the unknown under control. Even in contemporary literate cultures individuals can be ranked against each other, with degree of literacy (reading ability or level) used as a method of distinguishing the good from the bad, as a way of grading people. (One might agree with Flannery O'Conner at this point, who once wrote, "He had gone to a country school where he had learned to read and write but that it was wiser not to.") The question of what to do with the people who do not make the grade becomes important, particularly given that some scholars have argued that illiterates are prone to dangerous tendencies. As recently as 1956, in a frequently quoted passage, Freeman and Kassebaum suggested that when illiterates group together, certain institutionalized categories of behavior emerge:

> Their religion tends to follow a pattern of emotionalism and physical expression with the relative absence of abstract arguments. Probably a larger proportion of illiterates than literates are among the followers of charismatic religious leaders. Akin to their religious simplicity is their proclivity to be taken in by soothsayers, faith healers, and witch doctors. The extent, variety, and intensity of their superstitions are prodigious. (p. 374)

Freeman and Kassebaum argued that society denies illiterates success and its incumbent symbols. So, because "ornamentation, flash, and extremity of dress are easily perceived phenomena...conspicuous consumption stands out more unabashedly than in most of the sophisticated larger society" (1956, p. 375). This stereotype (albeit extreme) is an example of what happens to those ranked lowest on literacy achievement, and gives an example of what such people might have to cope with in their dealings with their literate culture. The meaning of illiteracy in such cultures includes notions of stigma as well as objective reading levels.

As the quotations above suggest, literacy was imbued with a moral flavor (and thus, by implication, illiteracy with an immoral flavor) from an early stage. In fact, religion has had an enormous influence on the historical development of literacy (Akinnaso, 1991; Duranti & Ochs, 1986; Schieffelin & Cochran-Smith, 1984). The first litterati were arguably the priesthood, and historical and anthropological texts often identify religious functionaries as the only people in local societies who could read. The earliest efforts at mass literacy were intended to develop mastery of a limited set of prescribed biblical or religious texts, rather than a generalized capacity to read. Centuries later, when public schooling was introduced, the old church education system was subsumed and it was difficult to separate primary education from religious education. For example, until the end of the nineteenth century in France, the responsibilities of the primary school teacher included encouraging attendance at mass, teaching prayers, and assisting the priest (Resnick & Resnick, 1977). As a consequence of these roots, as Olson argued, "Illiteracy is often listed along with malnutrition, disease, poverty and unemployment as a serious social ill. Hence, any threat to standards of literacy or any putative drop in literate competence is taken as the forerunner of a return to primitivism, ignorance, and savagery" (Olson, 1985, p. 1).

Illiteracy is often viewed not only as immoral, but also as expensive. In what appears, at least to British readers, to be a peculiarly American economic analysis, Kozol outlined the cost of illiteracy for the United States:

> The Senate Select Committee on Equal Educational Opportunity estimated a figure of $237 billion in unrealized lifetime earnings forfeited by men 25-34 years old who have less than high school level skills.... Direct costs to business and taxpayers are approximately $20 billion. Six billion dollars yearly (estimate: mid 1970s) go to child welfare costs and unemployment compensation caused directly by the numbers of illiterate adults unable to perform at standards necessary for available employment. $6.6 billion yearly (estimate of 1983) is the minimal cost of prison maintenance for an estimated 260,000 inmates—out of a total state and federal prison population of about 440,000—whose imprisonment has been directly linked to functional illiteracy.... Several billion dollars go to workers' compensation, damage to industrial equipment, and industrial insurance costs directly caused by on-site accidents related to the inability of workers to read safety warnings, chemical-content designations, and instructions for the operation of complex machines. (1985, p. 14)

This author claims on the cover that one out of every three American adults cannot read his book. These are dramatic statistics, delivered in a semi-hysterical tone. Somebody is guilty of something.

Who is to blame when literacy fails? The moral and religious flavor of literacy, the emphasis on the importance and centrality of the individual in Western cultures, and the need for society to find a way of categorizing and controlling those who do not meet the grade will all be internalized by the adult with reading problems, and the blame all too frequently becomes personal guilt. This might begin in school, for example. School, for most illiterate adults, remains the scene of former failure. Most illiterate adults have spent about 8 years in school listening to the message, "Jon and Ann could do better if they tried." The impression gained from cultural media such as newspapers suggests a tension between the responsibility of society and its schools to provide literacy and subsequent opportunities for employment, and the role of the individual in the failure to learn.

## THE INDIVIDUAL LEVEL

It is thus clear that the ways in which cultures, over the course of historical time, have used and made available written materials have had a powerful impact on cultural expectations about who should read and at what age. What, then, is the role of the individual? Individual and socio-cultural factors are so tightly enmeshed from the perspectives of theorists such as Vygotsy or Mead that it is difficult to talk about factors that are purely individual. Growing up in and coming to make sense of a social world means that individual characteristics are simultaneously self- and other-constructed. However, biological and genetic characteristics are, apart from their obvious socially derived foundations, relatively impervious to influence from the social world. At the simpliest level, age and developmental status are obviously critical, if only because infants and toddlers do not have the cognitive capacity to read in any currently accepted sense. No amount of cultural expectation or parental prodding will produce a two-year-old reader, although the ability to recognize the odd "flash card" might be taken as evidence of early maturing skill. Similarly, genetic, biological, and physiological factors (which we shall assume to be individual characteristics) may well have an impact on whether or not an individual turns out to be illiterate. At the most obvious level, a reader has to be able to see to read ordinary printed text (although it should be noted that blind people are not illiterate). Conversations with adults who are poor readers will sometimes lead to the revelation that the person had hearing problems or an undiagnosed need for glasses, or spent a large part of childhood outside the classroom suffering from asthma attacks.

The role of genes in reading problems is still a moot subject. There seems to be some evidence that reading problems are more common in boys and men than girls and women. Ratios in epidemiological surveys of 10 year olds suggests rates of 3:1 boys to girls with specific reading retardation (e.g., Berger, Yule, & Rutter, 1975). Large twin and family studies sometimes suggest a pattern of language and reading problems that may run in families (e.g., Decker & DeFries, 1981; DeFries, Fulker, & LaBuda, 1987). Attenders at adult literacy clinics tend to be more male than female: these statistics may simply reflect other sex differences apart from genetics, but the possibility that men and women treat their reading problems differently would also be an appropriate point to make in this section on individual contributions.

There is also some indication that some children seem "primed" for reading early, sometimes in the absence of special parental assistance and even at the expense of embarrassment on the part of the parents (Bissex, 1984; Clark, 1976; Fitzgerald & Needleman, 1991; Torrey, 1973), and sometimes even in cultures that do not encourage children's reading (Schieffelin & Cochran-Smith, 1984). Others will show little interest in the written word. Moreover, while some motivation for reading is undoubtedly a response to social and cultural factors, some is certainly an individual phenomenon. As children and adults, some people will simply like reading, and some will not.

It is thus clear that the cultural and the individual levels of analysis are necessary in order to make sense of the phenomena of both literacy and illiteracy. However, it would be quite incorrect to view either level as sufficient. The next section will consider the ways in which the individual and the culture *co-construct* illiteracy. In this regard, we should note that the culture exerts an impact both in the course of helping to construct the meaning of literacy and then by providing a reaction when people do not make the grade. Such reactions are a reality of the social world, and the impressions of any person held by others in society is something to which the person has to be able to adapt.

## THE INTERACTION BETWEEN INDIVIDUAL AND CULTURE, AND ITS IMPLICATIONS FOR ILLITERATE ADULTS IN LITERATE SOCIETIES

From the very start, reading itself is the product of interaction between what the culture contributes, assistance provided by those who are already mature readers, and what the child brings to the reading process. Although human infants are primed to learn the spoken language they will not do so unless in a language-speaking environment. The same is true of reading; children will not spontaneously learn to read unless they are exposed to written material. On the other hand, while all normally developing children will learn to speak if they are simply exposed to the spoken language, the same is not true of reading and written language. There are thus social issues relating to the written word that typically do not relate to speech. In an essay on the social context of literacy, Robinson wrote

> Language in all of its uses is an intimate part of human experience: Language is expressive of identity and personality, but it is also socially binding and expressive of collective values. Written language is peculiarly public, more so than speech, and as a consequence its forms are carefully scrutinized; reading and writing are highly valued activities and society monitors their acquisition. (1988, p. 243)

There are two ways in which we can consider the interaction between the individual and culture in constructing notions of illiteracy. First we shall consider the different ways in which people use literacy in different cultures. Second, we consider ways in which the person with reading problems internalizes and restructures society's messages concerning illiteracy.

There have been a number of ethnographic studies that focus on the functions, for people, of reading in different cultural communities, both across and within societies. (This is a different point from the consideration of the functions of literacy for society, considered above.) One such study, focusing on different cultural groups within one geographical region of one society (the Piedmont area of South Carolina) was conducted by Heath (1983) who examined reading and writing behaviors in the context of community life. The study had a particular focus on the literacy experiences of children in three U.S. communities, two of which were working class (one Black, one White) and one of which was middle class. Heath found quite distinct differences in the organization and meaning of literacy events in these different communities, differences that appeared to serve the different cognitive and social goals of each community. For example, in the white working-class community, Heath reported that reading was a social activity. Written material was used in conjunction with oral explanation, humourous narratives, and other verbal accounts. Heath described seven uses of literacy in this community, including its use in social interaction, in news gathering, and in providing information about practical problems of everyday life. She recorded that she did not find any evidence of uses of literacy for aesthetic, organizational, or recreational purposes, uses that were associated with literacy in the middle-class community she studied. Similar findings, namely that working-class White and African-American communities in the United States have different approaches to literacy than those found in middle-class communities, have been reported by Ogbu (1987) and by McLane and McNamee (1990). Not surprisingly, similar findings have been reported in the cross-cultural literature (Akinnaso, 1991; Duranti & Ochs, 1986; Schieffelin & Cochran-Smith, 1984; Scribner & Cole, 1981). Definitions of what constitutes literacy in these different cultural communities ranges widely, depending on the use to which reading and writing is expected to be put (Langer, 1987; Wagner, 1991).

Individuals within any given cultural setting react in different ways to the presence of printed material, cultural expectations of literacy and illiteracy, and so on. As we suggested above, for example, even in cultures in which reading is not at all encouraged, some people (adults and children alike) may be highly motivated to become literate. For example, Fitzgerald and Needleman, describing a study in which books were made available to parents who had no books at home, reported that one mother asked for a replacement copy of her book: "My daughter insists on reading it every night; by now it's in tatters" (1991, p.18). Similarly, Schieffelin and Cochran-Smith (1984), studying reading among the typically nonliterate Kaluli of New Guinea, described one child who worked to ensure that she was able to engage in reading with her mother even through in this culture children were not expected to learn to read (in fact, it was not considered desirable). The authors argued: "The length and frequency of these [reading] interactions...were determined by the child's persistence and interest, never the mother's" (pp. 14–15). The relationship between individual and culture is thus clearly not unidirectional. In the interaction, both sides are pushing for consistency and organization of the social world, trying to make a coherent pattern out of events and actions, and using literacy for certain functions. This happens both within a society and also within an individual. In the process, a place is found for illiteracy and reading problems that makes sense to the parties involved. We have identified some ways in which culture might find a place for illiteracy in its construction of the world. At the individual level, this push for consistency and control of the social world is identified in developmental theory and research as a drive to make sense of the world (Bruner, 1990; Trevarthen, 1980) at the same time that the world, organized typically in rather consistent ways, provides models of how the world works. Similarly, social-psychological theories identify the drive for consistency as the underlying motivation of social cognition. Social cognition at the individual level includes the development of personal theories relating to making explanations of the social world and to attitude formation and attitude change. The aim of this impulse to put together theories about our social worlds is knowledge, and knowledge allows individuals to feel that they understand their environment. In part, this process involves the "appropriation" (i. e., more active process of internalization in which what is internalized is transformed in ways that make sense to the individual who is internalizing—see Rogoff, 1990) of external explanations, reactions, or theories.

Thus, ideas concerning personal illiteracy are not created in a social vacuum. We need to consider the individual and social co- or jointly constructed "social representations" (Berger & Luckmann, 1966; Moscovici, 1981) of common ideas of illiteracy, within which people with reading problems learn to view themselves. Given the ways in which contemporary societies have portrayed literacy, the internalization of illiteracy often reflects on individuals with reading problems in such a way that they are likely to feel stigmatized. Generally, the literatures on stigma and social representations are quite separate, deemed to derive from two distinct sociological traditions of social psychology. However, in considering the experiences of the illiterate adult in literate societies, the two need to be related. The social representation of illiteracy may imply a negative self-esteem for people with reading problems, or they may discover ways of protecting their self-esteem. Various self-presentational tactics may be appropriate and specific coping strategies may be employed. These ideas suggest a more dynamic conception of stigma as the outcome of definitional processes arising from social interactions (see, for example, Ainlay, Becker, & Coleman, 1986).

Goffman only once mentioned illiteracy (1963, p. 19), but it is obviously open to a Goffmanesque construction. He outlined a series of phases that a stigmatized person will have gone through. These start with the initial incorporation of the standpoint of the normal, including the identity beliefs of the wider society. The individuals then become conscious of their possession of stigma, and of the negative connotations of these stigma. The stigmatized has to decide how to manage information about his failing. Although little attention has been directed at the stigma of illiteracy, there has been an interest in the experience of the stigma of obesity (Cahnman, 1968; DeJong, 1980). This is an example of a problem that includes a large component of moral reprehensibility, leading the obese adolescent to feel that he or she deserves the treatment received from society. This shame is then internalized, so that whatever avenue is chosen, the individual interprets his or herself in the way that is indicated, accepting dominant values and responding to expectation (Cahnman, 1968). The notion of internalizing the viewpoint of the "other" and learning about the self by seeing it reflected in eyes of the wider society, is, of course, rooted in Meadian symbolic interactionism (Mead, 1913, 1925).

This discussion leads us inevitably into questions of social comparison (Festinger, 1954). Illiteracy poses interesting questions in terms of social comparison. Unlike many other disabilities, reading problems are extremely common (whichever set of political statistics are adopted: a rate of 1:10 in men is often posited, in comparison to 1:2500 for blindness in both sexes). Yet, reading problems are often more easily hidden than other disabilities and it may be possible for reading-disabled adults to structure a world for themselves where reading is not a necessary skill. This is much less likely in the case of rarer and more severe handicaps. Because of these features, it may be more likely that poor readers compare themselves to the good-reading public, which is likely to have negative consequences for their feelings about themselves if they consequently find themselves lacking.

To some extent, the bottom line with respect to definitions of illiteracy lies with the individual, because these ideas outlined above are only really important as they are internalized and used by the person. However, the experience of the illiterate in a literate society is not solely the product of their internalization of society's messages.

## SOCIAL COPING STRATEGIES

How does it feel to be lacking in literacy? What happens to people who do not feel that they can "grab hold of the book," as Brecht put it? What are the consequences of the social co-construction of illiteracy for the individual in literate cultures?

In this section, we briefly consider various ways in which adult poor readers might be managing their interactions with their social worlds. The literatures on stigma and self-presentation suggest a number of possible ways in which people who are illiterate or semi-literate might manage their interactions with the social—and literate—world. In addition, we make some use of descriptions taken from a larger study of the adult psychosocial functioning of adults who had reading problems as children, conducted by the first author. It is not the intention to provide a full description of the research methodology of this study in this chapter, rather, we want to make use of the qualitative data in an illustrative way (for more details, see Hagell, 1992).

Our description of the co-construction of illiteracy in our preceding discussions was partly intended to raise the notion that the individual has a choice in how they experience and manage reading problems. People are not the passive receptors of cultural dictates concerning what is correct or incorrect. It is our experience that many poor readers arrange and manage their lives within literate societies in ways that limit the negative implications for them. Given our discussion of the different functions of literacy in different sections of societies, one way in which adults with reading problems might handle life in a literate culture is to select an appropriate section of the culture that lays relatively less emphasis on reading, and concentrate on functioning within this. For example, poor readers may be opting for more manual occupations and then deciding to stay in such work, rather than moving up the occupational scale into jobs that would imply more paperwork. In our sample of largely working-class inner London poor readers, there was some evidence that this group was failing to achieve the same rate of upward mobility as their comparison group. Some poor readers are explicit about their acceptance of certain occupational restrictions; thus one man who said, "I know that I'm not very clever, so I'm limited to what I can do with earning a living and certain scales of wage capabilities." Others report that it has never been an issue, some even turning the definition upside-down in their responses by suggesting that they believe that they do not have a reading problem because they never have to read anything. One poor reader, employed as an electrician, when asked if he though he had any current reading problem, replied, "I don't really know, I don't do a lot of writing anyway now." Asked if he could write a decent letter, he said, "I don't know, I haven't written one for 5 years." Poor-reading women who bear children may have the option not to engage in the work arena, and may stay instead within a family world at home where they feel competent and equal.

It might be argued that such people have, knowingly or unknowingly, selected a subculture that offers a more benign contribution to the co-construction of illiteracy, rather than having to face the harsher judgements of other more explicitly literate sections of society. These types of strategies are much easier to employ in adulthood than childhood. When they are at school, poor readers are defined by the system as failures, because the prevailing criteria are educational and schooling is compulsory. However, in adulthood, educational objectives are much less relevant. This strategy basically involves putting distance between yourself and the problem. This may or may not feel adequate, but poor readers suggest that it works. Thus, in answer to a question concerning coping with reading difficulties, one interviewee stated, "You can get by without it, but it's not very nice. You miss out on a lot of things and you're restricted. You can get by, but as I say, it's not very nice." An comparison adult who did not have reading problems similarly commented, "I think nowadays people can get through life better without having to do a lot of it, because there is so much information on television and radio."

Denial of reading problems may take place at several different levels. Some semi-illiterate adults may deny existence of their reading problems to themselves. Some theorists have argued that it is a beneficial tactic for people to be somewhat estranged from the actual circumstances, and have purported to the existence of healthy illusions and positive denial (e.g., Taylor & Brown, 1988). Alternatively, poor readers may deny that they have reading problems to their surrounding social world. In this way they can, at least, hold off the judgements of the culture. Thus, for example, one woman with reading problems told her research interviewer, "What's worrying me is that my boss is thinking of opening a shop in the U.S.A. and he wants me to go there and teach them, but I couldn't face up to them knowing [that I couldn't read]. That's what I've been doing since I left school—running away. I look back to the look on my Mum's face when I told her and the look on the girl's faces at school—it's a nightmare."

Goffman referred to such techniques of concealing or hiding stigma as "passing" (Goffman, 1963). A small group is confided in, but the "secret" is kept from the wider world. It is likely that a substantial proportion of adult illiterates are relying on close others for help with day-to-day tasks demanding literacy skills. In the example of the electrician cited above, all of the respondent's domestic correspondence was coped with by his wife, so that, "She does all the forms, I just sit down and work out the figures, and tell her what to put in them." This inner London sample were in their late 20s at the time of the research interviews, and virtually all the interviewees were living with, supported by, or supporting other people, members of their family of origin or of a newly acquired family, and it was generally these people to whom they were turning for help. Approximately half of those who said that they were relying on others for help went on to confess that they were concealing their difficulties from people outside this close circle.

However, in literate cultures, functional illiterates will not always want to or be able to rely on other people, and it is likely that they will sometimes have to employ alternative strategies for getting the task done. For example, one woman reported that she will not write checks in shops because of the embarrassment of making mistakes. Instead, "I have to go and get cash out, use Access, or whatever." South east London is an example of a literate culture that also has a strong oral tradition, and, as evidence of this, these adult poor readers suggested that they supplemented their knowledge of current events (often acquired by others through newspapers) with information gained through social interactions. These included discussions with workmates, chats in the local pub, conversations with neighbors, and so on. In addition, they were more likely than their average reading peers to report that they used the radio news broadcasts for learning about current events. Many of these people, with or without reading problems, reported that they acquired manual jobs through social contacts rather than through written advertisements and application forms.

For those who do not manage to select a benign subculture, or fail to successfully conceal their difficulties, interactions with the literate society can have various negative consequences. One of the most obvious and interesting phenomena at this level is the high level of personal guilt felt by people who have difficulty reading and, in fact, this is reported by those who are otherwise successful, as well as those who seem to be in difficulty. These feelings of guilt are frequently reported in an anecdotal nature by people working in the adult literacy field. They are also documented in more systematic studies of adult illiterates (e.g., Hagell, 1992; Malcolm, Polatajko, & Simons, 1990). Given the strong societal interest in imposing literacy, and the relative and transactional nature of definitions of illiteracy, it is a testament to the power of the Western notion of the autonomy of the individual that people feel so personally responsible for their reading problems. We would suggest that this reflects the internalization of the co-construction of illiteracy that takes place between the individual and society. The majority of poor readers in the inner London group explained their difficulties as their own fault, stating, for example, "It might have been lack of concentration on my part," "Laziness at school, I suppose, that's where it all stemmed from," "Maybe if I took a bit more interest in it, I would have been all right." The comments of these individuals also showed some evidence of awareness of the moral and personally beneficial notions society has attached to literacy. Thus, for example, in response to a question concerning the importance of reading, one subject replied, "You have to read material to gain knowledge, and gaining knowledge makes you a better person, makes you more informed, makes you more equipped, especially nowadays," and another replied, "You gain a lot personally."

This section simply serves to illustrate some of the ways in which illiterates might be managing and experiencing their interactions with a literate society. Systematic research on adult illiterates is rare, partly attributable to the difficulties of recruiting representative samples from groups that are practiced at concealing the very thing that is of interest. However, the fact that we know very little about the adult experiences of people with reading problems hinders the provision of adequate support and remedial help, and this issue warrants further attention.

## CONCLUSION

It is clear, no matter what characteristics an individual possesses, he or she will not become a reader while living in a culture that has neither access to nor use for printed material. On the other hand, a person who has severe neurological or physical difficulties may have difficulty learning to read no matter how literate is the surrounding culture or his or her significant others. Similarly, one would not expect a 12 month old to be able to read. Thus, purely individual factors, just like purely cultural factors, may exert a large independent role on definitions and experiences of adult illiteracy. However, in the previous sections, we have sought to argue that, for the most part, one needs to consider the interaction of both individual and cultural levels in order to understand illiteracy in literate societies. In so doing, we suggested a model of illiteracy based on the Vygotskian cultural-historical approach.

We have also suggested that one of the important reasons for taking such an approach is that it will have implications for making improvements in the experiences of adults with reading problems. As Robinson dramatically stated, "We teachers of literacy meet students in a charged atmosphere. We need to be sensitive to the prevailing currents, if for no other purpose than to avoid electrocution" (1988, p. 234).

## ACKNOWLEDGMENTS

This chapter was prepared while the first author was at the University of North Carolina at Chapel Hill. The support of the Fulbright Commission is gratefully acknowledged. Preparation of this chapter was also facilitated by the award of a National Academy of Education Spencer Fellowship to the second author.

## REFERENCES

Ainlay, S.C., Becker, G., & Coleman, L.M. (1986). Stigma reconsidered. In S.C. Ainlay, G. Becker, & L.M. Coleman (Eds), *The dilemma of difference: A multidisciplinary view of stigma.* New York: Plenum Press.

Akinnaso, F.N. (1991). Literacy and individual consciousness. In E.M. Jennings & A.C. Purves (Eds.), *Literate systems and individual lives: Perspectives on literacy and schooling* (pp. 73–94). Albany: State University of New York Press.

Berger, M., Yule, W., & Rutter, M. (1975). Attainment and adjustment in two geographical areas II: The prevalence of specific reading retardation. *British Journal of Psychiatry, 126*, 510–519.

Berger, P.L., & Luckman, T. (1966). *The social construction of reality.* Garden City, NY: Acre Books.

Bissex, G.L. (1984). The child as teacher. In H. Goelman, A. Oberg, & F. Smith (Eds.), *Awakening to literacy* (pp. 87–101). London: Heinemann.

Bruner, J. (1990). *Acts of meaning*. Cambridge, MA: Harvard University Press.

Cahnman, W. (1968). The stigma of obesity. *The Sociological Quarterly, 9*, 283–299.

Clark, M.M. (1976). *Young fluent readers*. London: Heinemann.

Decker, S.N., & DeFries, J.C. (1981). Cognitive ability profiles in families of reading-disabled children. *Develop. Med. Child Neurology, 23*, 217–227.

DeFries, J.C., Fulker, D.W., & LaBuda, M.C. (1987). Reading disability in twins: Evidence for a genetic etiology. *Nature, 329*, 537–539.

DeJong, W. (1980). The stigma of obesity: the consequences of naive assumptions concerning the causes of physical deviance. *Journal of Health and Social Behavior, 21*, 75–87.

Duranti, A., & Ochs, E. (1986). Literacy instruction in a Samoan village. In B. B. Schieffelin & P. Gallimore (Eds.), *The acquisition of literacy: Ethnographic perspectives* (pp. 213–232). Norwood, NJ: Ablex.

Festinger, L. (1954). A theory of social comparison processes. *Human Relations*, 7, 117–140.

Fitzgerald, K., & Needlman, R. (1991). Reach out and read: A pediatric program to support emergent literacy. *Zero to Three, 12*(1), 17–20.

Freeman, H.E., & Kassebaum, G.G. (1956). The illiterate in American society. *Social Forces, 34*, 371–375.

Freire, P. (1972). *The pedagogy of the oppressed.* Harmondsworth, U.K.: Penguin.

Goffman, E. (1963). *Stigma: Notes on the management of spoiled identity.* Harmondsworth, U.K.: Penguin.

Goody, J. (1977). *The domestication of the savage mind.* Cambridge, U.K.: Cambridge University Press.

Hagell, A. (1992). The social psychology of illiteracy: An attributional perspective. Unpublished PhD thesis, Institute of Psychiatry, University of London.

Heath, S.B. (1983). *Ways with words: Language, life, and work in communities and classrooms*. Cambridge, U.K.: Cambridge University Press.

Heubner, T. (1987). A socio-historical approach to literacy development. In J.A. Langer (Ed.), *Language, literacy, and culture: Issues of society and schooling* (pp. 179–196). Norwood, NJ: Ablex.

Kozol, J. (1985). *Illiterate America.* Garden City, NY: Anchor Press/Doubleday.

Langer, J.A. (1987). A sociocognitive perspective on literacy. In J.A. Langer (Ed.), *Language, literacy, and culture: Issues of society and schooling* (pp. 1–20). Norwood, NJ: Ablex.

Levine K. (1986). *The social context of literacy.* London: Routledge & Kegan Paul.

McLane, J.B., & McNamee, G.D. (1990). *Early literacy.* Cambridge, MA: Harvard University Press.

Malcolm, C.B., Polatajko, H.J., & Simons, J. (1990). A descriptive study of adults with suspected learning disabilities. *Journal of Learning Disabilities*, *23*, 518–520.

Mead, G.H. (1913). The social self. *The Journal of Philosophy, 10*, 375–380.

Mead, G.H. (1925). The genesis of self and social control. *International Journal of Ethics*, *25*, 251–277.

Moscovici, S. (1981) The phenomenon of social representations. In J. Forgas (Ed.), *Social cognition*. London: Academic Press.

Ogbu, J.U. (1987). Opportunity structure, cultural boundaries, and literacy. In J.A. Langer (Ed.), *Language, literacy, and culture: Issues of society and schooling* (pp. 149–177). Norwood, NJ: Ablex.

Olson, D. (1985). Introduction. In D. Olson (Ed.), *Literacy, language and learning: The nature and consequences of reading and writing* (pp. 1–15). Cambridge: Cambridge University Press.

Resnick, D., & Resnick, L. (1977). The nature of illiteracy: An historical exploration. *Harvard Educational Review, 47*, 370–385.

Robinson, J.L. (1988). The social context of literacy. In E.R. Kintgen, B.M. Kroll, & M. Rose (Eds.), *Perspectives on literacy.* Carbondale, IL: Southern Illinois University Press.

Rogoff, B. (1990). *Apprenticeship in thinking: Cognitive development in social context.* Oxford: Oxford University Press.

Schieffelin, B.B., & Cochran-Smith, M. (1984). Learning to read culturally: Literacy before schooling. In H. Goelman, A. Oberg, & F. Smith (Eds.), *Awakening to literacy* (pp. 3–23). London: Heinemann.

Scribner, S., & Cole, M. (1981). *The psychology of literacy.* Cambridge, MA: Harvard University Press.

Street, B. (1984). *Literacy in theory and practice.* Cambridge, U.K.: Cambridge University Press.

Taylor, S.E., & Brown, J.D. (1988). Illusion and well-being: A social psychological perspective on mental health. *Psychological Bulletin, 103*, 193–210.

Torrey, J.W. (1973). Learning to read without a teacher. In F. Smith (Ed.), *Psycholinguistics and reading* (pp. 147–157). New York: Holt, Rinehart, & Winston.

Trevarthen, C. (1980). Instincts for human understanding and for cultural cooperation: Their development in infancy. In M. von Cranach, K. Foppa, W. Lepenies, & D. Ploog (Eds.), *Human ethology: Claims and limits of a new discipline* (pp. 530–594). Cambridge, U.K.: Cambridge University Press.

Tudge, J.R.H., Putnam, S.E., & Valsiner, J. (1996). Culture and cognition in developmental perspective. In B. Cairns, G. Elder, & J. Costello (Eds.), *Developmental science* (pp. 190–22). New York: Cambridge University Press.

Tudge, J.R.H., & Winterhoff, P.A. (1993). Vygotsky, Piaget, and Bandura: Perspectives on the relations between the social world and cognitive development. *Human Development, 36*, 61–81.

Tulviste, P. (1991). *Cultural-historical development of verbal thinking: A psychological study.* Commack, NY: Nova.

Turman, M.C. (1987). *A preface to literacy: An inquiry into pedagogy, practice and progress.* Tuscaloosa: The University of Alabama Press.

UNESCO. (1970). *Functional literacy: Why and how.* Paris: UNESCO.

Valsiner, J. (1988). *Developmental psychology in the Soviet Union*. Brighton, U.K.: Harverster Press.

Vygotsky, L.S. (1978). *Mind in society.* Cambridge, MA: Harvard University Press.

Wagner, D.A. (1991). Literacy as culture: Emic and etic perspectives. In E.M. Jennings & A.C. Purves (Eds.), *Literate systems and individual lives: Perspectives on literacy and schooling* (pp. 11–19). Albany: State University of New York Press.

Wertsch, J.V. (1985). *Vygotsky and the social formation of mind*. Cambridge, MA: Harvard University Press.

Williams, R. (1983). *Keywords: A vocabulary of culture and society.* London: Fontana.

chapter 8

# Schooling, Literacy, and Social Change: Elements for a Critical Approach to the Study of Literacy

Angela B. Kleiman
State University of Campinas (UNICAMP), Brazil

## ON BECOMING LITERATE AND BECOMING ALPHABETIZED

Literacy studies in Brazil have been linked, for a long time, to studies on the acquisition of writing at school, a context in which learning to use the alphabetic system (a process called *alfabetização*) is viewed as an individual achievement. Becoming literate, in the school context, is a matter of developing a series of skills, among which the acquisition of the alphabet is paramount, enabling the individual to use the writing system. Partly to disassociate new studies on literacy from this rather narrow view of school writing practices, literacy studies in Brazil that examine the larger social impact of the written word have come to be known by a new term, *letramento*, first coined a decade ago (in Kato, 1986), etymologically unrelated to the word for alphabet. The new term reflects a shift in the focus of literacy studies, from the individual to the social dimensions of the phenomenon.[1]

In truth, it cannot be said that the focus on the social impact of writing represents a new theoretical and practical concern for researchers and educators in the Brazilian context. As far as 30 years ago, Paulo Freire (1970) gave a new meaning to the practice of alphabetization, by stressing the need to develop adult literacy programs that, by building upon the social and cultural worlds of the students, freed them to engage, as critical subjects, in an action that might permit them to question their social reality. Such questioning might then become the basis for social change and transformation. The focus of literacy campaigns, therefore, stressed an important aspect of the social dimension of literacy: The empowering effect of writing in technological societies, an effect that could bring about the development of the subject's critical awareness of his own role in society, and, most important, liberation from the confining boundaries imposed by a literate society on its nonliterate members.

The impact of writing in countries where large segments of the population cannot read or write[2] is just beginning to be understood. Of particular interest are those effects on urban groups who have been excluded from school, and who have, consequently, developed a variety of strategies in order to deal with the literacy demands of their surrounding world. Literacy studies in this context are tied up with important social concerns, many times related to the practical needs of groups committed to the transformation of the existing social conditions, which make large segments of the population whose primary socialization took place in oral, nonliterate families increasingly marginal.

In consonance with those concerns, these literacy studies examine what it means, cognitively and socially, to be unschooled in a literate society; what strategies unschooled subjects develop for dealing with the literate world; what conflicts and misunderstandings emerge when literate and nonliterate groups interact; what type of identity is defined, through schooling, for those teenagers and adults who enroll in adult literacy classes; and what conflicts and misconceptions a view of literacy traditionally associated with school has helped perpetuate in a society profoundly divided along class lines, where lack of schooling is one of the elements that makes that line indelible.

These are some of the questions that occupy literacy researchers in Brazil today. This paper will present a general overview of those concerns, and of important results of that research. In order to make the issues involved clear, we will also review some important mainstream theoretical issues regarding literacy, such as the existing research paradigms for the study of literacy, and their theoretical and empirical claims regarding the attributes and effects of literacy.

In order to understand the literacy practices of a society that has failed to bring large parts of its population to the universal literacy ideal, the dichotomy between autonomous versus ideological models of literacy proposed by Street (1984, 1993), though not semantically transparent, because all literacy practices constitute and are constituted by ideologies, has been crucial. This is why we will start this review with a presentation of the models and their implications, with particular attention to their implications for school literacy.

In the remaining sections of this paper we will examine critically some of the beliefs and myths that constitute the mainstream thinking about literacy, in the context of results from Brazilian literacy research in general and from oujr group in particular.[3] The basic assumption of this research is the validity of the theoretical distinction between models of literacy on the basis of the ideological assumptions that underlie them. The researchers in these projects subscribe to the view that literacy can best be understood in the context of the cultural and social characteristics of the groups that engage in literate practices.

One of the most pervasive and widespread beliefs regarding literacy, or rather, school acquired literacy, is the belief that learning to read and write has a general effect on cognitive development and functioning. After reviewing some of the most important empirical studies that have contributed to this claim, we present counter evidence from the oral and written production of schooled subjects—highly schooled, if we consider the high illiteracy rates in our context. The consequences of these claims about the general effects of literacy, both at the cognitive and social levels, on those who cannot read and write are worth examining because they bring important insights about other effects on the constitution of the subjective realities of participants in school literacy practices. A comparison of literacy practices and literacy acquisition inside and outside the school context permits a re-analysis of the effects of school literacy in intercultural contexts—of the types of practices it fosters—on subjects belonging to social groups within a predominantly oral tradition. The consequences of school literacy practices for matters such as the collective identity of the subjects who participate in them can then be evaluated.

Such evidence also raises questions about an unspoken assumption in literacy studies, that literacy is an all-or-none attribute of groups or individuals. There are, as a matter of fact, degrees of literacy (see Kleiman, 1992a), not only because unschooled individuals have strategies for dealing with the literacy requirements of their environment, but also because not all schooled individuals incorporate in their oral and written discursive modes those characteristics of literacy that are considered constitutive, which would mark them as bona fide representatives of the literate culture. This question is particularly important when those individuals in the periphery of literacy, so to speak, must act, by force of their profession, as representatives of the literate culture in a particular domain, such as the case of literacy teachers in the school.

After examining some samples of the reproduction of dominant ideologies of literacy, we present evidence from the interaction in youth and adult literacy classes of the conflict that these dominant ideologies, when translated into teachers' attitudes and practices, may cause for the members of the oppressed[4] classes, who make up practically all of the students enrolled in the literacy programs we have researched. The uncritical reproduction of these beliefs by the teacher in the classroom explains a great deal about the step-by-step construction of failure in youth and adult literacy classes we have observed, through ethnographic methods, in our research. The individual, disorganized, unpoliticized, and unsuccessful efforts at resisting the dominant ideology by the students, especially the male teenagers, are strong evidence of the need to re-examine our thinking about literacy and about the ways to introduce teenagers and adults into the literate world.

Less dehumanizing ways to be introduced to the world of writing are examined in the last section of this paper, by looking at subjects who have become literate through the action of another literacy agency, the grassroots, popular, social, and political movements. We present results from studies that look at the discourse strategies that unschooled leaders have developed in order to deal with the literate bureaucracy and the dominant class.

It is assumed in these studies that since unschooled, nonalphabetized individuals in urban technological societies have to function in institutional settings that require some familiarity with the written language, they have developed literacy practices to act in these settings. Because these subjects exhibit those characteristics that have been correlated with the mastery of writing, much more so than many highly schooled individuals, we have further evidence that the use and acquisition of a formal writing system can no longer be the defining criterion for inclusion or exclusion in a literate community, making many of the claims about the effects of writing on the reflexive capacity of individuals and social groups untenable.

## THE AUTONOMOUS VS. IDEOLOGICAL MODELS OF LITERACY

The autonomous model of literacy, according to Street (1984, 1993), is a research paradigm in which the ideological basis of the claims it makes about literacy are concealed. This opaqueness is due to the nature of the object it studies: Rather than studying people and what they do about writing when they need it, it studies the product, the written object, its characteristics and its apparent effects on the people who use it (also see Barton, 1994).

In this model, writing is seen as a self-sufficient product that is not dependent on its context of production for its interpretation. The production and interpretation process would be defined by the internal logical functioning of the written text, since the text does not depend, and, consequently, does not reflect, those strategic reformulations that come about in oral discourse due to the specific needs of speaker and hearer, such as changing the orientation of an argument, improvising, and other mechanisms not solely determined by rational, logical principles aimed at obtaining internal consistency (see, for example, Olson, 1981, 1984; Olson & Hildyard, 1983). Written discourse, free from such contextual constraints, would represent a symbolic order of communication substantially different from oral discourse, because in the written text the identity of the participants and the social relations they build during communication would not play an important role. The acquisition and use of this abstract, internally logical system would also have important cognitive and social consequences, as we shall see below, because of a line of reasoning that extends the characteristics of one type of writing to the people who use it.

The ideological model of literacy, on the other hand, explicitly recognizes the fact that no literacy practice is neutral; all practices of literacy are the product of culture and of the power structures in a given society. Literacy practices vary according to the social and cultural characteristics of the institutions in which they are acquired: family, school, church, business. Unlike the autonomous model, the ideological model of literacy does not presuppose a causal relationship between literacy and cognitive development, economic progress, social mobility, and increased democratic rights.

Although the profound changes that the development of writing systems have brought about in modern society cannot be denied, researchers who make the ideological basis of literacy transparent in their studies and who seek to understand these changes (cf. Tfouni, 1995; Oliveira, 1992, 1995) examine the particular contexts of use and acquisition of literacy practices in so far as some of them, especially those favored in the school context, represent the dominant ideologies in the society, which are then reproduced through the language and discourse practices of these institutions. Therefore, the particular cognitive strategies and discursive practices that dominant institutions teach become privileged ways of organizing and structuring reality, and an important instrument for social reproduction (or, in principle, transformation), but they do not constitute the only means that the members of a society have at their disposal either for accomplishing cognitive tasks or for acting through language. Works in the area of mathematical thinking have reached similar conclusions regarding practical, contextually acquired mathematical knowledge versus formal, school knowledge (Carraher, Carraher, & Schliemann, 1988; see also Knijnik, 1996).

If we define literacy as a set of social practices which make use of writing, both as a symbolic system and as a technology, in particular contexts for very specific contextually differentiated purposes, then the dominant literacy practices of a particular institution, such as the school, can be analyzed as one type of practice, the effects of which contribute to the separation of two different groups in society: those who have been alphabetized, and those who have not. School literacy practices are opaque as to the ideological foundations that sustain them because, being dominant in the society, they have come to be regarded as natural, not socially determined practices (cf. Clark, Fairclough, Ivanic, & Martin-Jones, 1987).

In this light, the failure of the school system to abolish one of the differences between the subordinate and oppressed classes and the rest of society can be accounted for: Those who are already literate even though they are as yet unschooled, that is, who are familiar with literacy practices in the family institution, have a better chance of acquiring school literacy practices, because the school presupposes a familiarity with home, family literacy events (that is, events whose interpretation involves somehow—a knowledge, awareness, or presupposition of—writing) (Heath, 1982, 1983). School literacy practices build upon this knowledge, a particular practice that emphasizes the progressive decentering, distancing, and abstraction of the written language from everyday matters.

Through an ethnographic study of the literacy events in small communities in southern United States, Heath (1982, 1983) has shown that the universal model of literacy oriented by school practices represents an opportunity to continue the linguistic development of children who had their primary home socialization among highly literate groups, such as teachers, doctors, and the like, but it represents a major break in the familiar discursive patterns of making sense of the world for children outside those groups, whose parents have lower schooling.

The recognition of underlying ideological differences determining the surface characteristics of a given literacy practice creates an important field of inquiry for better understanding the effects of literacy on modern society: This field of inquiry examines the literacy practices of both majority and minority groups in industrialized societies, and the effects of the dominant school practices on such groups. That is, literacy studies in the ideological paradigm no longer assume a universal literacy effect independent of a community's cultural practices, nor do they admit as sufficient proof of that effect the differences between literate and nonliterate subjects' performance in cognitive tasks during formal test situations.

## Literacy and the General Cognitive Effect Hypothesis

The assumption that literacy promotes profound changes in the cognitive functioning of individuals is a belief that cuts across different social classes, being stated, in different forms, in all types of discourses, from the academic to the popular. The model of writing used to make claims about the cognitive changes that writing would bring about is the essay type (cf. Gee, 1990). Because essay writing involves producing a text that is free from the determinants of the immediate context of production, with no real interagent in mind but rather with an image of an ideal reader, and, furthermore, because it deals with complex subject matters whose understanding necessarily involves the understanding of other texts already produced (that is to say, essays are strongly intertextual), it is indeed a product that is much more abstract than, say, letter writing, in which the immediate context of situation is relevant, the addressee is known, and the subject matters are affairs that relate to the spheres of action and thought shared by the writer and his intended reader (cf. Chafe, 1982; Chafe & Danielewicz, 1987).

Essay writing is a particular practice of one particular domain, the school. Most of the literacy practices that concentrate on step-by-step, everyday teaching have, as their final objective, the production of an essay. Competence in essay writing, for example, has to be demonstrated for students to pass the highly selective exams that determine whether or not they can enter the university. Being dominant, the characteristics of this particular text-type have come to define the literate person. Thus, it is claimed that being literate means having an increased capacity to deal with abstract matters, as well as an increased capacity to analyze a situation using rational rather than emotive arguments, and an increased reliance on the logical cogency and internal consistency of an argumentation rather than on external factors (see Ong, 1982).

The emphasis on abstract thinking ruled by logic is the most salient claim of the autonomous model of literacy. Some related claims, many of which are incorporated into commonsense ways of thinking about literacy, are the existence of a causal relation between literacy and cognitive development; the existence of constitutive differences between oral and written discourse; and the attribution of certain intrinsic "powers," so to speak, to writing, and, by extension, to the societies that use writing.

The different ways used by literate and nonliterate groups to organize and use their knowledge, and the differential empirical basis for that knowledge have resulted in the postulation of a Great Divide

(Gee, 1990; Street,1993), which used to serve as the basis for separating primitive, traditional, prelogical societies from the modern, progressive, "logical" ones, and which today has been transformed into a line that divides abstract versus concrete thought (see, for example, Goody, 1986; Olson, 1981). Goody, who criticizes several of the former parameters of the Great Divide, postulates that abstraction is directly dependent on literacy:

> When people speak of the development of abstract thought out of the science of the concrete, the shift from signs to concepts, the abandonment of intuition, imagination, perception, these are little more than crude ways of assessing in general terms the kinds of processes involved in the cumulative growth of systematic knowledge, a growth that involves elaborate learning procedures (in addition to imaginative leaps) and which is critically dependent upon the presence of the book. (Goody, 1986, p. 150)

The classical studies of Luria (1976) and Scribner and Cole (1981) have shown that there does exist a difference in the types of cognitive strategies used by literate and nonliterate people in problem-resolution tasks such as classification, categorization, and deductive reasoning. Working among the peasant population of the Uzbekistan and Kirghizia regions of the former Soviet Union in the 1930s, Luria showed that older peasants, who could not read or write and who subsisted using traditional means of farming the land, used contextually defined strategies in the resolution of decontextualized problems, whereas the young rural workers, who were undergoing profound changes in their socialization process, due to their participation in a learning situation that included learning to read and write, learning new techniques of farming, and developing collective communal methods of production, used strategies that did not use practical, empirical, contextualized evidence for solving those same problems. For example, the abstract problem par excellence, the syllogism, was differently solved by both groups: The nonliterate group used empirical data, refusing to draw inferences from the major premise; thus, their solution to a syllogism of the type "Metals do not rust. Gold is a metal. Does it rust?" might be something like "I wouldn't know, because I don't own any gold jewels but people say gold is precious." Young farmers who could read and write, on the other hand, arrived at the conclusion of a syllogism without resource to personal experience (Luria, 1976, pp. 100–116).

Scribner and Cole (1981) carried the study several steps further and were able to isolate the variable schooling from literacy in their study among the Vai people of Liberia. According to the authors, the evidence from the answers the schooled literate subjects (who knew the English script) or unschooled literate subjects (who used the Arabic or Vai scripts) gave in the experiments does not seem to support the correlation hypothesis, that is, the existence of a general effect of literacy on cognitive performance. The findings show one important effect from schooling on verbal strategies: the schooled subjects' increased ability to provide verbal explanations for the principles involved in the performance of the tasks (pp. 130–133).

From studies of reading, there is also counter evidence from the other side of the spectrum, the performance of schooled individuals, to the general literacy effect hypothesis. If the general cognitive effect claim were valid, it should be the case that highly schooled (and presumably highly literate) people should be able to use abstract inferential strategies to determine if a given piece of information explicitly stated in the text was inconsistent or contradictory to some other information in the text. In a reading experiment carried out by Carraher and Santos (1984), research subjects were given a newspaper article in which the headline ("Children from the Northeastern backlands are well nourished") was inconsistent with other pieces of information explicitly stated in the body of the same article ("50% of Northeastern children are anemic...10.7% of Northeastern backland children are undernourished to a second degree," and so on). The authors tested Brazilian undergraduates on a reading task that asked them to find out the contradiction. Their results show that the students did, in fact, resort to empirical evidence to solve the task, which may be solved on the basis of logical inferencing only, by analyzing the internal consistency of the text. In the task, students not only failed to detect the internal contradiction, but also justified their answers on the basis of their previous experience, knowledge, and beliefs: "The child who stays in the Northeastern backlands is well nourished because his family has the economic means to stay there: resources, money, land..." (p. 143).

There is also counter evidence to the general cognitive effect of literacy hypothesis from the writing performance of students in the Brazilian university entrance exam, a part of which consists in writing an essay. Every year the media takes up the subject of the students' lack of expression which is revealed, over and over, in their essays; such poor performance has also been the theme of numerous academic theses. Even if we take into the consideration the conditions in which these texts are produced, where the high degree of tension might prevent the student from achieving his best, the analysis of such texts leaves little room for defending the position that literacy allows the writer to free himself from the contextual restraints of empirical evidence, in order to produce an object that is abstract, internally consistent, and logically organized. The text below, one of many of that type analyzed by one of our research students (Moreira, 1991), produced by a candidate after at least 11 years of formal schooling, shows none of those traits. The task required that the students produce an argumentative text in response to the statement "Work not only guarantees the bread that man eats, but, especially, ennobles his character and gives him dignity":

> Work, a question of courage, good will, learning.
>
> All those who work, whatever is their job, is (*sic*) contributing in some way to himself and to everybody.
>
> Today machines are substituting the jobs of many people and on the other hand giving jobs to many people as well.
>
> If thou work honestly, with good will, with perfection in everything that you do you will be worthy of attention, trust.
>
> Whoever works honestly has the right to disagree, debate something.
>
> Work, even if it is the simplest job, and ennoble each time more your capacity to do and get what you want.[5]

It could be argued that even though these students do not seem to be able to produce an abstract object in writing, they might do so orally. In other words, there might be evidence of literate orality as a corollary of 11 years of schooling, because the production of an internally consistent piece of written discourse would involve other elements, as for example, the student's individual history of readings. However, the oral production of the schooled does not necessarily bear traces of the cognitive general effect of literacy, as evidenced in a study carried out by Milanez (1993), which involved the production of a 2-minute oral presentation, prepared in advance, on a voluntary basis, based on the reading of a newspaper or magazine article, by third-year students in a high school with a teacher training option, that is, students who would be, in the following year, introducing children to the world of the book. Among the various linguistic problems (at the sentence and word level) and textual problems (related to organization, theme development, adequacy) that the author analyzes in the students' oral presentations, several of them relate to the cognitive domain: contradiction, lack of local coherence, lack of internal consistency.

In one of our studies (Signorini & Kleiman, 1994), evidence from primary school teachers' attempts to use explanatory discourse in the classroom points strongly to the conclusion that it is not possible to maintain the existence of a general literacy effect as a consequence of schooling. In the case of the teachers whose classes we observed, their schooling amounts, in all, to 11 years—including the 3 years of teacher training school after the eighth grade. As I said before, in our context they are highly schooled.

The sources of classroom explanatory discourse are embedded in a literate tradition: They can be traced back to both scientific literary discourse and didactic, or pedagogical, discourse, which aims at popularizing, making accessible to students, the scientific source. Explanation is a discourse genre in which a speaker elaborates, through language, a meaning. Such elaboration may start from a situation or experience but does not stop at the empirical level. The initial, situational, or empirical meaning gets successively re-elaborated into a logical structure that organizes the knowledge sources tapped by linking the initial structure with other meaning structures, not necessarily built upon experience, through a reasoning process. The effect aimed at is that of objectivity and neutrality, a concern for truth. It is highly interactive, for in the pedagogical setting the speaker must calculate his listener's knowledge in order to choose those elements that will help him construct new knowledge (see Borel, 1981; Miéville, 1981).

In the following example (reproduced from Kleiman, 1993), recorded in an adult literacy class, the students are reading a newspaper article that tells of the conviction and sentencing of a school principal because of racism. The reading text stated that one of the discriminatory practices of the school principal consisted in segregating black students from games with other children, and insulting them. One of the students in the classroom asked for the meaning of the word "segregationist." In the transcription, we have the teacher's attempt at explaining:

> Teacher: Segregation is ... to be a segregationist means that you take away a person, right? from a toy, from a given place.
>
> Student: Ahhh!
>
> Teacher: Let us suppose, I'd take away, if I were a segregationist, I'd take Leandra, right? (approaching Leandra, a black student, until she stands next to her desk, and touching her on the shoulder) she wouldn't be able to play with you ... then a separation would be needed, right? among you.[6]

In the above exchange, there is no transformation of the concept that is the object of the explanation. In other words, there is no linking of the initial object of experience with a generalizing concept (for instance, segregation is an action, an attitude, a policy based on prejudice); there are no discursive reformulations using elements from other referential networks (such as racial, religious, social minorities; or separation of activities such as drinking, eating, bus riding for members of different races). This lack of structure makes the explanation unintelligible unless we consider the intertext being built through the reading of the newspaper article (which, we must remember, stated explicitly that the segregationist practice involved playing and games). That is to say, the teacher's explanation will not be recognized as such unless we consider the immediate context of experience as part of its structure, and unless we reduce this genre to the elaboration and re-elaboration of a contextualized structure, with no abstraction and no linking, through reasoning, with other elements, absent in the immediate context.

The results of these studies point overwhelmingly to the conclusion that school acquired literacy may contribute little to the "abstract" rationality progressively acquired because of an extended incursion into the world of the book.

## The Reproduction and Transformation of the Literacy General Effect Hypothesis—The Literacy Myth

The thesis that writing would have the power to make human beings freer to pursue new intellectual heights has been advanced by Ong (1982), who argues that having a writing system enables those who have it to devote their mental faculties to higher order intellectual operations, unlimited by memory constraints. Orality would be restrictive, and this restriction would manifest itself in the discourse patterns of those who do not read and write. This is to say, nonliterate peoples, or unschoooled people in literate societies, would be impeded from realizing their full human potential, which may be defined by their ability to engage in conscious and reflexive action. Should we take this to mean that the use of a writing system is essential for people to engage in reflexive action? Before we bring evidence that this is not the case, let us look further into some of the consequences of this attribution of such powers to writing.

Adherence to the autonomous model of literacy focuses on the undeniable differences between literate and nonliterate members of a same society, or between literate and nonliterate societies. These differences help to characterize these two groups as expressing opposite values with regards to a social, symbolic, and technological commodity—writing—possessed by some and not by others. By focusing on the difference, and because writing is but one aspect in a long list of differentiating characteristics in technological societies—in Brazil those who are fully literate also send their children to private schools, hold white-collar jobs, live in houses, are rarely black, are physically taller and stronger, and live longer—writing can easily come to be viewed as being the instrument needed to transform not just our mental structures, but social structures as well.

Once a comparison is made between oral and literate traditions, be it the primary orality of groups whose culture is untouched by writing, or the secondary orality of groups in technological societies (Ong, 1982), a comparison of the people who favor oral or literate patterns for organizing knowledge, and for expressing that knowledge, becomes inevitable. Since the positive side of the comparison that becomes dominant in a society that has both schooled and unschooled groups co-existing is inevitably that of the legitimate literate groups, a judgmental, evaluative characterization of the literate tradition as intrinsically superior to other forms is also inevitable (see Soares, 1986, for a discussion of deficit hypotheses in the Brazilian school context). Thus social myths are formed, and the "literacy myth" (Graff, 1979, 1987) is one of them: a 200-year-old ideology that attributes progress, economic development, social mobility, and a series of other social effects to literacy.

The social effects attributed to literacy are wide-ranging and widespread: They range from the religious to the economic; they are voiced in practically unchanged form by the industrialist and by the most oppressed worker, who have learnt to see the social order as natural (Kleiman, 1995, Matencio, 1995, Ratto, 1995). The media presents its version of this social effect in memorable, though sometimes brutal, images. In a particularly effective television ad used to promote the 1990 alphabetization campaign in the country, the face of a young child gradually turned into the face of an ape while a voice off screen told us that in order to be fully human every human being needs education and instruction. Another of the ads in the campaign depicted a man trapped in a car that was slowly sinking underwater; despite his efforts he could not break free because his hands were tied up, and therefore he drowned; meanwhile a voice off screen stated the need to read and write to be a fully functioning member of society.

The idea of an inferior citizen, who is not self-sufficient or productive because of his inability to read and write, is a recurring theme in newspaper reports, as the examples below show. The first example, attributed to a woman in domestic service, stresses the low self-esteem of the unschooled:

> To take one, two, three buses in the wrong direction in the same day and at midnight to be still far away from home is just one of the problems faced by 39-year-old Maria do Socorro Pereira, because she cannot read. The others range from dealing with money, going to the supermarket and to the drugstore, up to feeling embarrassment and discrimination. But above all, what humiliates her the most is her feeling of dependence, because she has to ask for help even to fill in the forms when she asks for a job.[7]

The same theme, in a variant that stresses the limited perception and language skills of those who cannot read or write is expressed by another editorial on the need for universal literacy: "The illiterate understands poorly what he hears and answers in a very imperfect way to the messages so received. The illiterate needs even more applied attention to what he sees."[8] The next newspaper report, attributed to an industrialist, stresses, as we would expect, productivity: "Without education and training, the worker is a disaster for himself and for the company."[9]

Graff (1979, 1987) has presented convincing arguments that there is no historical evidence in support of the literacy myth. The major universal literacy campaigns at the beginning of the century in countries in the Northern Hemisphere did not have a statistically significant effect on social mobility. On the contrary, while some individuals managed to move up the social ladder, the great majority of the poor became poorer. There does not seem to exist any evidence for the often stated correlation between universal literacy and economic development, social equality, modernization. That is to say, merely providing universal schooling without any other measures to bring about social change will not result in social transformation.

The dominant literacy ideology has a further, extremely pernicious effect in that the responsibility for being unschooled is attributed to the already oppressed individual. It is this perception that comes through in many of their statements: They lament the fact of not having frequented school because they were not good students, because their parents were not interested in their study, and so forth. When questioned further, several other facts come to light: The nearest school was 15 miles away and in the rainy seasons it was impossible to navigate the roads, their parents needed the extra hand which would increase, to a subsistence level, the amount of cotton, or sugar cane, or cocoa they picked for the landowner, and so forth. The contradiction is perceived only by some, who become literate under very particular conditions, as we will see below, in the last section of this paper.

## EMPIRICAL CORRELATES OF LITERACY MODELS: FROM SOCIAL REPRESENTATIONS TO ATTITUDES

Is the literacy myth accepted, then, without conflict? When we examine a cross-cultural context in which social representations are acted out, are translated into specific behaviors, conflict emerges. That is, instead of rational cooperation among the participants—the guiding rational principle presupposed in mainstream pragmatic analysis of language use—which would enable communication and understanding, we find a series of misunderstandings—systematic distortions of communication (Habermas, 1982, 1984)—resulting from the conflict between the beliefs of the groups in contact.

One such conflictive context of interaction among literate and nonliterate groups is that of the adult literacy classroom. Its examination permits us to see the construction of failure, in the effort to alphabetize, as a consequence of (a) the conflict that accepting the dominant literacy ideology as reproduced by the teacher represents for the unschooled; (b) the students' individual efforts to resolve the conflict and, sometimes, to resist the dominant beliefs; and (c) the teacher's perceived need to enact the dominant role attributed to her by the school power structure (see Bourdieu & Passeron, 1970, in relation to the issues of power in teaching).

Let us begin by examining the misunderstandings resulting from beliefs that center around the nature of the object to be taught, that is, about the written text. Focusing on the differences between the oral and the written text, a school practice that aims at introducing the student to the world of writing should be based on an accurate analysis of those differences, in order to develop a comprehensive set of activities to introduce them gradually. An obvious place to begin would be those differences that are a consequence of the medium, from the phonic to the visual: ephemerality versus permanence; online, concomitant to speech planning, versus advanced planning; online repair strategies versus possibility for revisions; and as a consequence of this, the possibility to choose, among lexical and structural linguistic options in the system, for that which best—more economically, more accurately, more elegantly—represents the meaning intended. And above all, teacher and students should explore the differential functions of writing and speaking practices in specific communities.

The view that literacy practices are dependent on the communities in which they are acquired (see Heath, 1982, 1983)—that they are, in fact, cultural forms acquired in those contexts in which the use of writing is necessary—might prevent situations such as the following, in which students are at a loss to understand what the teacher wants, which would seem to be a transformation of knowledge acquired in everyday practice—cooking—into formal school knowledge. The teacher is trying to engage the students in the collective production of a recipe. If we examine the issue purely from the viewpoint of the pedagogical strategy involved, the basis for such an exercise would seem relatively sound: The classroom students are mostly women who work in their homes or in domestic service; because they have experience in cooking, we can interpret the activity as an attempt, on the teacher's part, to build the new on the old, presupposed, previous knowledge (see Kleiman, 1995). Yet the problem is not just pedagogical, because it involves questions that have to do with the ways practice helps us structure our social knowledge, the ways we experience and perceive reality:

Teacher: /.../What do we still need to know? ... I'll give you an example. Pay attention to this.... I have a recipe for corn cake, here. And I say like this, the ... What's the title of the recipe? Corn cake. What goes into it, right? What are its ingredients? Well, we put ... two cups of corn meal, ehh ... three spoonfuls of flour, one spoonful of baking powder, two eggs, one and a half cup of sugar ... is the recipe finished then?

Students: (very low) No.

Teacher: What's lacking?

Student Ne: Milk.

Teacher: No, pretend that I said all the ingredients, milk also. What else do we still have to know?

Student Ne: Margarine.

Teacher: No, I am not saying that we still need an ingredient. What else do we have to know?

Student Ne: How to make it

Teacher: That's it! And how are we going to get to know that?

Student Vi: Well, we get to know that ... by making it.[10]

The analysis of the exchange above shows that the teacher is trying to introduce mnemonic and archival functions for written discourse which, for the students, had been fulfilled up to that moment by orality. No contexts are being introduced that might demonstrate to the students the need for such a change; furthermore, the emphasis is on the form of the text, since the teacher's words center around the introduction of a genre—the manual—as a sequential, ordered set of steps, as her use of words such as *title*, *ingredients*, and the targeted *directions* indicate. In other words, it is not the procedural contents of a recipe that is unfamiliar to the class, as the students' answers show, but the specific elements of the decontextualized written genre. In another class observed in this project, where the students were all women, a much more complex task was successfully introduced without causing perplexity among the students, even though it necessitated that the students themselves organize the sequential steps of the written recipe. After making cleaning soap for use in their homes and modeling dough for their children to play with, teacher and students would write the recipes not to forget them, or to hand them to absent classmates. Soon, other recipes, no longer supported by a classroom activity, were being brought—sometimes already written out, other times yet to be dictated to the teacher scribe—by the students themselves, who wanted to share some knowledge with their classmates.

The first, unsuccessful activity presupposes that the mnemonic and archival functions of writing are universal and neutral. Yet as Heath (1982, 1983) has shown, not even all groups that use writing with familiarity (for instance, high school graduates) verbalize the steps involved in a procedure, nor do they use writing as a support to memorize the steps in a given procedure. It is therefore a safe assumption that groups that favor an oral tradition for the acquisition of knowledge will have developed other strategies to remember relevant information. To present a culturally determined function of writing, through a practice that does not go beyond a transmutation of speech into a written form, to those groups who are in the process of being introduced to writing is a consequence of an uncritical acceptance of the autonomous model of literacy. The transmutation is no simple matter: It means abandoning one symbolic system, that of our mother tongue and therefore the one that permitted us to create our cultural identity, for another symbolic system, which represents the alien values of the dominant class.

It is important to note that in highly stratified societies such as the Brazilian one, with huge masses of people who cannot read and where the differences have a historic reality (having arisen as far back as the 16th century with the emergence of the dominant religious and administrative bureaucracy, "the city of letters," as Rama, 1985, calls it), the linguistic situation in which the oral and written varieties of a language coexist can be characterized as a type of conflictive diglossia between two discourses, or ways of representing reality through language. (See Ferguson, 1959, for the concept of diglossia to describe a situation of languages in contact; Hammel & Sierra, 1983; Martin-Jones, 1989; and Ninyoles, 1975, for the concept of diglossia to describe the relationship between languages in a society deep in intercultural conflict.)

With regards to the uses and functions of the oral and written discourses, we find the coexistence of two modalities that are varieties of the same language, but have very different status and prestige, and quite different functions in society. Such differences are manifested at all levels of the linguistic system: phonological, morphological, syntactic, and semantic. The differences are also present at the sociolinguistic level: Only one of the modalities has a prestigious literary tradition, which codifies and reproduces the values of the dominant groups in the community, and only one of them has gone through the processes of grammaticalization, dictionarization, and standardization; the standard variety, the only one acceptable in writing, is acceptable and adequate for all social situations. Adding these differences to the socio-historical elements first mentioned, the claim that the relations between the oral and the written languages is diglossic is quite reasonable.

When two languages, or forms of discourse, exist in a conflictive diglossic situation, the subordinate language is in constant danger of being displaced and of disappearing. Language identity, not the mere acquisition of a form, is at play in a situation like the one analyzed. The use of the new written form for the old oral function entails a functional language loss, and the consequent destructuring of what, until that moment, constituted an efficient oral discourse practice. The students' perplexity, and the ensuing failure in communication, are but the surface signs of the deeper conflict. To deny the existence of conflict, through the prompt comprehension and assimilation of the new form, would be a perfect case of what Ninyoles (1975) has called *auto-odi*, self-hate, a situation in which the culturally alienated abandon the values of their cultural identities. These students' perplexity, we believe, is akin to the escape attitudes of the backlander that Ribeiro (1995, pp. 343–361) describes: They are beginning to gain awareness of the situation they are immersed in, though they are still nonrebellious, that is, they are essentially inactive and reproductive of the system.

Similar situations emerge whenever the claims of the autonomous model of literacy are presupposed as universal by the teacher. Let us consider the belief in the general effect of literacy on cognitive functioning, which is reproduced in the teacher's discourse in the example that follows (taken from Kleiman, 1995). The exchange was recorded after the students had finished reading a small text (an excerpt from a major work) in their textbook. In the text, the unschooled wife of an also unschooled, inarticulate migrant worker had saved him from being cheated by the land and cattle barons, by helping him figure out the accounts through her adding and subtracting skills. There are several issues that could have been focused here, the most notable being the misuse of literacy (numeracy) skills by the dominant class, as one of the instruments for cheating the poor. Instead, the teacher chooses to focus on the inferior status of the unschooled, and the following dialogue occurs among the teacher and three teenagers in the class:

> Teacher: Why would it be good to be able to read and write as Sinha Terta does? Is it true that it helps people not to be cheated? Are you cheated, Everton?
>
> An: I don't think so. You don't have to. It is all the same thing!
>
> Ev: You just have to use your head. It is all the same, a person who cannot read, need not be cheated. It's all the same.
>
> Ade: He was smart because he canceled the sale.
>
> An: But he perceived that he was being cheated. Not being able to read doesn't mean that one/he is stupid.[11]

Ananias' answer is a response to an unspoken statement which is implicit in the teacher's question. The student reacts by denying it, just as if it had, in fact, been stated: "People who can read and write are more intelligent, smarter, cannot be cheated as easily as illiterates can." Though the form is crude, its gist corresponds to the cognitive general effect hypothesis which has fostered, as we saw, a built-in bias in favor of literate people, who would thus be cognitively superior.

His classmates, Everton and Ademilson, continue the process of meaning construction along the same lines, finalizing their remarks with the explicit denial of the unspoken general effect claim. As they engage in this process, they become more categorical in their answers: Whereas the use of a verb of opinion (*I think*) by the first student expresses subjective modality, and therefore does not commit the speaker to the truth of the proposition, his classmates use the categorical forms of the verb in the present tense, a form that is typical of axioms, definitions, and other eternal truths, statements that are valid for all times. It has been noted elsewhere (see Fairclough, 1992) that when people are interacting, the use of modalities that imply an increasing commitment to the truth of a given proposition is not necessarily evidence of a stronger, increasing belief in its truth, but of the ongoing construction of a chain of solidarity among the participants of the interaction.

The building of solidarity ties is a strategy that helps members of a group keep their collective identity intact in situations that involve a threat to that identity, that is to say, in situations involving conflict. There are, however, two problems that thwart the students' attempts at solidarity. The first one has to do with the fact that their attempt is undirected, disorganized, and ineffective because it is not a part of a collective social action; they are impromptu responses motivated by some aggressive stimulus in the context. The second problem we see in this strategy in this particular context is that it plunges the students into another, extremely conflictive situation: It makes their participation in the literacy course dysfunctional, since such participation is usually motivated by exactly the same values they feel compelled to deny here, because the nondenial would imply accepting the teacher's (and other dominant group member's) evaluation of them as minor, less intelligent, easily duped subjects. They come to class because they are aware of their need in order to compete in society and because they believe in schooling as the instrument needed to change their social status; they come looking for instruments that will let them, in the words of a student, "sit at a desk and count the loads being carried from the warehouse to the truck instead of carrying those loads on his back," yet they must deny the value of the instrument. Unlike the successful history of the politically engaged (see Knijnik, 1996, and the discussion in the last section of this paper), where the individual's insertion in an organized social movement resolves the individual conflict because of the collective gain, these teenagers' history usually ends with their abandonment of the course.

When we consider other differences the autonomous model of literacy helps to constitute, such as that between legitimate, book knowledge and traditional, popular knowledge, we find that conflict again arises when dominant values are imposed, by force of the institutional context, on the subordinate groups, as we will see in the next example.

This exchange takes place during a reading lesson, and the text being read consists of a list of precautions against self-medication (in Kleiman, 1992b, there is an analysis of the whole lesson). In addition to that text, the teacher had brought a sample of the warning slips that come with pharmaceutical drugs. Self-medication is a common practice, because there are no enforceable restrictions against purchasing almost any kind of prescription medicine over the counter. The teacher's presupposition, which, as we shall see below, is not borne out, is that the purchase and use of pharmaceutical drugs is a universal practice in the society, regardless of social and economic class. After 75 minutes of reading, paraphrasing, and commenting on the small text, 15-year-old Gilvan, an orange picker, contests the teacher's premise, and the following dialogue takes place:

Gilvan: There's times when home medicine is better than the doctor's.

Teacher 1: No, it's not, Gilvan, what's that you're saying?

Gilvan: I think so.

Teacher 1: Isn't it better at the doctor's? You go there you get an orientation.

Gilvan: No.

Teacher 2: NO?

Gilvan: For me, I don't think so.

Teacher 1: You're gonna know exactly what the medicine is for.

Gilvan: No. Bush medicine is better.

Teacher 2: Huh?

Gilvan: Today's medicine is no good.

Teacher 2: What do you mean it's no good?

Gilvan: (in a low voice) I don't know.

The teacher then switches her line of argumentation, trying to justify her opinion by appealing to the legitimacy of the medical institution:

Teacher 2: Today's medicine? And why do you think doctors study?

Gilvan: No:::. They study just to be there sitting. To make money out of the poor.

Teacher 2: Ahhh! They study to sit there. Aha. And you think that he will ... that when you go to consult him he's gonna give you that medicine wa:::::y back, from 1900 or he's gonna give you a medicine that ...

Gilvan : A medicine from today.

Teacher 2: Aha. Didn't you say medicine was garbage?

Jair: No teacher, he said...

They continue at odds, until Gilvan, already exasperated, changes his line of argumentation, offering a specific example for his claim:

Gilvan: I have an aunt (inaudible) that nobody gave her medicine. Her medicine is bush medicine

Teacher 1: Natural medicine?

Gilvan: (Nods affirmatively)

Teacher 2: And isn't that medicine?

Gilvan: It's not a medicine [that was prescribed], it's just plant medicine.

Teacher 2: So ... that plant ... she's using it as medicine. And you don't think it's medicine?

Gilvan: But it is not given by a doctor![12]

Notice that Gilvan does not deny the value of prescription drugs initially, but merely points out that sometimes (for some types of illnesses) homeopathic medicine works best. He successively rephrases his original lexical choice—*home medicine, bush medicine, today's medicine* and *plant medicine*—in an effort to make his meaning clear to the teachers, showing considerable communicative flexibility (Gumperz, 1982). His statement does not represent an idiosyncratic, isolated belief but one that is shared by literate and nonliterate groups alike.

In spite of the universality of the practice he defends, the teachers do not have much choice but to refute his opinion, since they are representing, in that context, the literate values to which the student has to be introduced and, in consonance with the conceptions that make up the autonomous model of literacy ideology, those values are superior:

Modernity and progress characterize prescription drugs, values notably lacking in traditional, old wives' remedies. Therefore, the relevance or the validity of the student's comment must be denied. This refusal to acknowledge the student's point triggers an escalation of the argument in which Teacher 2 and student get further and further apart until agreement is no longer possible. The student's initial statement, which consisted of a circumscribed and noncategorical comment about drugs, escalates to a rejection of the medical profession before it finally gets reduced to the absurd, through this teacher's manipulative reinterpretation of the student's words. In the context, the expression *today's medicine* was used by Gilvan to mean prescription medicine in opposition to old, traditional medicine; the expression gets reinterpreted by the teacher as medicine produced by the pharmaceutical industry today in opposition to obsolete pharmaceutical medicine. In addition, the overgeneralization of the student's remarks makes his argument untenable, because of the idiosyncratic interpretation of the student's comment about drugs as meaning that no medicine, whether it is a prescription drug or natural medicine, does any good. Through these deceptions, the student is finally silenced.

The teacher's argumentation strategies are quite revealing in their ruthlessness; yet they make perfect sense when we consider the matrix of beliefs that determines her action. Uncritical, unreflective acceptance of the literacy myth makes it imperative that two prestigious institutions of literate and technological society which represent the modern and the progressive—medicine and pharmaceutical research, on the one hand, and erudite, modern literate practices, on the other—be upheld as intrinsically superior. The fact that for large groups of people who are marginal members of that society those institutions are not surrounded by the mythical prestige to them attributed by literate communities seems to come as a surprise to the teacher.

And yet just a small amount of reflection would show that the reliability and objectivity that literate groups attribute to these institutions is a social construction made possible because of the dominant groups' social and cultural practices, who can afford to go to private doctors and buy prescription drugs. Any doubts we may have about these institutions, or about the literate tradition itself (for instance, regarding the strange form and function of prescription warning slips, cf. Gee, 1990) are not easily voiced and rarely find echo given the prestige and authority of these institutions. It can be convincingly argued that the layman's belief in these institutions is a matter of faith, not a matter of logic, or internal consistency, or independent knowledge. For example, it is a fact that the medical knowledge about many areas is still incipient, and that much research is still needed to develop cures, drugs, or vaccines against some diseases; furthermore, as laymen, we have no empirical evidence about the existence of the agents to whom diseases are many times attributed. Yet, if a disease is diagnosed by a physician as being caused by some such agent, it is most likely that this verdict will be accepted, and that his instructions to alleviate the symptoms of said disease will be religiously followed.

It is unreasonable to expect that such a relationship based on faith and trust will have been developed by those large groups for whom, first, the inaccessible written text is not a reliable source of information, making face-to-face interaction with those trusted ones the preferred mode for the transmission of knowledge, and, second, for whom the medical profession is not trustworthy since, in the context we are describing, the contacts between a physician and a member of the subordinate classes take place in the worst imaginable conditions, having become a matter of national scandal. Given these facts, it is not surprising, then, for the teenager who raises his voice against these institutions to say at one point that "doctors are sitting there to make money out of the poor."

When the dominant literacy conceptions get translated to the level of attitudes and behaviors, without analysis or reflection, when they are taken to belong to the natural rather than the social order of things, the outcome can be dehumanizing: A presumably well intentioned teacher, who seems to have thought she had something important to show her students, turns into an ruthless authoritarian who does not admit cultural diversity and must silence opposing views at any cost, regardless of the ethical consequences of her action, both at the intrasubjective and interpersonal levels (for example, the student's lowered self-image through her abuse of language through manipulative, specious arguments and the lack of understanding).[13]

It is difficult to characterize their interaction as communicative action, that is, an action in which participants "can mobilize the rationality potential (...) expressly for the cooperatively pursued goal of reaching understanding" (Habermas, 1984, p. 99); an action which, furthermore, according to the same author, would have to be coherently based on the actor's relations to his referential, ethical, and subjective world. Rather, it is a manifestation of what Habermas calls strategic action, not oriented towards understanding but to success, situations that result in systematically distorted communication, and in which "at least one of the parties is deceiving himself about the fact that he is (...) only keeping up the appearance of communication" (p. 332). In another article, which analyses clinical psychology data, the author calls cases of systematically distorted communication such as this "pseudo-communication" that "produces a system of reciprocal misunderstanding which, due to the false assumption of consensus, are not recognized as such" (1982, p. 311). In our example, the structural power vested on the teacher does not even require an appearance of consensus and rationality.

At the interpersonal level, the situation is bad for everybody involved. The rest of the students are extremely uncomfortable throughout the episode (shifting constantly in their chairs, avoiding eye contact with the teacher, some of them throwing away the sheet of paper with the text, others trying to interfere in order to explain their classmate's viewpoint to the teacher). In terms of learning literate values, concepts, customs, and habits which are certainly necessary for their life in the urban environment, their knowledge and beliefs seem to emerge untouched and unchanged, given the fact that, at the very end of that lesson, not one but three adolescents state their skepticism towards the medical institution, and the teacher (T2) must once again use the institution structural power in order to continue making her unheard point: One student states that to take or not to take medicine does not make any difference whatsoever; another says that he refuses to take medicine on the principle that diseases, their cure, and death are all preordained; the third one states that he prefers herbal teas over prescription drugs. The teacher must talk louder and faster in her summation to override the students' voices, insisting that what the students are saying has nothing to do with the topic of her lesson: "What we are speaking about here, students, is whether we should medicate ourselves. That's what we are talking about."

We conclude, then, that the literacy general effect hypothesis, a natural outcome of the autonomous model of literacy research, cannot be sustained when we consider evidence from the performance of schooled subjects. As we shall see below, it is also questionable when we consider the performance of a particular group of unschooled subjects.

## SOCIAL MOVEMENTS AS LITERACY AGENCIES

An examination of the literacy practices of the nonalphabetized, that is, those who have not acquired alphabetic writing through schooling, makes sense in a context such as ours, with large masses of unschooled people who have to cope daily with all sorts of literate institutions in various kinds of literacy events. Such a situation practically dictates new research objectives for the study of literacy from an applied linguistics viewpoint such as ours, in order to examine both the unschooled subjects' practices in these events and the effects they have on their discursive practices, which we take to be both constitutive and constituent of their cultural identities.

As an example of context determining research designs, we mention the analysis of a literacy event particular to our society, the civil service public exam, analyzed by Descardeci (1992), one of the graduate research students in our project. In any urban setting, we find a large number of unschooled public servants in almost every federal, state, and municipal institution. In 1989, due to a new constitutional exigency that required that public servants be able to read and write, they had to submit themselves to a written test to prove their literacy skills. The research analyzed both the form of the exam (practically a prototype for an autonomous model literacy event) and the strategies used by unschooled subjects—those already in the institution and those trying to enter into civil service—in the test situation. Unlike the event aimed at by the dominant groups, the bureaucrats who made up the exam questions, a new literacy event was created by the people involved in it. The impossible exigency placed upon the unschooled was resolved by their demand, and the examiners' compliance, that the exam questions be read aloud to those who could not read and that their oral answers to the questions be then written down, thus confirming one of the claims of the ideological paradigm: Literacy practices must vary according to the needs of those involved in a situation which necessitates the use of writing for it to make sense to the participants.

Several studies reported in the literature confirm the view that literacy practices are creative responses to the groups' practical needs, varying according to those needs and to the contexts in which they take place (Tfouni, 1995; also Knijnik's description of traditional mathematical practices, 1996). One group is of extraordinary interest because of its exceptionality with regards to the generalized failure of adolescents and adults (and, as we saw, a great number of high school graduates) to become literate according to the criteria of autonomous academic literacy. Leaders of social movements—such as rural, union, and community leaders—who have come from the poor and subordinate classes engage in a process aimed at social transformation that necessarily involves reflexivity and awareness and which seems to guarantee their success in becoming literate.

Knijnik's ethnographic study (1996) of a continuous education experience involving primary school teachers who were directly involved with the rural movement "dos Sem Terra" (the landless ones) is striking in this respect. The ethical and pedagogical problems that prevent the socially unengaged teachers in our project from developing a relevant and efficient practice, and that prevent our words and actions from making sense except to a small number of them, were not an impediment to those teachers, who, through debate and reflection, could arrive at coherent action. This was not a result, as the author shows, of any particular success in her efforts to break the constitutive asymmetries of the situation: "We should not have illusions about the process of insertion of the intellectual in a social movement," which is the site of a "permanent tension between autonomy and commitment" (p. 123). Nor could we say that it was only due to her deliberate efforts to symmetrize the weight of the discourses by legitimizing the other involved in the process, because this is a process in which all progressive educators, ourselves included, engage (Freire, 1980, 1991). The difference, it seems to us, lies in those rural educators' commitment to a social movement that neutralized the tension and ambiguity inherent in their appropriation of the dominant, academic, legitimate culture[14] and the partial or complete abandonment of their own, in order to attend the practical needs created by the social movement.

When popular movement leaders take the floor, their words reveal, even to the most cursory examination of their contents and organization, their capacity to decenter and to distance themselves from their social condition in order to analyze it. It would seem, then, that through their engaged action in popular social movements, they have developed a reflexive awareness of the symbolic power, or symbolic violence (Bourdieu, 1993), of ideologies such as the autonomous literacy and the mythical nature of the beliefs thereof associated. Thus, whereas most unschooled subjects blame their status on their inaptitude for learning, or on their parents' lack of interest in keeping them at school, thus legitimizing this power by reproducing the stigmatizing majority views, political activists attribute their status to lack of political will, refusing to displace, to the discursive level, other forms of power exercised by the dominant groups, thus reducing the impact of stigmatization on their cultural identities.

This is particularly clear in an recently published interview of a rural leader who has risen to national prominence.[15] Like most, if not all, members of his class, José Rainha Junior never went to school as a child but learnt to read as a teenager, while working the land, through the action of the Liberation theologues of the Catholic Church (Comunidades Eclesiais de Base). Both the theme and the language in the report have a very marked bias against the leader: The article is about the fact that, "even though he owns 4 hectares of land," he does not live in the land occupied and "*assentada*" (distributed among the rural workers and in the process of becoming productive) but dwells in a small house that belongs to the state government, in the city of São Paulo, free of rent, "*hardly*" paying for the water and electricity he and his family use, and which he failed to pay one month. He obtained the house through the intermediation of a state congressmen, who, we are told, is the brother of a former small-town mayor "who lost his mandate because he was accused of irregularities in his administration." The article also informs us that in his piece of land in the collective farm "he himself did not plant anything. He didn't even erect a house." In addition to the argumentation strategy of presenting the information as contrary to what we, readers, would expect, through the use of the operators "*even though,*" "*hardly,*" and "*not even,*" which signal argumentative scales in which a host of other, worse things are implied, the newspaperman reports that the leader *admitted* and *had to acknowledge* facts that could have been simply *said* or *explained*, as when the leader *admits* that he would like to buy the house he is living in, carrying the presupposition that the fact had been denied first, because of culpability or need for secrecy, both having negative connotations.

Yet if we leave aside the interviewers' interpretation of the leader's words, and look instead at his own words in the direct quotations, what we find is the picture of a man who is not living an ambiguity or a contradiction, because he has restructured his discourse as an element of a social reality that does not recognize the legitimacy of the symbolic power the reporter tries to exercise over him during the interview. As part of his analysis of the place of language in the relationship between dominant and subordinate classes, he has adopted both the literate standard variety and literate argumentative strategies: Through his appropriation of the legitimate culture, his answers cannot be said to reproduce the relationship between the dominant and subordinate classes. The rural leader does not assume the blame for the oppressed classes' social conditions, "I worked in the coffee farm since I was seven. As I had to work in order to eat, I couldn't go to school, which was very far away;" later on in the interview he argues against the limited, ethnocentric, and logically inconsistent views of the majority press: "The other day, a reporter asked me a stupid question. He wanted to know if I would give away land if I was a land baron. I said I wouldn't. But it so happens that I am the produce of another context, that of the workers, and I fight for my class."[16]

It is interesting to note that the man achieves a coherence between his actions and their representation through discourse which his wife, also a rural leader in her own right, seems to have difficulty achieving in this interview (pointing to another dimension through which power is exercised, that of genre); she recognizes the reporter's questions as legitimate by trying to justify the situation, a fact that is explored by the reporter by using her own words as a running commentary on the "facts" he chooses to report. The following is the relevant excerpt: "The Rainha couple has all the goods that are typical of a middle-class family:

television, parabolic antenna ('donated by a priest,' says Deolinda); a sound equipment ('second class,' she warns), refrigerator, washing machine, and telephone ('the telephone bills are paid by the MST,' the woman announces)."[17]

Two researchers in our project, Signorini (1994, 1995), and Ratto (1995) have focused the discourses of unschooled leaders of social movements. Through their analysis, a very clear picture emerges of a type of literate orality without alphabetic support.

I call this type of orality literate, in order to distinguish it from schooled orality, though both would be types of what Ong (1982) calls the secondary orality of technological societies, that is to say, a type of orality that has been transformed and is sustained by writing technologies, such as the press, television, the book. Unlike the schooled type of secondary orality, which is many times a peripheral approximation to the legitimate, academic literacy, literate orality would have, as constituent features, those that have been put forward as constituent of written discourse: a sustained, decontextualized, decentered, "objective" analysis of a matter, using cogent, internally consistent arguments. We would maintain that the presence of these features would mark any type of orality as literate, be it academic—or school acquired—or popular, emerging from the social transformation needs of a popular social movement. Like other popular systems, this discourse practice may be linked to the practical needs of constructing a legitimate representation of the subordinate class in their dealings with the dominant institutions, such as the press, or management, or the established political forces.

The concept of literate orality proposed here ties closely with the notion of popular, versus academic, cultural forms. As several authors have pointed out, this is a dangerous concept because it can lead to Romantic or populist views, which either deny the social facts by accepting all folk cultures as legitimate, or reinforce elitist views because by necessity popular cultures have to be analyzed through the prism of the academic, socially legitimate forms. Furthermore, it is a difficult concept because it carries to the analytical field the struggles in the social world (see Bourdieu, 1993; Knijnik, 1996).

It is important, however, to characterize these leaders' public discourse as a popular form of literate orality because to continue to describe the needs of the unschooled leader as the acquisition of literacy is misleading, one more instance in the exercise of power of the academic institutions. Furthermore, the "neutral," "objective" mainstream linguistics discourse which insists on the equivalence of all dialectal varieties is inadequate. Just as inadequate is the school practice that reduces literacy acquisition to the learning of new forms and of a system to encode those forms and register them permanently. All these inadequate analyses of the situation add one more complicating element to an already complex, ambiguous, and tense event which involves the adoption, for a practical purpose, of the dominant-class discursive practices, while remaining true to the needs and interests of another class.

The academic recognition that literate discourse is not just a product of book learning but that it is a discursive practice characterized by increased power to verbalize issues relating to the social world, by the reflexivity, distancing, and decentering that create the effect of a discourse that sustains itself internally, without recourse to contextual meanings, is a step towards recognizing popular solutions in a society that has historically fragmented the concept of people and their productions (cf. Ribeiro, 1995).

In order to describe the elaborate discourse practices that are the product of these subjects' increased capacity to verbalize their experience, it is necessary to make a distinction between the systemic, structural aspects and the rhetorical aspects of that discourse.

At the systemic level, their language retains many of the archaic features that characterize the stigmatized varieties, and it is fragmented by a large number of hesitations, false starts, and ongoing repairs (which has been compared to the effect produced by a "speaker who speaks a foreign language he doesn't know well," Payer, 1993, p. 28, following Pecheux). There are two elements at work here: One is a very pronounced, continuous monitoring, or epilinguistic activity, a product of the reflexivity on his linguistic action; the other is a product of self-censorship, since as a member of a subordinate class, he must conform to the "demands of the market" in a society which has historically deprived him of linguistic and cultural capital (Bourdieu, 1993). In a study of the language of rural social movements, Payer (1993), working from a discourse analysis perspective, analyses these features as the manifestation, in the hetereogeneity of their discourse, of the emergence of a historical rural subject position still remnant in the leader's discourse.

Formally, the phonological, morphological, syntactic, and lexical features used by these representatives are variable, alternating between the standard and the nonstandard varieties, thus continuing to constitute a source for stigmatization (Ratto, 1995, pp. 283–284). These representatives, some of whom were enrolled in the adult literacy classes we observed in our research project, had incorporated features of the standard variety (such as number agreement) but they used these rules variably, except in the case of ready-made set phrases related to their political speech-making activities (such as "os direitos dos trabalhadores": the [plural] rights of the [plural] workers); in addition, they tended to use complex syntactical patterns (like nominalizations and passive voice) and erudite vocabulary with either a hesitant control of the rule ("that man had a lot of ... he was very much represented ... he represented many people") or, perhaps, with a semantic decomposition of the lexical item which did not correspond to the legitimate, dictionarized form (a confluence, for example, of separate meanings of the word "represent", reflected on the number and type of arguments of the verb: "be the representative of"; "to mean"; "be a symbol of").

The great part of the hesitancy, false starts, and hypercorrections observed comes from the fact that the subjects interviewed by Ratto (1995) consistently incorporated, in a mirror-image effect, the pronunciation patterns, the structure, and the wording of the questions posed by the interviewer, who was the representative of the legitimate, literacy institution in that context, in a systematic effort to reproduce the "correct" forms of speech. This linguistic strategy indicates that these subjects are taking concrete measures in order to deal with what they see as inadequacies in their speech, so as to legitimize themselves as representatives of their class in their dealings with the dominant classes. The phenomena also show that these concrete steps do not come easily for these subjects, both in operational terms, since they cannot match the fluency and security of one who was born speaking standard Portuguese (cf. Mey, 1985), and from a cultural viewpoint, because of the conflict and tension resulting from the inherent ambiguity involved in the appropriation of the other's discursive practices and the displacement of their own.

At the rhetorical level, on the other hand, the general effect produced is that of a highly literate text—that is, a text characterized by its internal consistency (see the interview above)—by decentering and distancing from the immediate personal concerns through the use of general categories ("the worker's rights" instead of "my rights"), producing an effect of objectivity and neutrality typical of academic discourses. Furthermore, the unschooled subjects in Ratto's study produce the literate genres necessary to their practical needs with familiarity, constituting themselves as authors of a complete text in all relevant intersubjective and organizational aspects, since the only exceptional feature lies in their inability to use the alphabetic system, and this they accomplish through the use of secretaries, that is to say, by adopting the literate practices of literacy events in the business world.

The example below (reproduced from Ratto, 1995, pp. 285–286) is particularly interesting because it involves the production of a written text by a syndicate leader. Since he cannot read or write, he adopts the expedient of dictating the letter to his secretary. The secretary's specific decisions do not involve academic, literate aspects of text production, but only decisions related to alphabetization, registering the text in the standard form according to the alphabetic rules: spelling, application of the standard-dialect obligatory verb and number agreement rules, and spatial display on the page are the issues that come under the responsibility of the secretary. The grammar and lexis of the letter are practically faultless, even though, as Ratto points out, there are still traces of idiosyncratic cohesive ties (in the paragraph starting with the use of connector *in addition to,* the workers would be demanding irregularities, and not the solution of irregularities). The discursive organization, which shows the leader's familiarity with the letter-writing practices of literate business and bureaucratic tradition, are his own. The logical consistency between the interplay of claims (negotiations are necessary), warrants (the demands are true to the workers' needs and desires), and data and facts (list of attested problems) is impeccable, from the point of view of the structure of an argument. (We used Toulmin's model of argumentation, 1958, for the description.)

> The Union Board of representatives, in a meeting with the workers of the firm, verified the following irregularities:
>
> 1) janitors have a 6 day working load, with one free period per week; therefore, there should be, obligatorily, two free periods on Sundays. They are working four extra hours a day.
> 2) lately, the food has been bad
> 3) there are discounts in the pay envelopes justified as "Accounting Payments"
> 4) lack of job classifications in the firm
>
> In addition to the above irregularities, the workers also demand:
>
> 1) Saturdays off
> 2) medical insurance
> 3) job transportation
> 4) drinking water fountains
>
> In light of the above, we ask that a meeting be scheduled between the Syndicate Board of Representatives and the firm representatives, with the indirect participation of a workers committee, with the sole purpose of witnessing these negotiations.[18]

Signorini (1994, 1995) has investigated the penetration of the literacy myth among unschooled rural workers, with particular reference to regions in the interior of the Northeast, where the illiteracy rate raises above 50%, in small towns that only recently have had access to television, and where writing, according to the author, is rare and practically unnecessary. In the versions of the literacy myth among the rural workers living in these distant and isolated villages, what stands out is their faith in the power of writing to bring about individual success and social progress by bringing about an improvement in their general language and communicative skills, in their knowledge, and in their overall behavior ("dom de ser," gift of being). Only in the political site, in city councils where the overwhelming majority of elected representatives has 1 or 2 years of schooling, such general powers are contextualized in relationship to the need for legitimacy and the practical needs of their office: to be the majority whip, to introduce a project, to participate with pertinence in the legislative debate.

In their talk, these unschooled politicians show an analytical stand in relation to the situation in which they participate, not in relation to the legitimacy of the social situation that makes them inadequate. That is, it is the situations in which they live that are problematized as involving issues of legitimacy in their representation, and as potential circumstances for being "maneuvered" by others who can "do more than just listen" but who can also express themselves (Signorini, 1995, p. 24). That is to say, the political site itself permits them to contextualize the problem, but does not lead them to interrupt the process of legitimization of their subordinate role; there is no break with the legitimate ways of thinking about the problem, because, after all, in an elective democracy, it is not necessarily class solidarity that gets politicians elected.

Quite different is the situation of the leaders who got their representation by working with their class in a popular grassroots movement, even when they have no formal schooling at all. Unschooled leaders in that context do not adhere to this commonsense, universal view of literacy, and they question the myth of literacy on ethical grounds. They see the written word as having both a positive and a negative side: Not being able to speak "right" deprives them of legitimacy, but, at the same time, it does not create solidarity conflicts through distancing them from their class. Literacy may create identity and acculturation problems for those who become full members of the literate society which is the one that has oppressed them: "Those who could give, who could share what they have do not, those who want to cannot" (Signorini, 1995, p. 26).

By identifying the written word as one of the instruments for abuse of the powerless by the powerful, they are in fact questioning the universal status of the literacy myth, even though they acknowledge, at the same time, its place in bringing about change. In a particularly lucid statement, a rural leader who cannot read or write expresses the paradoxical nature of literacy: "The letter gives life and kills at the same time."[19]

Since writing is seen as unequally distributed among the social classes, its appropriation and use is not seen as an individual's ethical option; it is a question that has to do with social class interests. The rural worker's analysis of literacy contrasts sharply with the analysis of primary school teachers who, by force of their profession, are the representatives of the literate culture at school. In the example discussed previously, the teacher's interpretation of similar ethical questions places the dilemma at the level of the individual's capacity to deal with the demands of modern society, reproducing the autonomous ideology of literacy as a universal panacea for social problems. The leader's view also contrasts sharply with the apathetic unschooled subjects, who recognize the social stigmatization of their discursive practices, and through this legitimization, make it a part of their linguistic identity: It is not uncommon for these speakers to preface their words, stating that they cannot speak Portuguese, that is, by denying their identity as native speakers because their speech does not conform to the norm.

## CONCLUSIONS

The acquisition of literacy through political engagement in popular grassroots movements, political parties, and labor union movements, in order to participate fully in events where literacy is required, leads to success in the acquisition of the literacy cognitive (and technological) apparatus, but not to empowerment and legitimacy. As we saw in the newspaper interview discussed above, the press contributes to the reproduction and imposition of the dominant view, regardless of the cogency, articulateness, internal consistency, and even the presence of standard formal features in the speech of the representative of the subordinate class. This power was redundantly exercised by the press throughout the last two presidential campaigns, in order to disqualify the representative of the popular workers' party, whose speech still retains, occasionally, stigmatized features. What he said was consistently disregarded by focusing on how he said it, every time he used a nonstandard form. It was, to use Bourdieu's words, "a labor of dissimulation and transfiguration (...) capable of producing real effects without any apparent expenditure of energy" (1993, p. 170).

The same power may be exercised by teachers with respect to the oppressed students they teach, and by any others who socially represent the role of the literate person in any interaction. As actors in that role in our dealings with those teachers, and in a larger social context as well, as members of the academia, we must take a stand with regards to this issue. If, on the one hand, it is important to avoid what Bourdieu calls the "canonization" of the popular forms, espousing a Romantic view that these forms are as "good" as any other because socially they are not; on the other, we have to stop contributing to the reproduction of the dominant views about literacy.

One measure in this direction is, as Street (1984) puts it, to make the ideological basis of our conception of literacy as clear as possible, which in turn determines that literacy practices, not literacy, be the object of research. It is the study of social practices linked to the uses of reading and writing that makes it possible to show the relation that exists between power, class structure, and the dominant views of literacy, a relationship that endows literacy as the symbolic expression of oppression. A research program that focuses on the study of the social practices in which reading and writing play a part will permit us to challenge some of the literacy myths on an objective basis, as well as the ideology sustaining those beliefs on an ethical basis.

Another measure is to engage critically in the analysis of local, micro situations in agencies whose purpose is to disseminate the dominant conception of literacy. An analysis along these lines will most likely show the failure of school literacy practices, that is, of practices that are not contextualized with respect to the identity of the participants and their social relations, which are opaque as to their specific purposes, and that lead to almost inevitable distortion in communication and to symbolic violence because of the uncritical adoption of the dominant model of literacy. Such a critical treatment may contribute to changes in those practices. This does not mean that we naively believe that social change will take place, but simply that the almost pathological nature of school communication might change, with less traumatizing effects for the students.

Another step in the general direction against uncritical reproduction of dominant views about literacy is to achieve greater descriptive accuracy with regards to the teaching and learning tasks involved in the acquisition of literacy. One of the elements of such a description is an adequate examination of the discourse practices of literate groups; one danger in trying to accomplish this task is to fall into what Bourdieu calls the canonization of the popular forms, which he exemplifies through efforts to legitimize that which is not socially legitimate (e.g., Black English) on the basis of its greater consistency, coherence, logic, or economy. We do not feel, however, that the efforts to rehabilitate "popular forms" should be abandoned because they will be difficult, if not impossible, to impose, since they contradict the dominant, universally accepted views. Dominant views are structured upon preconceived beliefs which, at any moment, may be transformed into attitudes in the world of action. Unchecked, uncontested prejudice may easily lead to harassment, as our data show. In order to avoid the acting out of prejudices, the opposing views of academia, among other institutions, with regards to social issues such as the "neutral" superiority of some social dialects, or of some practices associated with reading and writing, must be heard. These views may filter into the classroom, even if slowly, through teacher preparation courses, creating—by making some things unspeakable—some checks on the structural power of the institution on the students.

In order to be descriptively accurate, it will be also necessary, for language and interaction studies, to examine, at the microanalytical level, the discourse practices that make some literacy agencies successful, while others, most notably the school, are not. Both are important objectives for applied research that aims at saying something of relevance about how to become literate. What microanalysis of the interaction so far tells us is that, in order to teach reading and writing to those who are not engaged in popular movements, it is essential to create contexts where writing is the answer to a practical, material need: in other words, where students read and write in order to do and to learn something else, thus replacing today's context, where the students engage in learning activities in order to write, an end in itself (cf. Heath, 1986). Echoing Foucambert's explanation (1994) for the increasing numbers of those merely alphabetized, it is the absence of needs regarding the written word what excludes them from the social world constituted by the written discourses, and their answer, absence of learning, is simply a reflection, an echo of this exclusion. It is only when the school manages to transcend its narrow objectives based on a narrow view of what it means to be literate, when it critically examines the social implications of the literacy acquisition process, and when it offers programs that will attend to its students' needs and purposes as already constituted and participating members of the literate society, that we may hope to see some success in school literacy programs.

## NOTES

[1]Another neologism, *alfabetismo* tries to separate the social from the individual aspects of literacy. The term, related to *analfabetismo*, illiteracy, was coined by Soares (1994).

[2]As much as 25% of the adult Brazilian population cannot read, according to the last 1990 census, reaching as high as 68% in some Northeastern States, according to UNICEF.

[3]The projects Literacy and Interaction, and Literacy and Intercultural Communication of the literacy research group at the State University of Campinas (UNICAMP) are funded by the CNPq and FAPESP Brazilian funding agencies. They combine research and action. Our group is interested in the academic question of intercultural communication, and for this we use the classroom as a site for the observation of teacher-student interaction. We also have a commitment for progressive education. Therefore, we work regularly (3 hours a week) with the teachers of these students, in a reading and writing program the aim of which is to introduce these teachers to the world of writing as understood in the

academic world: ability to read a wide variety of types of texts (from short stories to newspaper editorials) and ability to write an argumentative text on a matter related to their practice. These teachers' reading experience previous to their training was reduced to reading classroom texts and the excerpts of works therein, and to writing school papers, which can best be described as a series of statements about a theme. Our sessions with these teachers also include the problematization of both literacy and specific classroom literacy practices we observe.

[4]Following Ribeiro's (1995, p. 211) four-class social stratification model, we distinguish the oppressed from the subordinate classes. He classifies as members of the oppressed class seasonal rural workers, itinerant workers, domestic servants, occasional odd-jobbers (biscateiros), criminals, prostitutes, and beggars. The first four make up over 90% of the declared professions of the students in the adult literacy classes in our project. There are a few members of what Ribeiro classifies as the subordinate classes—salaried farm and industry workers—but no "meieiros" (rural workers who give the landowner part of their crop as payment for the use of the land) or minifarm owners. The other two classes in Ribeiro's model are the intermediate (comprising both the independent liberal professionals and small industry and commerce owners, and the dependent white collar workers and civil servants), and the dominant class (comprising the oligarchy of land owners and modern industrialists and the first echelon in the political, military, and technocratic bureaucracies).

[5]This translation, as well as all other translations of data presented in the paper, is mine. The Portuguese original runs as follows:

"Trabalho, questão de coragem, boa vontade, aprendizado.
Todos aqueles que trabalham, seja seu trabalho qualquer que seja, está contribuindo de alguma forma consigo mesmo e com todos.
Hoje em dia as máquinas estão substituindo o trabalho de muita gente e por outro lado dando trabalho a muita gente também.
Se trabalhas honestamente, com boa vontade, com perfeição em tudo que faz você será digno de atenção, confiança.
Trabalhe, mesmo sendo o mais simples trabalho e enobreça cada vez mais sua capacidade de fazer e conseguir aquilo que quer." (Anonymous)

[6]We have used conventional Portuguese spellings in the transcripts, with three exceptions: a) the spelling of infinitives, pronounced without the final /r/ in all Brazilian Portuguese dialects; b) the spelling of *estar* and *não*, prounced *tá* and *num* in informal speech in all dialects; and c) the spelling on nonstandard forms of the stigmatized variety of rural Portuguese, used by the students.

The other conventions used in the transcript are the following:
/.../: Passage not transcribed;
...: Pause;
Repeated colons: Long vowel;
Capital letters: Emphasis

Teacher: /.../ uma segregação é ... se ... segregacionista significa você tirá uma pessoa, tá, de um brinquedo, de um determinado lugar.

Student: Ahh!

Teacher: Tá? Vamos supô, eu tiraria, se eu fosse segregacionista, eu tiraria a Leandra, tá? (approaching the student) ela não poderia brincá com vocês ... então precisaria fazê uma separação, tá? entre vocês.

[7]The original text was published in Jornal da Tarde, 1/8/1990:

"Tomar um, dois, três ônibus errados no mesmo dia e à meia-noite ainda se encontrar longe de casa é apenas um dos problemas enfrentados por Maria do Socorro Pereira, 39 anos, por não saber ler. Os outros vão desde lidar com dinheiro, ir ao supermercado e à farmácia, até o constrangimento e o sentimento de discriminação. Mas, sobretudo, o que mais a humilha é a sensação de dependência, por precisar ajuda de outras pessoas até para preencher as fichas nas empresas onde procura trabalho".

[8]The Portuguese original was printed in O Globo, 10/27/1990:

"O analfabeto compreende mal o que ouve e responde de maneira bastante imperfeita às mensagens assim recebidas. O analfabeto precisa até de atenção mais aplicada ao que vê."

[9]The Portuguese original was printed in Folha de São Paulo, 7/3/1993:

"Sem educação e treinamento, o operário é um desastre para si mesmo e para a empresa."

[10]The Portuguese version is the following:

T: /.../ Que que vai (faltar) a gente sabê? ... Vou dá um exemplo. Presta atenção aqui ... Eu tenho uma receita de bolo de fubá. E eu digo assim, o de ... Qual o título da receita? Bolo de fubá. Que que vai, né? Quais são os ingredientes? Ah, vai ... duas xícaras de fubá, ahmmm ... três colheres de farinha de trigo, uma colher de pó royal, um copo e meio de açúcar ... cabou ai a receita?

Ne: (very low) Não.

T: O que que tá faltando?

Ne: O leite.

T: Não (faz de conta) que eu falei todos os ingredientes, tinha leite também. Que que vai faltá a gente sabê ainda?

Ne: Margarina.

T:Não, eu num tou falando que tá faltando ingrediente. O que que vai faltá a gente sabê?

Ne: Fazê.

T: Isso! E como que a gente fica sabendo?

Vi: Eh, fica sabendo é ... no jeito de fazê ela todinha.

[11]The Portuguese version we recorded is the following:

Teacher: Por que seria bom sabê lê e escrevê como Sinhá Terta? É verdade que ajuda a gente a num sê enganado? Você é enganado, Everton?

An: Eu acho que não. Num precisa. É a mesma coisa!

Ev: Tem que usá a cabeça só. É tudo igual, uma pessoa que num sabe lê, num pode sê enganada não. É tudo igual.

Ade: Ele foi esperto porque ele desmanchou o negócio.

An: Mas ele percebeu que tava sendo enganado. Não sabê lê num significa que é bobo.

[12]There were two teachers in this classroom, T1 and T2. The original Portuguese version goes as follows:

G: Tem vei que tomá remédio em casa é mió que no médico. Tem vei que remédio em casa é mió que do médico

T1: Num é não, Gilvan, que que é isso?

G: Eu acho

T1: Mas no médico num é melhor? Você vai lá tem uma orientação

G:Não

T2: NÃO?

G: Pra mim eu acho que não

T1: Vai sabê exatamente pra que que é o remédio

G: Não

T2:Não?

G: Remédio de mato é mió

T2: Hã?

G: Remédio de agora num presta

T2: Como que num presta?

G: Num sei /....../

T2: Remédio de agora? E por que ceis acham que os médicos estudam?

G: Nã::::o. Eles estudam pra ficá lá sentado. Ganhá dineiro dos pobre

T2: Ahh. Estudam pra (ficá) sentados. Ahhh. E você acha que ... que que ele poder-/ quando ele vai consultá ele vai dá aquele remédio lá:::: de 1900 ou vai dá um remédio que ...

G: Um remédio de agora /............/

G: Eu tenho uma tia ... (inaudible) que num deu remédio pra ela. Remédio dela é remédio do mato. /.../

T1: Remédio natural?

G: Nods affirmatively

T2: E não é um remédio?

G: Não um remédio (curá ela), só remédio de planta

T2: Então .... essa planta .... ela tá usando como um remédio pra ela. E você num acha que é remédio?

G: Mas num é passada por médico!

[13]It is interesting to point out that outside the classroom these teachers share several of the social and economic characteristics of their students' class: All of them are women, and therefore in a subordinate genre position, many of them are the first literate member in their families, their profession carries

no social prestige, and their salaries are lower than that of women in domestic service.

[14]We use culture in the sense defined by Geertz (1973, p. 363), as the the ordered sets of significant symbols through which man makes sense of the situations in which he lives.

[15]Folha de São Paulo, 22/10/1995.

[16]The Portuguese original goes as follows: "Trabalhei na roça do café desde os sete anos. Como tinha de trabalhar para comer, não pude ir à escola, que era longe"; "Outro dia, um jornalista me fez uma pergunta idiota. Queria saber se eu daria terra se fosse fazendeiro. Disse que não. Mas acontece que sou fruto de outro meio, o dos trabalhadores, e luto por minha classe."

[17]MST: Movimento dos Sem Terra, Movement of the landless ones.

The relevant passage is the following: "O casal Rainha dispõe de todos os bens característicos de uma família de classe média: televisão, antena parabólica ("doada por um padre," diz Deolinda), aparelho de som ("de segunda mão," adverte ela), geladeira, máquina de lavar e telefone ("quem paga as contas é o MST," avisa a mulher).

[18]"A Diretoria desta entidade, reunida com os trabalhadores desta Empresa, constatou as seguintes irregularidades:

1) os trabalhadores da Portaria trabalham 6 dias na semana, tendo uma folga semanal, portanto, obrigatoriamente duas folgas deveriam ocorrer no domingo. Estão fazendo quatro horas extras diárias.
2) a alimentação está péssima
3) descontos nos envelopes de pagamento a título de "Pagamento para Caixa"
4) inexistência de classificação de cargos na empresa

Além das irregularidades acima, os trabalhadores reivindicam também:

1) sábado livre
2) convênio médico
3) transporte
4) água potável

Diante do exposto, solicitamos a V.S. que seja marcada uma reunião entre a Diretoria desta entidade e os representates desta empresa, com a participação indireta de uma comissão de trabalhadores, ou seja, somente para acompanhamento das negociações.

Certos de podermos contar com a colaboração e bom senso desta empresa, aguardamos um pronunciamento."

[19]The relevant excerpts of the interview are the following:

"é o seguinte: se eu tivesse estudo… talvez eu não fosse tão esforçado quanto eu sô";

"porque quem tem pra dá num dá";

"a letra dá (vida) mas também pode matá."

## REFERENCES


Barton, D. (1994). *Literacy. An introduction to the ecology of written language.* Oxford: Blackwell Publishers.

Borel, M. J. (1981). L'explication dans l'argumentation. Approche semiologique. [Explanation in argument. A semiological approach]. *Langue Française, 50,* 20–38.

Bourdieu, P. (1983/1993). *Language and symbolic power.* Cambridge: Polity Press.

Bourdieu, P., & Passeron, J. C. (1970). *A reprodução. Elementos para uma teoria do sistema de ensino.* [*Reproduction in education, society and culture*]. (2nd ed.). Rio de Janeiro, Brazil: Francisco Alves Editora.

Carraher, D., & Santos, S. L. (1984). Leitura e senso crítico. [Reading and critical sense]. *Anais do I Encontro Interdisciplinar de Leitura.* Londrina, Brazil: Universidade Estadual de Londrina.

Carraher, T., Carraher, D., & Schliemann, A. L. (1988). *Na vida dez, na escola zero.* [*Success in life, failure at school*]. São Paulo, Brazil: Cortez Editora.

Chafe, W. (1982). Integration and involvement in speaking, writing, and oral literature. In D. Tannen (Ed.), *Spoken and written language: Exploring orality and literacy.* Norwood, NJ: Ablex.

Chafe, W., & Danielewicz, J. (1987). Properties of spoken and written language. In R. Horowitz & J. S. Samuels (Eds.), *Comprehending oral and written language.* New York: Academic Press.

Clark, R., Fairclough, N. L., Ivanic, R., & Martin-Jones, M. (1987). Critical language awareness, *CSL Working Papers 1.* University of Lancaster: Centre for Language in Social Life.

Descardeci, M. A. (1992). O concurso público. Um evento de letramento em exame. [Civil service exams. A literacy event under examination]. (M.A. Thesis). Campinas, Brazil: UNICAMP

Fairclough, N. (1992). *Discourse and social change.* Cambridge: Polity Press.

Ferguson, C. A. (1959). Diglossia, *Word, 15,* 325–340.

Foucambert, J. (1994). *A leitura em questão.* [*Reading in question*]. Porto Alegre, Brazil: Artes Médicas. French edition published 1989.

Freire, P. (1970). *Pedagogy of the oppressed.* New York: The Seabury Press.

Freire, P. (1980). *Educação como prática da liberdade.* [*Education as the practice of freedom*]. (10th. ed.). Rio de Janeiro, Brazil: Paz e Terra.

Freire, P. (1991). *A educação na cidade.* [*Education in the city*]. São Paulo, Brazil: Cortez Editora.

Gee, J. (1990). *Social linguistics and literacies. Ideologies in discourses.* Hampshire: The Falmer Press.

Geertz, C. (1973/1993). *The interpretation of cultures.* London: Fontana Press.

Goody, J. (1977/1986). *The domestication of the savage mind.* Cambridge: Cambridge University Press.

Graff, H. J. (1979). *The literacy myth: Literacy and social structure in the 19th century.* New York: Academic Press.

Graff, H. J. (1987). *The labyrinths of literacy. Reflections on literacy past and present.* Hampshire: The Falmer Press.

Gumperz, J. J. (1982) *Language and social identity*. Cambridge: Cambridge University Press.

Habermas, J. (1982). On systematically distorted communication. In E. Bredo & W. Feinberg (Eds.), *Knowledge and values in social education research*. Philadelphia: Temple University Press.

Habermas, J. (1984). *The theory of communicative action* (Vol 1). Boston: Beacon Press.

Hamel, R. E., & Sierra, M. T. (1983). Diglosía y conflicto intercultural. [Diglossia and intercultural conflict]. *Boletín de Antropología Americana, 8*, 89–110.

Heath, S. B. (1982). What no bedtime story means: Narrative skills at home and school, *Language in Society, 11*, 49-76.

Heath, S.B. (1983). *Ways with words. Language, life and work in communities and classrooms*. Cambridge: Cambridge University Press.

Heath, S.B. (1986). Critical factors in literacy development. In S. de Castell, A. Luke, & K. Egan (Eds.), *Literacy, society and schooling. A reader*. Cambridge: Cambridge University Press.

Kato, M. A. (1986). *No mundo da escrita. Uma perspectiva psicolinguística. [In the world of writing. A psycholinguistic perspective*]. São Paulo, Brazil: Atica.

Kleiman, A. B. (1992a). O letramento na formação do professor. [Literacy and teacher education]. *Anais do VII Encontro Nacional da ANPOLL, Porto Alegre 1991*. Goiânia, Brazil: ANPOLL.

Kleiman, A.. B. (1992b). The language of control: Teacher-student interaction in an adult literacy classroom. Paper presented at the 13th Forum for Ethnography in Education, Philadelphia.

Kleiman, A. B. (1993). Diálogos truncados e papéis trocados: O estudo da interação no ensino de língua materna. [Truncated dialogues and role exchanges. The study of interaction in mother tongue teaching]. *ALFA, 37*, 59–74.

Kleiman, A. B. (1995). Modelos de letramento e as práticas de alfabetização na escola. [Models of literacy and alphabetization practices at school]. In A. Kleiman (Ed.), *Os significados do letramento. Uma nova perspectiva sobre a prática social da escrita. [The meanings of literacy. New perspectives on the social practice of writing*]. Campinas, Brazil: Mercado de Letras.

Knijnik, G. (1996). *Exclusão e resistência. Educação matemática e legitimidade cultural. [Exclusion and resistance. Math education and cultural legitimacy*]. Porto Alegre, Brazil: Artes Médicas.

Luria, A.R. (1976). *Cognitive development. Its cultural and social foundations*. Cambridge, MA: Harvard University Press.

Martin-Jones, M. (1989). Language, power and linguistic minorities: The need for an alternative approach to bilingualism, language maintenance and shift. In R. Grillo (Ed.), *Social anthropology and the politics of language* (*Sociological Review* monograph, *36*) London: Oxford University Press.

Matencio, M. L. M. (1995). Analfabetismo na mídia: Conceitos e imagens sobre o letramento. [Illiteracy in the media: Concepts and images about literacy]. In A. Kleiman (Ed.), *Os significados do letramento. Uma nova perspectiva sobre a prática social da escrita. [The meanings of literacy. New perspectives on the social practice of writing*]. Campinas, Brazil: Mercado de Letras.

Mey, J. (1985). *Whose language. A study in linguistics pragmatics*. Amsterdam: John Benjamins.

Miéville, D. (1981). L'explication en mathématiques. [Explanation in mathematics]. *Revue européene des sciences sociales, XIX (56)*, 115–151.

Milanez, W. (1993). *Pedagogia do oral: Condições e perspectivas para sua aplicação no português*. [*Teaching the oral language: Conditions and perspectives in Portuguese teaching*]. Campinas, Brazil: Sama.

Moreira, T. M. (1991). A progressão temática na redação escolar. [Theme development in school essays] (M.A. Thesis). Campinas, Brazil: UNICAMP.

Ninyoles, R. L. (1975). *Estructura social y política linguística*. [*Social structure and language policy*]. Valencia, Spain: Fernando Torres.

Oliveira, M. K. (1992). Analfabetos na sociedade letrada: Diferenças culturais e modos de pensamento. [The unschooled in a literate society: Cultural differences and modes of thought]. *Travessia: Revista do Migrante V*(12), 17–20.

Oliveira, M. K. (1995). Letramento, cultura e modalidades de pensamento. [Literacy, culture and modes of thought]. In A. Kleiman (Ed.), *Os significados do letramento. Uma nova perspectiva sobre a prática social da escrita*. [*The meanings of literacy. New perspectives on the social practice of writing*]. Campinas, Brazil: Mercado de Letras.

Olson, D. R. (1981). Writing: The divorce of the author from the text. In B. M. Kroll & R. J. Vann (Eds.), *Exploring speaking-writing relationships*, Urbana, IL: National Council of Teachers of English.

Olson. D. R. (1984). See! Jumping! Some oral language antecedents of literacy, In H. Goelman, A. A. Oberg, & F. Smith (Eds.), *Awakening to literacy*. The University of Victoria Symposium on Children's Response to a Literate Environment: Literacy Before Schooling 1982. Portsmouth, NH: Heinemann Educational Books.

Olson, D., & Hildyard, A. (1983). Writing and literal meaning. In M. Martlew (Ed.), *The psychology of written language. Developmental and educational perspectives*. New York: John Wiley and Sons.

Ong, W.J. (1982). *Orality and literacy. The technologizing of the word*. London: Meuthen.

Payer, M. O. (1993). *Educação popular e linguagem. Reprodução, confrontos e deslocamentos de sentidos*. [*Popular education and language. Reproduction, conflict and meaning shifts*]. Campinas, Brazil: Editora da UNICAMP.

Rama, A. (1985). *A cidade das letras*. [*The city of letters*]. São Paulo, Brazil: Brasiliense.

Ratto, I. (1995). Ação política: fator de constituição de letramento do analfabeto adulto. [*Political action: A contributing factor in adult literacy development*]. In A. Kleiman (Ed.), *Os significados do letramento. Uma nova perspectiva sobre a prática social da escrita*. [*The meanings of literacy. New perspectives on the social practice of writing*]. Campinas, Brazil: Mercado de Letras.

Ribeiro, D. (1995). *O povo brasileiro. A formação e o sentido do Brasil*. [*The Brazilian people. The emergence and meaning of Brazil*]. São Paulo, Brazil: Companhia das Letras.

Scribner, S., & Cole, M. (1981). *The psychology of literacy*. Cambridge, MA: Harvard University Press.

Signorini, I. (1994). Unschooled councilmen in Legislative sessions: literacy and empowerment in bureaucratic settings. Paper presented at the 15th Annual Ethnography in Education Research Forum, Philadelphia.

Signorini, I. (1995). "A letra dá vida mas também pode matar"—Os sem leitura diante da escrita. ["The letter gives life but it may also kill"—Those without the alphabet talking about literacy]. *Leitura: Teoria e Prática, 24*, 20–27.

Signorini, I., & Kleiman, A. B. (1994). When explaining is saying. Teacher talk in adult literacy classes. In A. Alvarez & P. del Rio (Eds.), *Education as cultural construction, explorations in socio-cultural studies* (Vol 4, pp. 217–226). Madrid, Spain: Fundación Infancia y Aprendizaje.

Soares, M. (1986). *Linguagem e escola. Uma perspectiva social*. [*Language and school. A social perspective*]. São Paulo, Brazil: Ática.

Soares, M. (1994). Língua escrita, sociedade e cultura: Relações, dimensões e perspectivas. [Written language, society and culture: Relationships and perspectives]. Unpublished paper presented at the 17th Reunião Anual ANPEd, Minas Gerais, Brazil.

Street, B. V. (1984). *Literacy in theory and practice*. Cambridge: Cambridge University Press.

Street, B. V. (1993). Introduction: The new literacy studies. In B. V. Street (Ed.), *Cross-cultural approaches to literacy*. Cambridge: Cambridge University Press.

Tfouni, L. V. (1995). *Letramento e alfabetização*. [*Literacy and alphabetization*]. São Paulo, Brazil: Cortez Editora.

Toulmin, S. E. (1958). *The uses of argument*. Cambridge: Cambridge University Press.

chapter 9

# Conceptual Organization and Schooling

Marta Kohl de Oliveira
University of São Paulo, Brazil

"Man has much more development [than the animal], I don't know if it is more intelligence. It can only be in the organism, it must be different; other parts are alike: heart, etc.(...) The problem is in the head, something must be there; the brain must be a very fine box, like a computer: how can we remember things from 30 years ago?"

"The animal learns spontaneously, from its own development; it is different from the child, who we must teach."

"No [an animal doesn't make plans for the future]. He has a kind of reasoning very similar to man, but just for the moment."

These reflections about the differences between human beings and animals were produced by urban manual workers attending a literacy course for adults in São Paulo, Brazil. Do they indicate some specificity in their mode of thought or in the organization of their knowledge? Can we say these people show a *typically unschooled* (or illiterate) kind of reasoning, easily distinguishable from another, schooled, literate, kind? The present paper adresses the question of thinking and conceptual organization among adults of different instructional levels, aiming to discuss the possibilities of relating cognitive differences to cultural differences, or, more specifically, modes of thought to schooling (and literacy) levels.

The research on which this work is based is integrated in a collective research project about concepts and cognitive functioning, developed by the Núcleo de Estudos de Conceitos (Research Group for the Study of Concepts) of the School of Education of the University of São Paulo, Brazil. This group has as its central object of theoretical and empirical investigation the question of conceptual development and organization, based mainly on the so-called theoretical conception about concepts. (Núcleo de Estudos de Conceitos, 1994). According to this conception, a concept is constituted not only of properties but also of relationships with other concepts (see Carey, 1985; Murphy & Medin, 1985). These relationships, which articulate concepts with each other, constitute networks, seen as theories. The view here adopted, which takes concepts to be not isolated mental entities, but elements organized in some kind of structured whole, is prevalent in contemporary literature about many aspects of cognitive functioning. It can be found in theories about the nervous system that postulate neural networks, in the parallel distributed processing of the conexionist computers, and in many ideas within cognitive psychology, such as universe of knowledge, universe of meanings, semantic fields, conceptual networks.

The main question that directs the research of the group is: What is the nature of the theories in which, according to the theoretical conception, concepts should be seen as embedded? This main question is unfolded into more specific research questions, explored in different sub-projects: the distinction between common sense and scientific theories, the relationships between concepts and words and the importance of language development for conceptual organization, the problem of definition and its implications for lexicography, and the relationships between cultural differences and conceptual development.

The research here reported refers directly to this last question. It was planned to investigate the possible relationships between conceptual organization, that is, the mode of articulation of concepts into larger and more complex structures, and cultural differences, specially with respect to the confrontation of more- and less-instructed groups of adults in contemporary urban society. The basic question to be investigated was if adults with none or very few years of formal schooling have a mode of conceptual organization that would be different from that of schooled people highly integrated in the literate practices of literate society.

The theoretical support for this investigation is the approach in psychology that considers the genesis of psychism a result of the insertion of subjects in the history of their cultural group and of their interaction with objects of action and knowledge, with cultural signs and meanings, and with other subjects in situations of collective construction of meanings (Rieber & Carton, 1987; Van der Veer & Valsiner, 1991; Vygotsky, 1991). The understanding of the different cultural practices and of the different activity contexts in which subjects are involved, as well as the understanding of the relationships between cognitive processes and the semiotic tools created by human beings, are, in this approach, essential to the understanding of psychological development. In this theoretical context the school emerges as an important cultural setting in literate society, where an intense interaction of subjects with some specific cultural artifacts occur.

The point of departure for this research was previous research conducted in contemporary literate urban society about cultural differences associated with cognitive functioning (Oliveira, 1982, 1994, 1995a, 1995b), as well as other works about culture and thought (for example, Cole & Scribner, 1974; Goody & Watt, 1968; Luria, 1976), which have indicated that illiterate groups as well as low-instructional-level individuals tend to demonstrate a mode of intellectual functioning different from the one considered to be typical of more "literate" cultural groups. Literacy and schooling are pointed to as factors clearly central in the understanding of cognitive differences associated to cultural differences.

It is important to mention that although this volume is directed to the question of literacy development, in the present article the process of schooling is taken as more central to the proposed discussion than the process of literacy itself. This choice is due to many related factors. As pointed out in many studies about cultural differences and psychological processes, literacy and schooling are, in most cultures, confounded phenomena. They almost never occur separately. In the only well-known case where there is literacy without schooling, among the Vai of Liberia (Scribner & Cole, 1981), the psychological effects usually atributed to literacy-in-school were not present in people literate in the nonschooled written language. So, school, as a social setting where certain cultural practices are developed—these include the literacy practices but are not limited to them—seems to have some clear relationships to the promotion of a certain kind of cognitive development, usually associated with what is called the literate mode of cognitive functioning. Literacy in itself, on the other hand, if not associated with the context in which it is developed and used and to its shared meaning in a cultural group, is reduced to its technical dimension. To relate this technique to the promotion of psychological changes raises theoretical and methodological problems that have been discussed in the literature (see Street, 1984; Tulviste, 1991; and also Kleiman, this volume).

The main characteristics of the mode of cognitive functioning associated to predominant cultural practices in societies that are urban, schooled, industrialized, bureaucratized, and characterized by scientific and technological development seem to be the possibility of decontextualized thought, not referred to the immediate individual experience, and the conscious mastery, by the subject, of his own cognitive processes (meta-cognitive procedures).

Regarding the conceptual organization, then, it would be reasonable to hypothesize that a mode of thought more dependent on immediate perceptual data and on concrete context would operate with more fragmented modes of conceptual organization, subject to the influence of specific circumstances and peculiarities of individual history, with a smaller pressure for internal consistency and stability across time. The decontextualized mode of thought, on the other hand, would require forms of organization more similar to the very idea of "theory": with greater general applicability and greater independence from the subject's experience with particular instances of the involved concepts.

More or less prominence of meta-cognitive procedures could also be a factor related to the nature of theories that give support to concepts. These procedures consist of intentional actions of the subject on his own cognitive processes and allow for conscious operations on these processes. The presence of mechanisms of thinking about thought would give the subject the possibility of conscious access to the network of relationships that articulate his concepts with each other. With a basis of meta-cognitive operations, it would probably be possible for the subject to make explicit, for himself and for others, the relationships between his concepts and theories. Meta-cognitive action would then favor an organization of the content of theories in order to make them more consistent and more useful for prediction of events and control of reality. In the absence of meta-cognitive procedures, on the other hand, the subject would not be aware of the theories that underlie the organization of his concepts, being naively "submmitted to" theoretical conceptions that are, in a certain sense, ignored by himself.

Generally speaking, then, theories produced and used by more "typically literate" thinkers, that is, those who use a predominantly decontextualized mode of thought and rely on meta-cognitive procedures, would seem to be closer to the structure of scientific theories. The theories of the "less literate" thinkers, on the other hand, would be further away from the scientific model. The organization of this argument, quite important in the initial planning of the research, could be considered to correspond to the "autonomous" model criticized by Street (1984), which would suggest a great divide between literate and illiterate groups or individuals regarding their cognitive possibilities. As mentioned before and discussed throughout the chapter, the data obtained in the research here reported challenged this argument, showing much more complex relationships between cognitive performance and cultural practices related to literacy and schooling.

With a basis on these theoretical considerations, two general questions were then formulated to guide the investigation about the relationships among concepts, modes of conceptual organization, and cultural differences associated to literacy and schooling. Firstly, what is the nature of theories in which concepts are embedded when the main mode of thought is strongly based on the concrete context and on the individual experience (as seems to be the case among low-instructional-level adults)? Secondly, what would be the difference between theories accessible to the subject himself through meta-cognitive action and those that are not the object of this kind of action? That is, how would the access to one's own theories and concepts affect the mode of cognitive functioning of the subject?

## THINKING ABOUT PEOPLE AND ANIMALS—THE EMPIRICAL STUDY

For the empirical exploration of these questions a conceptual domain was selected: the domain of human thought—the peculiarities of the process of human thinking, especially when confronted with processes in animals. This conceptual domain was selected because, for the construction of theories about it, it is particularly relevant to rely on meta-cognitive procedures, to have a reflective attitude, and to have consciousness about cognitive processes.

Two groups of adult subjects were questioned about this conceptual domain. One of them consisted of low-instructional-level adults attending a special modality of school courses existant in Brazil, the so-called "cursos supletivos." These courses are equivalent to first through eighth grades and to high school, giving credits and certificates equivalent to the ones obtained in regular school, but are to be done at an older age and in a shorter period of time than the regular school courses. They provide an opportunity of late schooling for adult workers who could not study at the regular age, usually because of the poor social conditions of their families and the need to work full-time since childhood. Most of the students who go to these courses, especially to the initial grades (literacy class and up to the equivalent of fourth grade of elementary school), have migrated to the big city from impoverished rural areas, having worked, like their parents, as nonqualified agricultural workers.

The interviews done with these workers were conducted in the school attended by them. This school is a regular private elementary and high school that also maintains a low cost "supletivo" course in the evening, attended primarily by domestic servants (maids, drivers, gardeners, watchmen), who work at the high-social-class residences located around the school. The school teachers were aware of the research and allowed the students to leave the classroom for the interviews. With the teacher of the literacy class a collaborative work emerged as a sub-product of the research: The topics initially explored in the interview were further pursued in the classroom, as relevant school topics, during the whole semester, with the participation of the researcher and the research assistant. In the remaining classrooms there was no other activity besides the individual interviews with some students.

The main focus of the research with the low-instructional-level adults was the literacy class, of which the totality of students was interviewed. The intention was to obtain data about the conceptual organization of adults at the lowest possible instructional level. Students of other school levels were interviewed to provide some basis for comparison. Twenty-nine students were interviewed, being 13 of the literacy class, 4 of the fourth grade, 7 of the seventh grade, and 5 of the second year of high school. The interviews were conducted individually, by the researcher or the research assistant, in an empty classroom of the school during the school period. The subjects were informed that the researcher was an university professor, developing an investigation about thinking processes among adults. The main topic of the interviews was the differences and similarities between human beings and animals, especially regarding the question of thinking processes. (See Appendix A for the interview schedule.)

The second group of adult subjects questioned about the selected conceptual domain consisted of 69 junior and senior university students attending teacher training courses in order to get high-school teacher's credentials in different subject matters. Two questions to be answered in writing (see Appendix B for the questions) in the classrooom, were given to them in the context of an introductory course in education taught by the researcher in the School of Education of the University of São Paulo, one of the main public universities in Brazil. This was done in the first day of classes in the semester and the voluntary participation of the students in the task was asked as cooperation in an investigation conducted by the professor about the relationships between schooling and cognitive processes.

The two groups of adults included in this study were, then, very different, not only regarding their actual school experience (specially in the case of the contrast between university students and students of the adult literacy class), but also regarding their place in, and relationships with, literate society. One group could be characterized as low socio-economic-level *workers* who go to school at the adult age to compensate for their lack of schooling at the regular age; the other group is made of *students*, successful in their school career in a very selective social and school system, who go to one of the best universities in the country, and might or might not work. When contrasted throughout this paper, they will be referred to as "workers" and "students."

The data obtained from these two groups of subjects challenged the initial suppositions about different modes of conceptual organization of more- and less-instructed adults: There was no evidence of the existence of different kinds of "theories" about the explored conceptual domain that could be associated to literacy or schooling level. The interviewed subjects showed to the researcher, during the interview, the course of their reflection about the selected themes. This reflection was not a static picture of a mental content previously available, but a flexible set of meanings in construction during the interview itself. Crucial questions seemed to promote constant restructuring of the subjects' conceptions and to encourage the very process of thinking about the raised topics. Nuances of the concepts and meanings were negotiated all the time, and the resulting reflection provoked more precision and consistency along the interview.

The written discourse of the university students, on the other hand, contrarily to the expectations, showed that they solved the proposed questions by relying heavily on typical school devices (basically lists and tables), but did not demonstrate consistent theoretical formulations or deep reflection. The most prominent features of the material collected with the subjects are presented below so that a picture of what we could call conceptual organization could be drawn and some theoretical questions discussed.

## Reference to Personal Experience

Personal experience was clearly the point of departure for the reflection developed by the subjects. The main evidence of this were the choices made by the subjects in answer to the first question asked ("Think of an animal that you know well and tell me about the similarities and differences between this animal and man"). As it can be observed in Table 9.1, in spite of the great heterogeneity regarding the chosen animals, there were some strong tendencies within each group: Most of the subjects of the literacy class selected a farm animal (mainly a horse), in a clear reference to their rural experience. Personal experience was also the point of departure for the reflection of the urban university students: In contrast to their rural counterparts, almost all of them selected a pet (mainly a dog or a cat). The very idea of *animal*, then, seems to be

**TABLE 9.1. Animals Chosen by the Subjects as the Basis for Their Answers**

| | Literacy Class | Fourth Grade | Seventh Grade | Junior High | University |
|---|---|---|---|---|---|
| Monkey | 2(15%) | 3(75%) | 4(57%) | 1(20%) | 1(1.5%) |
| Farm Animals | 8(62%) | — | 2(29%) | — | 1(1.5%) |
| Dog | 3(23%) | — | 1(14%) | 4(80%) | 44(64%) |
| Cat | — | — | — | — | 14(20%) |
| Domestic Bird | — | — | — | — | 2(3%) |
| Garden Turtle | — | — | — | — | 1(1.5%) |
| Wild Bird | — | 1(25%) | — | — | — |
| Bee | — | — | — | — | 1(1.5%) |
| Ant | — | — | — | — | 1(1.5%) |
| Spider | — | — | — | — | 1(1.5%) |
| Fish | — | — | — | — | 1(1.5%) |
| Buffalo | — | — | — | — | 1(1.5%) |
| Animal Not Specified | — | — | — | — | 1(1.5%) |
| Total | 13(100%) | 4(100%) | 7(100%) | 5(100%) | 69(100%) |

mapped onto a different domain of experience, and consequently a different conceptual context, for these two extreme groups of subjects.

It is interesting to observe that the high school students of the adult school behaved very much like the university students, also choosing mainly the dog as the basis for their answers. With regard to the students of the intermediate level, most of them mentioned the monkey—or the ape—as their chosen animal (in Portuguese there is a single word, *macaco,* to name both apes and monkeys). It seems that, for some reason, the wording of the question lead these subjects to look for an animal as similar as possible to the human being, so they could talk about the "similarities" asked for in the question. One possible explanation for this is that they were studying in school some topic which made them specially aware of the relationships between apes and human beings.

Still regarding the role of personal experience, even though many workers have told stories about one particular animal as an illustration of something being said or as a way of proving a point, they refered to the chosen animal as a class ("the horse") and not as a known exemplar of a class (a particular horse or "my horse"). The wording of the question ("an animal that you know well") was, then, adequately interpreted as "a class of animals about which I have much information" and not as "a single animal which I know well as an individual."

The university students' arguments, on the other hand, were consistent with their choice of pets as their knowledge base: Many of them treated the concept of animal as an individualized creature and not as a class, frequently making explicit reference to their own pets as the main source of information on which their reflection was built, or mentioning the lack of experience with animals as a limitation for their possibility of reflection about the proposed topic. Some examples from their written answers illustrate this observation: "The comparison will be made between my two children and my two German shepard dogs, because I have daily, emotional contact with them" (M, history major); "I do not have a very broad knowledge about any animals, maybe because I have never had a pet" (F, physics major).

It is clear that different subjects resorted to different aspects of their personal world of meanings (be it originated in their immersion in concrete experience or produced through verbal reasoning) in order to face the demands of different aspects of the cognitive task proposed to them in the research situation. It seems, then, that with a basis on these data, it is not possible to talk about a stable relationship between schooling, subjects' experience with particular instances of the involved concepts, and conceptual organization.

## Animals Don't Talk: Selection of Relevant Items for Reflection

There is another characteristic of the ideas expressed by the workers during the interviews that is relevant for the understanding of their conceptual organization and their mode of reasoning about the proposed questions: They included in their speech many important theoretical dimensions of the topic "human thought," that is, dimensions that are relevant within scientific formulations about this topic. Right from the beginning of their discourse, very few subjects directed their attention to visible physical characteristics of the animals in order to compare them to human beings; most of them referred to some kind of psychological trait (language, thought, emotion) or mode of activity in the world (work, habitat, preparation of food). This initial approach to the problem, taken by the subjects themselves, probably provided a favorable context for the emergence of relevant dimensions of the domain in question.

Language was one of these dimensions: The lack of speech in the animals was often mentioned as an important contrast to humans ("The horse does not speak; its neigh does not make sense"—C, literacy class), as well as their communication through other means ("Among animals there is an understanding which is theirs, we don't comprehend it very well. [...] They don't speak, but they have an understanding, one understands the other. [...] They understand each other by licking, smelling, petting, communicating, understanding"—S, literacy class). The parrot was often mentioned during the interview, usually to somehow bring up the relationship between language and thought. Apes were also often mentioned, because of their impressive similarity to men, combined with their lack of speech.

Another important dimension that emerged in the workers' speech was the relationship between learning and development and, more specifically, innate and acquired characteristics. The main idea was that human beings are more dependent on learning than animals: "Animals don't teach their young; they are born the way they are, with the little gifts God gave them" (R, literacy class); "I don't think they teach the young; they develop and acquire the manners of their mother" (A, literacy class); "The animal learns spontaneously, from its own development; it is different from the child, who we must teach" (C, literacy class). Related to that is the conception of animals as more attached to the context than human beings: "The horse doesn't think, but if we teach it, it learns. [...] It does not learn everything: only things related to work, to paths to walk" (C, literacy class). "No [an animal doesn't make plans for the future]. It has a kind of reasoning very similar to men, but just for the moment" (E, literacy class).

Still another dimension often used by the workers in their characterization of animals was the relationship between thinking and feeling. Some peculiar ideas emerged regarding this question, not easily interpretable, but important to mention given their recurrence. The concept of ill-treatment ("judiação", in Portuguese) was often brought into the dialogue. The idea of an animal being ill-treated and not being able to react to it was related to the animal's ability to think. Somehow the fact that the animal perceives that he is being ill-treated (or well treated) is considered a mode of animal thinking. ("It does not make plans for the future; it thinks mostly about ill-treatment"—R, literacy class) Besides being related to animal thinking, ill-treatment is related to the animal's incapacity to talk: "If you ill-treat it, it seems the horse wants to speak. [...] The sheep groans when it is beaten; it is asking for the person to stop; there is something it wanted to say, but it is not able to." (D, literacy class); "There are animals that are innocent, I think the horse is innocent. People ill-treat it and it does not speak" (J, literacy class).

A better understanding of the meaning of this idea and specially of the importance of the concept of ill-treatment as associated with animal thinking probably would be developed through a better knowledge about the rural culture these subjects come from. It is important to work with it in the present context, however, as an evidence that the low-instructional-level subjects' performance was very complex and nonhomogeneous. If sometimes their reasoning and discourse approached the structure and content of scientific theories, sometimes they demonstrated to be at an enormous distance from a supposed literate mode of thought. Simultaneous proximity and distance from a certain theoretical model of thought show that the conceptual organization of subjects is not monolitical, not corresponding to one or another "kind of thought."

## Dogs Have Fur and Are Friendly: Attention to Superficial Features

The university students also showed heterogeneity in their thought about the proposed questions, but what calls for attention in their discourse, specially given the contrast with the performance of the workers, is the absence of meaningful concepts for a theoretical discussion of the question about the specificity of human beings. The use of concepts like language, symbolic representation, culture, consciousness, emotion, planning, anticipation, and ethics, which could be considered central for the discussion of the differences between man and animals, was restricted to 50% of the students.

The other half of the students were mainly concerned with the consideration of physical differences ("the dog is a quadruped, man is biped; man hears in a different frequency level than dogs; dog's hair is important to it, while man's is not essential, etc."—B, no information about major), the presentation of some temperamental or attitudinal attributes ("the dog is an animal that knows how to reciprocate all friendship, care, attention that a man gives to it, being not false, while a human being, independently of the friendship you give him, is capable of betrayal, of being false"—A, physics major), or the reflection about philosophical questions, usually involving some judgement about the possibility of animals being somehow "better" than man, in spite of the supposed superiority of human beings ("I think [my birds] may be even happier than me, since I should also be a prisioner, even though I am still not able to see the dimensions of my cage" C, no information about major). A theoretical approach, based on school knowledge or on scientific concepts, was virtually absent from the presented answers.

Also absent from the answers of the university students was an elaborated reflection about the proposed questions; they produced superficial texts, with evident structural and conceptual problems. Simplified analysis, contradictions, and inexact meanings can be seen in the following examples: "No, [the animal] presents reflexes. Thought may be identified when the animal has and perceives two or more alternatives for behavior or action. This may be expressed by the movement of the dog's eyes, which are kept static as the head moves, as a reflex act and not an act of thinking" (G, no information about major); "There is not doubt that the animal should think, we can notice that by observing its way of acting, its thought is more limited than ours.(...) Everything an animal does is related to its thought, even when it is irrational" (F, physics major); "If, to define thought, we take human being as a parameter, few (or none) animals would think. If, however, thought is the awareness of one's acts or the planning of actions, we can say they think" (E, no information about major).

It is interesting to observe that the students wrote rather extensively about the proposed questions, responding to a request from the professor in a classroom situation. In that sense the task was adequately accomplished. But the content of their answers, as exemplified above, indicate that the students were not intellectually challenged by the questions: They seemed to be just performing a routine school task. This is also evident in the format adopted to structure the answers, as it will be discussed in the next item.

### Use of School-Like Resources

Sixty-five percent of the university students used a pattern of response that corresponds to a school-learned mode of treating information: lists, tables, and schemes. A high level of schooling seemed, then, to promote a homogenization of the format of thinking, or of communicating thought, independently of its content. The main format used was an answer organized in three parts: name of animal, list of similarities, and list of differences. Thirty-three percent of the university students answered in *exactly this same format,* with variations only in the animal selected and in the characteristics chosen as similarities and differences between the animal and the human being. An example illustrates this favorite format of answer:

*Animal*: Spider
*Similarities*: —may take care of offspring
—feel afraid
—show behavior that is not learned (instinctive)
*Differences*: —lonely, never constitute a family
—does not vocalize (suposedly does not communicate)
—for being lonely, nothing is taught by other individuals.
(E, no information about major)

Different kinds of tables and lists were used by the remaining 32% of the university students who chose to use a school format, with the same result of synthetically and graphically presenting the differences between the chosen animal and the human being. Many of the subjects who used a school pattern to organize their answers did it in an inadequate way, producing nonexhaustive lists of similarities and differences (seemingly generated at random, not planned listings), and working with non-mutually exclusive categories when proposing their criteria for comparisons. Many also showed a confused spatial distribution of the information, ambiguous references to what is being compared, or "false tables," where lines and columns are present, but there is no real crossing of information between variables. Another example illustrates this inadequacy in the use of formal resources:

| CAT | MAN |
|---|---|
| Does not bath, cleaning itself with the tongue | Takes showers frequently |
| Gets some illnesses similar to human illnesses. Ex: bronchitis | Gets illnesses, like bronchitis |
| Feeds itself from different kinds of foods (like man's: fish, meat, but usually uncooked) | Feeds from meat and other food like cat's, but not uncooked |
| Has some sensibility to supernatural things and a misterious aspect (not proved) | When he has these aspects, tries to deal with them somehow |

(H, history major)

## Meta-Cognitive Procedures

Given the characteristics of the content and of the format of the university students' answers, one could say that meta-cognitive procedures were apparently absent from these answers. The university students seemed not to have distinguished relevant from irrelevant aspects of the questions proposed, nor to have selected appropriate intellectual instruments to think about them, nor to have selected adequate tools for the organization and communication of their thoughts.

The workers interviewed, on the other hand, showed a clear meta-cognitive attitude in the process of reflecting about the themes proposed in the interview, demonstrating to be consciously working on a thinking activity. Many of them verbally manifested their worries about not having much to say or not having an elaborated answer, saying that they were taken by surprise and had not had the time or the conditions to be well prepared ("If I had thought about it before I would have prepared myself"—S, literacy class; "You took me by surprise, I have never thought about that before"—M, literacy class). Some declarations about the difficulty of some—but not all—of the questions ("I don't know how to explain that"—A, literacy class or "This is too complicated"—D, literacy class) also show the awareness of the relationship between different aspects of the task to be faced and oneself as a thinking subject.

Other evidence of meta-cognitive activity was the awareness of the existence of different bodies of knowledge for different people (the contrast rural-low-instructional-level/urban-schooled being the most relevant one for these subjects). When questioned about the meaning of the word *animal,* one of the subjects explained that it refers to farm working animals (mainly horse, but also ass, mule, pig, and cow), mentioning that he had learned in school that animal applies to "everything" (meaning all kinds of living animals) and that he has a lot of difficulty with this new school knowledge. Another subject, having mentioned the word *mare,* spontaneously explained its meaning to the interviewer, supposing that this was a specific piece of information, not necessarily part of the knowledge of an urban university professor.

Still another aspect of the meta-cognitive activity was the demonstration of a genuine interest in the topic, which was afterwards taken into the classroom by the teacher and kept the students extremely active in seeking for systematic information about apes, human evolution, human thought, and other related subjects. The attitude of openly wanting to know more about a domain of knowledge was also clearly present in the interview, being evident in comments like "This is something I would like to know" (M, literacy class); "If I was a researcher, that's what I would study first" (D, literacy class); "At home I'll find out, observing the animals" (D, literacy class).

## NOT ALWAYS SCHOOLING HELP TO THINK BETTER

The analysis of the empirical data indicates, more than the hypothezised presence of different modes of conceptual organization between higher- and lower-instructional-level adults, the importance of the process of joint construction of meanings in situations of dense verbal interaction. There was no evidence, in the obtained data, of different types of "theories" about the conceptual domain in focus, which could be examined regarding its larger or smaller consistency, stability, and independence from personal experience. The most relevant difference observed distinguishes subjects who where involved in an oral dialogue with the researcher, throughout a long open interview, from those who individually answered written questions.

The interviewed subjects, workers who attend the adult "supletivo" courses, showed to the researcher, during the very process of interview, the path of their reflection about the conceptual domain being investigated. This reflection was not a static picture of a mental content previously available, but a flexible set of meanings in process of elaboration during the interview itself. Crucial questions formulated by the investigator seemed to promote a constant restructuring of subjects' conceptions and to encourage the process of thinking about the topics proposed. Nuances of concepts and meanings were negotiated all the time and the joint reflection promoted more and more precision and consistency along the course of the interview.

Good examples of the process that occurred during the interviews can be seen in the following excerpts of dialogs:

> *Subject*: That's why I say the ape has and does not have a brain, because at this moment it thinks. It is capable of knowing that people want to harm it.
> (...)
> *Researcher*: So, what do you think, the ape thinks or does not think?
> *Subject*: In a certain sense it thinks. If it did not think it would not learn.
> *Researcher*: Do all animals think?
> *Subject*: Yes, they do, differently from us.
>
> (J, 4th grade)

> *Researcher*: Does the dog teach something to its offspring?
> *Subject*: It teaches, it conveys the instinct very much, the mother's instinct.
> *Reseacher*: What does it teach?
> *Subject*: I don't know if teaching is really the right word. I think it is its instinct which commands.
>
> (S, high school)

The first excerpt corresponds to the very last part of an interview along which the subject stated, at different moments, that animals think and do not think, that they have a brain and that they do not have a brain. At the end of the interview the subject is trying to contemplate these two possibilities simultaneously. He seems to have gone from unthoughtful contradiction to the acceptance of the complexity of a phenomena which cannot be understood in a simplified manner and which depends on a refinement of nuances of meaning. In the second excerpt, the ideas of "teaching" and "instinct" were initially grouped in a single process. After a question posed by the researcher, which certainly promoted reflection, these two ideas had their meaning refined.

The university students, on the other hand, tended to present answers apparently more "well finished," which could correspond to the existence of a theory giving support to their concepts. Contrarily to the expectations, however, they did not demonstrate as much density in their reflections as the interviewed workers. Dominant in their answers was the use of a typically school-like format, rather homogeneous throughout the whole group of subjects, but without the corresponding conceptual sophistication. It is reasonable to suppose that the fact that the questions were answered in writing, without the opportunity of an interpersonal construction about the topics in question, made these students express themselves in a brief way, with no commitment to a more consistent theoretical formulation, nor with a true personal involvement in the process of intellectual elaboration requested. With no possibility of questioning the intentions of the researcher, of asking different things about concepts and ideas, of exploring nuances of meaning, the university students seemed to have chosen to solve the formal problem, without investing in the reflection task: for a school task, a school answer.

The most interesting result of this analysis was, then, the displacement of the axis of diferentiation between systems of conceptual organization. The initial hypothesis of the investigation was that the axis of "degree of literacy" (or of schooling) would differentiate adults with a high level of instruction (supposedly with a conceptual organization more consistent, precise, and subject to meta-cognitive analysis) from adults with a low level of instruction (possibly with a more fragmented elaboration, more vulnerable to the peculiarities of individual history). Instead, the axis of "modality of interaction" was the one that differentiated those subjects placed in a situation of dense intellectual interaction from those submitted to a formal individual task. The former were truly provoked to reflect about the proposed questions, and to refine and re-elaborate their conceptions during the very process of interaction; the latter could accomplish their task with no reference to a body of previous consistent knowledge or to a conceptual articulation in process.

As mentioned in the beginning of this chapter, the view here adopted takes concepts to be not isolated mental entities, but elements organized in some kind of structured whole, complex systems of interrelations. To think about concepts as embedded in networks of meanings, therefore going beyond the notion of concepts as isolated entities defined by a set of fixed properties, may lead to the attempt of identifying supposed "conceptual states" of subjects in given moments of their development, and of mapping their network of concepts in a certain domain of knowledge. There is, in this conception, a nonexplicit assumption about the existence of a previously given conceptual network that can be accessed as such.

The point of departure of the research here reported was the understanding of the route of human development along cultural history through the understanding of the relationships between cognitive processes and the semiotic tools created by human beings. This lead to the attempt to identify different kinds of conceptual organization as related to people's interaction with different cultural artifacts: Concepts and theories produced and used by higher- and lower-instructional-level subjects were, then, hypothezised as having different natures. The data obtained clearly challenged the idea of a divide between more and less instructed groups or individuals, showing much more complex relationships between cognitive performance and cultural practices related to literacy and schooling.

Conceptual organization showed to correspond not to a complete and stable theory, but to a flexible set of meanings, open to constant restructuring on the basis of interpersonal situations that promote reflection. Actually this idea is much more consistent with the theoretical postulates that initially oriented the present work. By accepting the presupposition of a constant, intense, and complex relation subject-subject-sign-meaning-object, one cannot accept the existence of finished concepts and conceptual networks: They would be always subject to transformations, specially in situations of social interaction. This statement has important implications for the investigation in cognitive psychology: The very process of collective construction of meaning would be a more relevant object for the understanding of cognitive mechanisms than a supposed "state," even if acknowledged as temporary, of conceptual organization. The notions of transformation, of dense intellectual interaction and of promotion of real reflection would become central in the understanding of human cognitive functioning, rendering it closer to the very idea of cognitive development.

## APPENDIX A: SCHEDULE OF INTERVIEW WITH LOW-INSTRUCTIONAL-LEVEL SUBJECTS

(1) Introductory Question—proposed to generate a spontaneous listing of characteristics relevant for the comparison human being/animal:

- Choose an animal that you know well and talk about differences and similarities between this animal and the human being.

(2) Open set of questions—proposed in a different combination to each subject, according to the aspects included in their spontaneous listing given as the answer to the first question. The researcher conducts a discussion with the subject, exploring the reasons for the given answers and the arguments used by the subject.

- Does the [name of selected animal] look for food when it is hungry?
- Does it build a house to live in?
- Does it know how to speak? Could it learn?
- Does it know how to read and write? Could it learn?

- Does it take care of its offspring?
- Does it remember the time when it was young?
- When it is born, is it different from when it is an adult? How?
- Does it make plans for the future?
- Does it teach things to its offspring?
- What are the most important things that it teaches its offspring?
- Is it able to invent different things, which no other [name of animal] had invented before?
- Does it run away from dangerous things?
- Could it know that it does not know something? (for example, if it gets lost, does it *know* it is lost?)
- Could it want to learn something new?
- Could it perceive differences between itself and the human being?
- How does it choose the best way out of a difficult situation?

## APPENDIX B: WRITTEN QUESTIONS GIVEN TO THE UNIVERSITY STUDENTS

1. Select an animal that you know well and make a comparison between this animal and the human being, listing the main similarities and differences between them.
2. Do animals think? Justify your answer: How would you define thought to give support to your answer?

## REFERENCES

Carey, S. (1985). *Conceptual change in childhood*. Cambridge, MA: MIT Press.

Cole, M., & Scribner, S. (1974). *Culture and thought*. New York: John Wiley and Sons.

Goody, J., & Watt, I. (1968). The consequences of literacy. In J. Goody (Ed.), *Literacy in traditional societies*. New York: Cambridge University Press.

Luria, A. R. (1976) *Cognitive Development: its cultural and social foundations*. Cambridge, MA: Harvard University Press.

Murphy, G. L., & Medin, D. L. (1985). The role of theories in conceptual coherence. *Psychological Review, 92*(3), 289–316.

Núcleo de Estudos de Conceitos. (1994). *Conceitos e Teorias [Concepts and theories]* (mimeo). Research project presented to CNPq (Brazilian National Research Funding Institute).

Oliveira, M. K. de. (1982). *Cognitive processes in everyday life situations: An ethnographic study of Brazilian urban migrants*. Unpublished doctoral dissertation, Stanford University, Stanford, CA.

Oliveira, M. K. de. (1994). From graphic-functional to categorial mode: A qualitative turning point? In J. Wertsch and J. D. Ramirez (Eds.), *Literacy and other forms of mediated action.* Madrid: Fundación Infancia y Aprendizaje.

Oliveira, M. K. de. (1995a). Letramento, cultura e modalidades de pensamento [Literacy, culture and modes of thought]. In A. Kleiman (Ed.), *Os significados do letramento [Meanings of literacy].* Campinas, SP: Mercado de Letras.

Oliveira, M. K. de. (1995b). The meaning of intellectual competence: Views from a favela. In J. Valsiner (Ed.), *Child development within culturally-structured environments*, Vol. 3. *Comparative-cultural perspectives*. Norwood, NJ: Ablex.

Rieber, R., & Carton, A. (1987). *The collected works of L.S. Vygotsky.* New York: Plenum Press.

Scribner, S., & Cole, M. (1981). *The psychology of literacy.* Cambridge, MA: Harvard University Press.

Street, B.V. (1984). *Literacy in theory and practice*. Cambridge: Cambridge University Press.

Tulviste, P. (1991). *Cultural-historical development of verbal thinking: A psychological study.* New York: Nova Science Publishers.

Van der Ver, R., & Valsiner, J. (1991). *Understanding Vygotsky: A quest for synthesis.* Oxford: Blackwell.

Vygotsky, L. S. (1991). *Obras escogidas: Problemas teoricos y metodologicos de la psicologia [Selected works: Psychology's theoretical and methodological problems].* Madrid: Visor/Centro de Publicaciones del MEC.

chapter 10

# Learning to Write Letters: Semiotic Mediation in Literacy Acquisition in Adulthood*

Simone Gonçalves De Lima and Maria Helena Fávero
University of Brasília, Brazil

## INTRODUCTION

Current research on literacy in the socio-cultural tradition demonstrates a trend that points to the abandoning of the search for absolute and universal impacts of literacy acquisition on cognition. This trend was perhaps dominant in the 1970s (cf. Greenfield, 1972; Olson, 1977) and constituted the so-called great divide theory, which contrasted literate and illiterate groups as homogeneous blocks, only the first of which were believed to possess higher mental functions. In this tradition, the investigations, mostly cross-cultural, failed to identify logical, formal, and abstract thought in illiterate or unschooled groups. Literacy was then heralded as a sufficient and necessary condition for consequences ranging from "logical and analytical modes of thought; general and abstract uses of language; critical and rational thought; a skeptical and questioning attitude…" to "complex and modern governments (…) political democracy (…) economic development…" (Gee, 1988, p. 196).

*Abstracted from the MSc thesis submitted by S. G. De Lima to the post-graduate program in Psychology of the University of Brasília. (Advisor: M. H. Fávero) These investigations were partially supported by grants from CNPq and CAPES.

The 1980s brought about reactions to this view, in studies like the classical one by Scribner and Cole (1978, 1981), which failed to identify sweeping consequences of literacy on cognition in the Vai group of Liberia. Also along these lines, and in an attempt to demonstrate the universality of abstraction and logical reasoning, a great volume of empirical work has come from groups in Third World countries like Brazil. This is probably due to the proximity to the problem of illiteracy and as a reaction to the inferiorizing attitude towards illiterate groups derived from the previous approach. In the Brazilian literature, for example, Carraher, Carraher, & Schliemann (1985) investigated cognitive processes in unschooled street children in everyday activities that had been previously overlooked by psychological research and educational institutions. Other authors who developed work along these lines were Oliveira (1982) and Tfouni (1988). They defended the need for methodological changes in the assessment of the cognition of the illiterate and criticized earlier, conventional, First World, and literate-oriented tests.

A drawback of some of this reaction was that, in the attempt to prove that the illiterates think logically and abstractly, a certain tendency arose to underplay the potential role of symbols—or more specifically, of symbolic mediation—in the development of consciousness. In an egalitarian effort, symbolic and motor acquisitions are equaled and no differences in the complexity (or level of formalization) of tasks are admitted. An example is the work of Cagliari (1985): "Writing is no more difficult than playing football, scoring a goal is not easier than solving math. Actually, scoring a goal is also a question of math, of ballistics" (p. 52, author's translation).

Differences in the level of abstraction involved in writing and orality are dismissed: "The fact that writing is a representation of a representation does not mean it is more abstract or formal or complex or demands superior capacity" (p. 53).

A problem remained open in this approach, spurring further research: a homogeneous view of thought. In one approach, the illiterate and the literate were seen as two distinct but internally homogeneous groups. In another, researchers sought to prove that thought processes—whether in industrialized, literate or traditional, illiterate societies—were universal and homogeneous.

It was in conceptual studies set forth in the late 1980s and in the beginning of the 1990s (cf. Tulviste, 1987, 1989, and 1992; Valsiner, 1988, 1989a; and Wertsch, 1991) that the question of whether literacy changes thought started to be identified as inappropriate, as, in these authors' views, the view of homogeneity in human thought processes was erroneous.

In a review of his and other groups' data, Tulviste (1989) finds the evidence to show that, in some activity settings, scientific, abstract thought was also to be found in illiterate societies. What is more important, he points out that the dualistic view of units of thought (logical, abstract *v.* concrete thought) is based on the false assumption that individuals in industrialized, literate societies think in a consistently logical, formal manner, ignoring the fact that the literate populations maintain forms of concrete or mythical thought alongside logical, abstract thought. According to Tulviste, thought is heterogeneous in any given time and culture, both across and within individuals, because the activity that gives rise to it is also heterogeneous. Wertsch (1991) argues similarly, defending the idea of a "tool kit" of heterogeneous mediational devices which are constituted culturally and used according to the activity the individual is engaged in.

At the heart of the question seems to be the definition of development adopted in mainstream psychological research: that of a linear, inexorable development from prelogical, concrete thought to logical, abstract thought, and scientific thought. Valsiner (1988) argues for the need to adopt a multilinear view of development. In evolutionary biology, which originally influenced developmental psychology, the search for a new, multilinear concept of development is in motion, spurred by recent archeological findings (see Gould, 1991). Tulviste (1992) argues that in sciences of culture heterogeneity of thought has long been recognized, and although not a new idea in psychology, its assimilation by research has been limited.

In psychological phenomena, multilinearity arises from the diversity and heterogeneity of cultural and social activities human beings engage in, which constitute culture, itself in a constant process of historical change. A key to the disentanglement of the literacy/cognition dilemma seems to be the introduction of history in the analysis, one of Vygotsky's main contributions to psychology. Following Scribner (1985), we understand history in various levels: not only the history of a society, but of the individual, of the tools used by the individual and of the cognitive function. From this, we can conclude that not only thought processes vary, but also literacy. However, reading, writing, and being illiterate are often viewed as invariable concepts. Frequent comparisons are established between being a child in a literate society who has not yet learned to read and write and being an illiterate adult in a literate society. Oliveira (1991) reminds us of the important distinctions, for example, in being illiterate in literate and traditional societies. In the first, society is organized through literate uses of the language and literacy becomes thus a requirement for integral participation in the society.

The different uses to which reading and writing are put (even within the same time, individual, or institution) constitute different tools with unique potentials for cognition. In the domain of literacy, the need for an ethnography of writing—a thorough survey of the diverse uses and meanings attributed to reading and writing—has started to be recognized by several authors as a requirement for the understanding of the literacy/thought relation. Francis (1987) and Torrance and Olson (1987) criticize the divisions of oral and written language and argue that any cognitive influence of writing is not to be found in any inherent property of written language but in the uses to which it is put. An example is the metalanguage on written language present in preschool children in highly literate societies (Olson & Astington, 1990). Rockwell (1985) and Scinto (1985) have identified quite differentiated uses of writing even in the same context of schooling (cf. Ferreiro et al., 1986). Freire, normally pointed to as the herald of the proposal that emphasizes the role of literacy in "conscientizaçao" (growing political awareness) and liberation, has admitted that the role of literacy as a generator of critical sense may have more relation to the mechanism through which literacy is acquired than in the mere use of written language (1981).

The differentiated impact of the heterogeneous uses to which writing is put is also related to the values associated with these tools. In the related area of mathematics, for example, Fávero, Tunes, and Marchi (1991) studied the influence of the kind of information presented to children solving logical mathematical problems. The performance is linked not only to cognitive stages, but also to the interpretation of the task, in which social values interfere. Holland and Valsiner (1988) have argued for the necessary contemplation of the system of beliefs associated with literacy.

This brings us back to the question of culture. In the advances in the socio-cultural tradition, understanding how culture constitutes behaviour has stopped being a synonym of cross-cultural comparison (in which the variables to be observed end up being a compromise between the variables in one culture and another, frequently resulting in a loss of the integrity of the phenomenon) and have started to mean diving into a culture, through the contemplation of how culturally constituted uses, beliefs, and values interact with the task being carried out (Valsiner, 1989b).

The literacy/cognition debate can thus be reworded as follows: What culturally constituted and meaningful literate activity is this group or individual involved in, and what forms of thought does this activity engender? Underlying the idea of an activity *engendering* a specific type of thought is the idea that studies must adopt a genetic, developmental stance to their object: to understand the process, its history must be investigated.

## PSYCHOLOGY AND MEANING

This leads us to one of the initial problems Vygotsky tackled, namely, what is specifically human in human activity? The Vygostkian proposal was to go against the behaviorist tendency to reduce all behavior and semiotic functioning of the human to the signalization process, shared by humans and animals. Signals trigger off automatic responses, they do not mean or communicate—they dispense with dialogue. On the other hand, signification—the creation and use of signs—involves comprehension and a dimension of will.

It is exactly this use of the sign that inaugurates the line of cultural development (as opposed to the line of biological development) that allows the individual to conceive, plan, communicate, and coordinate conduct. Combining the elements of a finite code, he expresses and signifies in an infinite manner. In a dialectical relation, signs are created by social forms of life and at the same time allow for the genesis of new ones.

An important concept that arises in the Vygotskian notion of sign and later developed in Peirce (cited in Parmentier, 1985) is that of mediation. In the Peircean sign the introduction of a third element to the Saussurean dyad of significant and signification adds its mediational character. In mediation, a third element is a bridge between the other two. The importance of the concept of semiotic mediation lies exactly in the fact that "humanity" lies in the capacity to carry out semiotic mediation. Plants and animals are tied, to a greater or lesser extent, to the immediate. Through the use of signs—psychological instruments of representations—human beings can mentally manipulate concepts that either refer to objects in the physical and cultural world, or to internal representations. In this way, experience is free from the immediate. From semiotic mediation arise intersubjectivity and the construction and transmission of knowledge. We can thus conclude that semiotic mediation is at the root of the social and historical being. This tripartite logic of symbol highlights its active role, on the one hand, and, inserting it in the historical process, defines it in its diachronic axis. In other words, the sign becomes an instrument that acts on the genesis of other signs and mental structures.

In his discussion of the analogy of the sign as a tool, Vygotsky (1960/1977; 1929) distinguished the use of instruments, which are oriented externally and transform nature, and signs, which are oriented internally and transform mental operations: "The same problem, if solved by different means, will have a different structure...a sign or an auxiliary means of cultural method forms thus a structural center, which determines the whole composition of the operation and the relevant importance of each separate process" (1929, p. 421).

A genetic analysis of this transformation indicates that it moves from the social, or intermental, plan to the intramental one. That is, the sign, originally a form of influencing the other, subsequently takes on an intellectual, self-regulatory function (cf. Wertsch, 1985). This constitutes the dialogue with the self, the sign as a mediator between the individual and himself.

We then reach the important relation between the communicative process and psychological functions:

> If the primary function of psychological tools such as language is to communicate, it is reasonable to expect these mediational means to be formed in accordance with the demands of communication. If these means also play an important role in shaping individuals' mental processes, we can expect such processes to be indirectly shaped by forces that originate in the dynamics of communication. (Wertsch, 1985, p. 81)

Returning to the question of literacy, the relations between literacy and cognition may be brought to light if one investigates the mediational potential of the instrument of writing, especially from a genetic point of view. In other words, it seems important to investigate how the symbolic system being acquired interacts with previously existing systems and what functions exist and arise in its genesis and development.

In an attempt to delve deeper into these questions, we have worked (Fávero & De Lima, 1989) with the articulation of the text typology proposed by Luria (1981) and the semiotics of culture of Lotman (1988a and b), which elaborates the proposition of symbolic systems as subtexts in the wider text of culture.

The text typology elaborated by Luria (1981) has its roots in the work of Vygotsky (1987, 1962), who in turn was influenced by Yakubiinski's ideas on the differences between monologue, dialogue, writing, and direct verbal interaction (1932, apud Wertsch, 1985b). Luria (1981) systematized Vygotsky's contribution, analyzing the text in such a way that the pragmatic conditions of text constitution could be taken into account. He proposed a functional classification of language as follows: oral and written language manifestation and monologic and dialogic discourse organization. These forms are intercrossed, yielding four functional types of language: (1) oral, dialogic speech; (2) oral, monologic speech; (3) written, dialogic speech; and (4) written, monologic speech.

Luria's functional analysis involves not only the linguistic aspect, but also the psychological origins and varying mediational possibilities each functional type entails.

According to Luria (1981) one of the main characteristics of the dialogic organization of discourse is the lack of pre-planning, due to the shared control in this type of speech. Another characteristic is the shared knowledge of the communicative situation, which allows the text to contain nonverbal markers, resulting in grammatical incompleteness and ellipsis. The monologue, on the other hand, is autonomous, expanded speech generated from an internal project. This project, or motive, is generally in the speaker's exclusive control and tends to yield greater grammatical completeness and logical passages from one point to the next. (In more contemporary terms, cohesive links in the texts.)

As to the form of discourse organization, Luria (1981) goes on to point out that one of the characteristic aspects of the oral form is the presence of an interlocutor. This allows the speaker to use nonverbal markers and external prosodic elements and to omit certain words. Another point is the difficulty in correction: Once produced, an utterance can be amended, but not simply crossed out and reworded. Finally, oral language is primary in the sense that it is the child's natural form of communication.

Still according to Luria (1981), in the written language, in contrast, the absence of an interlocutor can be observed. This brings both limitations and possibilities. It becomes possible to plan and edit a text, since its control is in the hands of the writer. Besides, the absence of an interlocutor creates the demand for verbal markers to ensure comprehension. Written language, adds Luria, is not acquired primarily, but involves a learning process in which several conscious intermediary operations are present. Both Vygotsky and Luria attributed great importance to the written manifestation of monologic discourse. The high level of abstraction and volition involved in writing are believed to create a space that at the same time demands the complex development of abstraction and ensures greater liberty to the writer.

Contemporary studies in the fields of conversational analysis and anthropology have tended to relativize this importance and make the point that (Cook-Gumperz, 1991; Collins & Michaels, 1981) the differences are not restricted to oral *v.* written modes, but are linked to levels of formality and cultural origin of the text. Anthropological studies on the differences between writing and orality in nonindustrialized communities have, furthermore, highlighted the need to understand the use and values attributed to these modalities (Finnegan, 1988; Kullick & Stroud, 1990).

Nevertheless, we understand that in the construction of an ethnography of writing based on the pragmatic conditions of discourse constitution, the typology systematized by Luria provides interesting parameters, provided a genetic and communicational perspective is adopted. For, as Holman (in Scinto, 1985) points out,

> Language as written typically occurs within an act of communication in which the roles of communicant and target of communication are maintained throughout the transmission of the message...The high degree of organization characteristic of written communication is called forth by its primary function: the transmission of detailed information concerning a severely limited sphere of discourse. In the actual transmission of written communication the fact of spatial contiguity is of little importance...the fact of psychological contiguity assumes a crucial role in the organization of written communication. (p. 210)

In this sense, it seems impossible to consider the increase in structural complexity of a text when it ranged from oral dialogicality to written monologicality if one is to dissociate this from its socio-communicative function.

## TEXT AND COMMUNICATION

The concern with the functioning of texts and the relation of the concepts of text and culture has been a growing trend in modern semiotics and has given rise to the semiotics of culture. From this point of view, a text (Lotman, 1988b) to be considered as such, must be coded at least twice. This derives from the bilateral approach to texts. In one approach, the materialization of language is considered to yield a text that is unlimited, open, and constantly being built upon the time axis. The other approach focuses the text as the final, closed, discrete result of encoding which tends to panchronicity or to form its internal time. Thus, the relation between text and code is altered.

According to Lotman (1988b) when an object is conceived as a text, encoding is presumed, as part of its very concept. The code may be unknown to the reader, leading to the necessary reconstruction: an encounter between our previous encoding and the new code the reader is faced with.

This bilateral approach to texts stems from what Lotman has termed the functional dualism of texts in a cultural system, that is, the ability to communicate meaning adequately and to generate new meanings: "The text is a generator of meaning, a thinking device, which requires an interlocutor to be activated. This reveals the profoundly dialogue nature of consciousness as such. To function, consciousness requires consciousness, a text requires a text and a culture requires another culture" (Lotman, 1988b, p. 40).

Such a postulation is paralleled in the Bakhtinian notion of dialogism, and in the Vygotskian inter/intrapsychological relation. Bakhtin states that thought, or internal discourse, is better conceived of as internal dialogue. Thus, thought is composed of interrelated utterances: "No one utterance can be either the first or the last. Each is only a link in the chain and none can be studied outside this chain" (Bakhtin, in Holquist & Emerson, 1986, p. 136).

A deeply similar idea is defended by Vygotsky when he defines consciousness as "social contact with oneself."

> The social dimension of consciousness is primary in time and in fact. The individual dimension of consciousness is derivative and secondary, based on the social and construed exactly on its likeness. Consciousness thus has a dual nature: the idea of a "double" is perhaps as near as any notion of consciousness can get to reality. (Vygotsky, 1925/1979, p. 30)

Functional dualism implies that a text is a generator of meaning, in such a way that in the introduction of a text in a new cultural context it is transformed in an unpredictable manner. The transformed text constitutes a new message which intervenes in the semiotic situation of this new context. Lotman (1988a) goes on to define the processes involved in the socio-communicative function of a text. Five processes of communication are described: between addressant and addressee; between the audience and the cultural tradition; the reader with himself; the reader with the text; and between a text and the cultural context.

This takes us back to our hypothesis, formulated initially in Fávero and De Lima (1989). We consider that in the development of the elaboration of written text, the increase in its socio-communicative complexity is related to the transformation from oral dialogic forms to written monologic forms.

The communication between writer and reader is guaranteed by the introduction of verbal markers; grammatical constructs like indirect speech, and so on; and planning and editing procedures. This activity is directed towards an increase in the logical structure of the text. The communication between the reader and the cultural tradition is related to the writer's consciousness that the potential reader may not share the same context. This means that besides the concern with the logical structuring of the text, a new concern is added: that with the selection of vocabulary and structure adequate to the potential audience. A text that results from this activity may become a mediator transiting between the reader and his cultural tradition.

The restrictions imposed by the cultural tradition on the selection of vocabulary and on the content of the message are rarely received neutrally by the reader. A text, when read, may lead the reader to engage in a meta-metacognitive activity: speculating about the writer's assumption about himself, the reader. This potentializes the text as an interlocutor.

But not only does the reader "talk to" the text, the writer himself is an interlocutor of the text in the sense that in his planning and editing procedures, he engages in a dialogue with the addressee via the text—a process in the course of which the awareness of the lack of physical contiguity arises and the need for psychological contiguity prevails. This increasing awareness enhances the text's potential as informer of the cultural context. The increased complexity of a text allows it to function autonomously, not only as a source, but also as a receiver of information.

The processes described by Lotman are situated at the extreme of a continuum of potential complexification of a text. The same can be said of Luria's prototypical monologue. What, one may ask, is the epistemic potential of the articulation of these propositions in the process of initial literacy acquisition? We believe that the interest in this articulation resides in the abandoning of the possession metaphor of a determined type of thought (Wertsch, 1991). The articulation permits the analysis of how an instrument is acquired and what is transformed in this action. In this manner, a genetic analysis of the texts produced by a subject may, using the parameters outlined in this articulation, show us a path through which we can shed light on the underlying intramental processes. In the Vygostkian analogy, the texts (external structure) are the string that, tied to the fish, will help us understand its path when it submerges into the water (Vygotsky, 1929).

## A RURAL MIGRANT AND HIS TEXT PRODUCTION: A CASE STUDY

In this work, we present extracts from an exploratory case study of an adult's acquisition of the written language (De Lima, 1993). The process of acquisition was studied through the analysis of (a) his text production, (b) the interaction in the writing process, and (c) the subject's representations of the process. In an analysis in the diachronic axis of the semiotic functioning of the texts produced by the subject, the history of the structural complexification is highlighted and related to its dialogicality.

The subject was a 19-year-old man who had recently migrated from northeastern Brazil, a region known for high poverty and illiteracy rates, to Brasilia, the capital, where the study was held. The subject worked as a cleaner at a federal organ. An initial survey of his reading and writing abilities showed he could not understand his attempt at written production and that he could recognize individual letters but had trouble reading words of more than two syllables.

The subject took part in 90-minute tutoring sessions held twice a week with the first author for 5 months. All sessions were recorded and his written production photocopied.

An initial interview was held at the beginning of the tutoring sessions, in which we attempted to identify the values and expectations related to reading and writing or literacy skills. In this interview, the subject makes a qualitative distinction between being illiterate and literate—according to him, literacy guarantees the access to knowledge and advantages in the literate society, which he recognizes to be organized through the written media. He also attaches the condition of being literate to prestige, or, in other words, he finds it socially uncomfortable to be illiterate.

The subject identifies his illiteracy as a limiting factor as concerns his autonomy, life perspective and standard, and communication and access to information. He thus expresses his desire to learn to read and write, as this, he believes, will give him access to autonomy, information, communication with his hometown, better working conditions and a consequent improvement in living standard, and will lead him to happiness. It is when speaking of his hometown that he states his mother's wish that he should learn to write:

> When I learn to read (...) I'll be very happy, you know, my biggest wish is to learn to read and tell my mother, tell (somebody to) say/send her a letter, telling her everything, how it all started, 'til the end, you know? Really everything, then...she'll be very happy too, I know. I intend to do this.

Communication through letters is thus a junction of two expressed desires: becoming literate and communicating this to his mother, which will make her happy.

In the interview, the subject carries out in a consistent manner a metacognitive analysis in the areas of literacy, mathematics, and problem solving:

> No, I can't read well, but, but it's that...you know, many words, I know the letters, but in the joining of some letters I get confused, I don't know. I can stay there for hours and hours but I don't know the words...I think I'm not going to pass, and the reason, I think, is this: there are many letters I can't join, really many, then...there's no way.

Here, for example, his previous knowledge of the writing system is made clear, as well as his consciousness of what limits his access to a proficient use of it. It is noteworthy that his view of his difficulty is that of a fixed, unchangeable situation. This is based on his comparison with colleagues and in the evaluations of his ex-teachers.

**TABLE 10.1 Characteristics of Prototypical Oral Dialogue and Written Monologue (Lima, 1991)**

| | Oral Dialogue | Intermediary Form | Written Monologue |
|---|---|---|---|
| *Semiotic Activity* | | | |
| A | Spontaneous | | Conscious operation with means of representation |
| B | Primary | Vocal mediation | Secondary |
| C | Lack of pre-planning | | Motive, project |
| D | Irreversible | | Editing, correction |
| E | Spatial Contiguity | | Psychological contiguity mediated by text |
| *Mechanics* | | | |
| 1 | Nonverbal, simpraxic markers (gestures, pauses, intonation, speed, and volume) | | Verbal, simsemantic markers, Pausal signs, Melodic signs |
| 2 | Lack of discreet units/low distinction between discreet units | | Discreet units: letters, words, sentences, paragraphs |
| *Lexical Choices* | | | |
| 3 | Implicit context | | Lexicalization (explicitation of information) |
| 4 | Coloquial expressions, dialect, slang | | Forms adequate to writing |
| *Sentences* | | | |
| 5 | Lack of grammaticality: mazes, ellipses, pleonasm; simple, short sentences | | Grammaticality (completeness, correct choice of tense, person); complex, long sentences |
| *Text* | | | |
| 6 | Disconnected text | | Cohesive text |
| 7 | Word redundancy | | Substitution of complete NP by pronouns; use of synonyms |

In a country in which most of the working population does not have the access to a phone and in which a 10-minute call may cost up to a tenth of a monthly minimum wage, letters are still used by the population who have come to the cities in search of work to communicate with their families left behind in the poorer, rural areas of the country. A network of communication is thus established, informing on the person's adaptation to the new situation and work prospects for colleagues. These facts, added to the personal meaning attributed to the letters by the subject himself, as mentioned before, defined, both for the subject and for the researchers, that the axis along which the work was to develop was that of letter writing—understood as culturally and personally meaningful text production.

A selection of the 11 letters produced in the period of the tutoring sessions is presented[1] here. The letters were analyzed in the dimensions of text structure and semiotic activity. The parameters used for this analysis are summarized in Table 10.1, which contains a description of the prototypical forms of oral dialogue and written monologue. Previous and more extensive analyses of these letters are to be found in De Lima, 1993, and Fávero and De Lima, 1989.

**Letter A** (see Figure 10.1)

**mos** ro da mariana may 30 1 1989
**mother fo rthefir st time I a m writingtoyou I apologize.**
i **a mwell am wor king at empal** which??? **you.-**
**sentme? some lace** for**metosell** fo r **you** here-
**lace is veryexpensive I'llsell andsend** the ( ) to**you.**
how **i sluis Ifeelalotofsaudadeofyou.**
he reit i s verycold andhow**arethingsthere and myfather is** he wor.
**mother isitrainingalot** there - **Isaygoodbyewith**much -
**saudades Si gned Reginado**
**Raimuda nonato** da Silva
**Manueu mezes** da Silva

This letter was written before the beginning of the sessions and brought in by the subject. We can thus take it as a reference of the initial level of mastery of writing.

***Text structure***

There is an attempt to organize the text in the graphic space, reflected in the lines the subject himself traced and in the attempt to add information such as date, addressant, and addressee, however outside the conventions of letter writing. Melodic and pausal markers are absent, and the lack of a consistent separation of words and sentences reveals lack of awareness of words and sentences as discrete units. Words are either separated according to a syllabic division (this has been noted to happen in students heavily influenced by dictations in which syllables, not whole words, are dictated) or joined as in orality. There is an attempt to conclude lines (not sentences) with a marker, in this case a dash, which is not used consistently.

Some of the information is made explicit, such as the weather in Brasilia, as contrasted with that in his hometown. In contrast, terms—like Empal, the company he works for—are not explicated. It is interesting to note the beginning of a narrative of the author's action (I say goodbye...), uncommon in oral Brazilian Portuguese and found more often in formal texts. This is the genesis of a monologic tone in the letters.

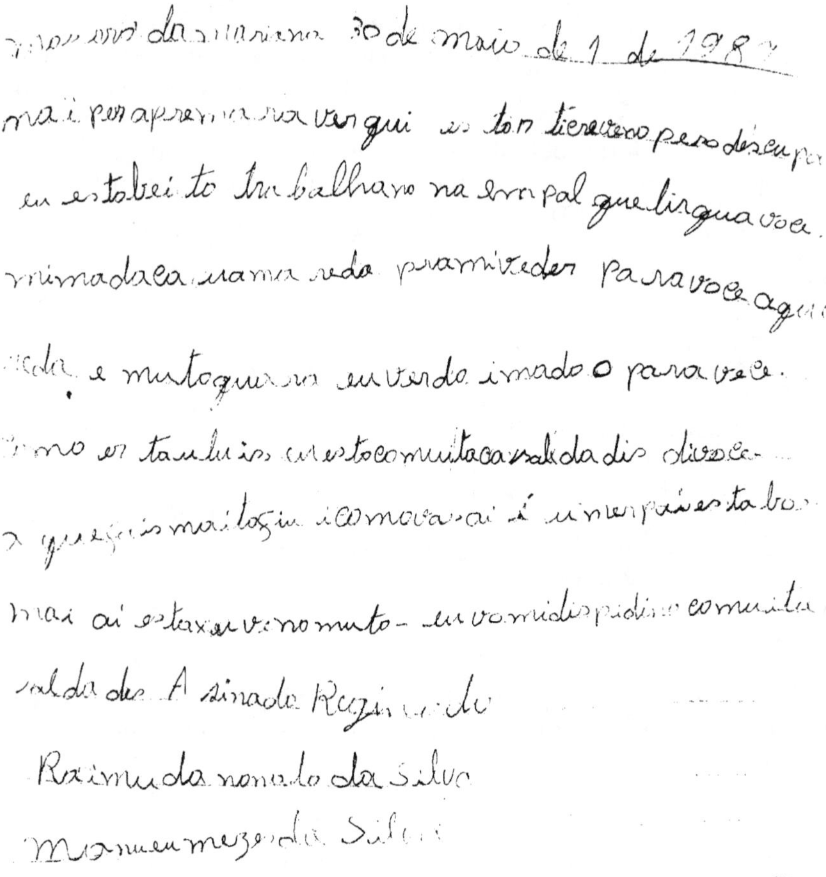

**FIGURE 10.1. Letter A**

Syntax is highly marked by orality, with exaggeratedly coordinated phrases; repetition of *ands*, ellipses, and sudden changes in sentence structure occur. Topics appear in a random order and there is little intralinguistic reference. No cohesive links mark the shift from one topic to another.

***Semiotic activity***

On being questioned about what it had been like to write the letter, the subject revealed it had involved a great amount of effort and a feeling of being lost: "I would do it, then I wouldn't know, if I would end it or start..."

These operations were limited to a first version of the letter: Editing and correction procedures were not possible as the faulty text mechanics prevented him from re-reading the text. This was possible only (and even then, in a limited manner) with the mediation of the tutor. Several sessions were devoted to the slow and difficult "deciphering" of the text.

At the time of the writing of the letter, all the subject's written production was necessarily mediated by orality: this means he had to speak while writing and reading. This seemed to hinder the separation of the two forms of discourse, "loading" the text with oral markers and forms.

There is no explicit project as how to go about writing the letter, although a motive (communicating with his mother and making her happy) was clearly present.

There seems to be very low awareness of the lack of spatial contiguity, demonstrated by the low and inconsistent explication of information. The subject uses the context of Brasilia in an indexical way, pointing to a reality that is not shared by the addresses. It was discovered in a later letter (analyzed in De Lima, 1992) that the sentence "I miss you very much" is directed not at his mother, the addressee, but to Luis, who he has recently referred to. That is, the subject shifts from one (explicit) addressee to another with no markers, just as one would do in face-to-face interaction, by directing one's fact towards the other person.

**Letter B** (see Figure 10.2)

29/07/89
Hi Luis how are you Luis?
What about your family are **all** well
Luis it'**s** good he re **but** you **can't .**
**have money** because here the cost ?"
of living **is** very expensive He re there are parties every
**saturday**
Luis I went fishing but I didn't **catch** anything..
He re I feel **saudade**[2] of you
I **wo uld like to know** how **theJune feastswere**
Luis **mando** dizer that I **am well but**
Iam **well. Because** here it is **not**
like it **is there He re it is different** because here I **work** from 7
to 3 **o'clock**
I am **working** at a **ministry** of education
Luis here I go **tothe swimmingpool** always on
sunday
I'll **end this with saudade** of **you.**

***Text structure***

The previous hypothesis that lines should be ended with a hyphen is abandoned and a division of sentences is attempted either through capi-

Brasila) 29/07/89/

Oi como está voce Luis?

E a sua familia estaõ todos bem?

. Luis aqui é bem mais nas da para
ter dinheiro por que aqui é muito caro o custo
de vida? Aqui tem festa todos sábados?

Luis eu fui uma pescaria mais não peguei nada.

Aqui tenho saudades de você?..

Eu queria saber como forma as festas Junina

Luis mando dizer que eu estou bem mais aqui..
não é como aí. Aqui é diferente por que eu trabalho
das sete hora até as três. Depois das três volto pra
casa e das sete hora até a dez eu estudo.
eu estou trabanhando num ministério da educação.

Luis aqui vou pra picina sempre ao domingo.

ou terminado com saudade de você. Reginaldo

**FIGURE 10.2. Letter B**

talization or punctuation. Words are separated more frequently, although some junctions and inadequate separations still occur. The presence of spelling mistakes drops. There is an increase in the lexicalization of information, shown for example in the explicitation of his workplace (Ministry of Education), which contrasts with the previous reference to a little-known firm that locates services to the ministry.

The initial text has faulty grammatical structures and incomplete sentences, but more complex sentences (with subordination, for example) do occur. Topics are still presented in a disorderly fashion. The text presents a great amount of redundancy (in words like "Luis," "here," etc.).

***Semiotic structure***

Despite its faulty text mechanics, this was a much easier text to read, allowing extensive editing procedures. Conscious operations when editing the letter concentrated on grapho-phonic equivalence (spelling), punctuation, and word and sentence separation. The editing procedures were, in general, initiated by the tutor, who pointed out mistakes and gave clues and hints:

*T*: Is this how you write dinheiro (money)?
*S*: I think so. Let me see. DIN-NHEI-RO.DIN-NHE-I.RO.
*T*: That NHEiro there. Remember we practiced it?
Dinheiro, banheiro (bathroom) Didn't you write that in your notebook? Where was that?
*S*: In the D. (Writes correctly on separate page, dictating to himself)
*T*: That's it!
*S*: Is it like this?
*T*: That H in the middle. Right! You'd forgotten the H.
*S*: Oh, so easy. Like this.

As can be seen, both reading and writing are still necessarily mediated vocally.

The subject starts to demonstrate his consciousness of problems in his writing, identifying his main difficulties. "Sometimes, I get confused. Look: Sometimes, if it's das, I put da. If it's der, I put des."

A planning procedure of how to go about writing the letter, especially in the second and third versions, in which the subject eliminates redundancies and fills in empty spaces, follows:

*S*: There's a space here now. Can I write more?
*T*: Yes. What do you want to write?
*S*: Like this: I go to work, when I arrive, I go to school. Then...I think it doesn't even make sense, does it?
*T*: No, tell him. Your life there is different, isn't it?
*S*: Maybe...**here** it's different, because...

In this episode one can note the subject requesting the tutor's authorization to write (as if the letter were not yet entirely his own space), her monitoring of his ideas, and the adoption of a lead-in the tutor introduced: the dissimilarities between his life in the country and in the city.

He also requests the monitoring of the tutor to eliminate word redundancy.

*S*: Here it's different because here...There's "here" there, already! Again?
*T*: Yes, you can take that out; you don't need to repeat it.
*S*: It's better.

Problem solving was involved in the planning of how to make the letter reach his friend, since the subject did not have the address. He decides to send the letter to his mother and ask her to hand it to Luis. He also adds a p.s. so that, from then on, his friend would go and check for correspondence at the post office: "Luis, I ask you to go to the post office always and check if there are any letters."

His concern with his mother's comprehension is highlighted in two passages: Since Luis is a common name in his hometown, he adds information on which Luis his mother should hand the letter to: "I'd better say one more word, so she doesn't confuse herself: Luis of Seu Raimundão."

Another instance in which this happens is revealed in his concern that his mother will think the letter is for herself and feel disappointed:

What can we do to send it to my mother and get her to hand it to Luis there? Send it...only in her name, and then, when she opens it, she'll: "Oh, letter!" She'll be so happy and when she sees: "Oh, it's not for you," she'll be: "Oh! It's not for me."

This imaginary dialogue with potential reader leads him to write a small note to his mother, too, explaining that the letter is for his friend and that his next letter will be for her (which he does in fact write).

This concern with the addressee's comprehension is also present in the high degree of lexicalization present in the text. The term "Eu mando dizer" is of particular interest. Roughly translated it means: I tell you to say or announce that: This term is rarely used in face-to-face dialogue and is more appropriate to the sending of an oral message through a third person—a messenger—in a mediated oral interaction. Consequently, it constitutes an interesting example of the interaction of forms of discourse in the genesis of written monology.

The correction and editing procedures in the two letters that preceded this one were all initiated by the tutor. In this letter, however, although most of the correction requires the tutor's mediation, some correction procedures start to be internalized, and self-correction strategies are initiated. Besides, he uses schoolbooks, other reference materials used in the sessions, and friends to help in his correction:

But I didn't ca...ca(tch)...here, I didn't know this, so I asked...I went and checked in my book...my schoolbook, you know? It has the consonants, the whole alphabet, to see if (...) then I didn't know this letter here. Then I wrote this one first, then I asked: "Is it this letter here? I don't know if it is." Then (she) said: "Yes."

**Letter C** (see Figures 10.3, 10.4, and 10.5)

This letter, written months after Letter A, and months after the start of the tutoring sessions, was written as a response to a letter he had received from a friend, which in turn had been a response to one of his letters. This is the text of his friend's letter:

5/8/89
Morros da Mariana
Saudade, friend
I am writing these few lines just to give you my news and at the same time to know about yours. Look, friend, how are you? Everything all right?? Here, everything is as it always was, slow, nothing very new, but every now and then something happens. Reginaldo, I apologize for not sending you anything, because I haven't been able to go hunting, because I am busy at work. There'll be a lot of cashew this year. There are a lot of nuts already. I am ending (this letter) with a lot of saudades of all of you. Give my regards to Dalva and Zuzuca and a hug. I'll write you soon.
Signed Luis.

This (Figure 10.3) is the first version of the letter he wrote. Two other versions of the letters (Figures 10.4 and 10.5) were later produced as a result of the editing procedures.

Luis I received the letter you **sent** me. I was very happy. Luis I ask you to send letters to me always so I can keep ~~always~~ corresponding." ~~So we~~ can keep always talking. Luis I ask if you have got **the** documents. After **the** problems in my house I will send for you. Here someone who has studied can find a job easily.
I ask you not to tell anyone I want it to be kept a secret. Luis I am going to ask you **a** favour. I ask you if po ssible to try and get Deuza's **phone** number.
Luís **there's** a cousin who can help to ask Celia what I **am** asking for. I hope that by the next corresponden **ce** you will have tried to **get** it.

***Text structure***

This is the first letter in which the notion of sentences as discrete units seems to have been consolidated: Since the first version, sentences are initialized with a capital letter and end with a period. The subject com-

Norte

Luis eu recebi a carta que você me mandau. Eu fiquei muito alegre.

Luis eu peço Por favor que você me mande sempre carta pra mim ficar ~~sempre~~ correspondendo. ~~pra genti~~ fica conversando. Luis eu pergunto se você já tirou os documentos Depois dos problemas na minha casa eu vou mandar buscar você. Aqui a pessoa que tem estudo é fácil de arrumar emprego.

Eu peço que você não fale para ninguém eu quero que fique em segredo.

Luis eu vou ~~tem~~ pedir o favor se for possível peço que você tenti conseguir o número do telefoni da Deuza.

Luis, tem uma prima que pode ajudar a pedir pra Célia o que eu estou pedindo. Eu espero que na próxima correspondência você tenha tentado consegue.

**FIGURE 10.3. Letter C—first version**

Luis eu recebi a carta que você mandou.

eu fiquei muito alegre.

Eu peço por favor que você vai mande sempre

carta pra eu ficar correspondendo.

Luis eu pergunto se você Já tirou

os documentos. Depois de resolver os problemas na minha

casa, eu vou mandar buscar você.

Aqui a pessoa que tem estudo é fácil de arrumar em-

prego. Eu peço que você não fale para ninguém

eu quero que fique em segredo.

Luis eu vou te pedir o favor, se for possível,

peço que você tente consegir o número do

telefone da Deuza minha prima célia.

tem uma prima que pode a Judar a pedir pra

célia o que eu estou pedindo.

Eu espero que na próxima correspondência você

tenha consegido.

consegrido

Figure 3B

**FIGURE 10.4. Letter C—second version**

ments on this acquisition of knowledge when he compared this to the first letter he wrote:

*T*: Did you use to do the beginning and end of sentences?
*S*: No.
*T*: How did you discover this?
*S*: I would do it and then when I reached a word I'd: "I think it's the end already," and then I'd start another (line).
*T*: And now, what do you do?
*S*: Now, when I reach the end, I think I sort of know, already, where the end is.
*T*: How do you know you've reached the end of the sentence
*S*: Because I've finished talking, I've finished writing what I was thinking, so the end is there.
*T*: The end of what?
*S*: The end...of the sentence.
*T*: Then...another thought...
*S*: Another thought, that's another sentence.

Here the subject's metacognition is made explicit: the criteria for sentence division are units of thought (or information chunks, to which Luria, 1981, refers). This is an important passage, in which we can highlight the flash of his transition from oral, intonational criteria for the separation of sentences to criteria based on the idea of sentence as a unit of meaning (I've stopped talking, I've stopped writing what I was thinking).

As to word separation, although in this letter there are no mistakes, they re-occur later on. The criteria for separation are not consolidated and are still heavily dependent on the tutor's monitoring. The need for separation is clear, but the concept of word as a unit is still unclear:

*T*: How do you know the words are separated?
*S*: I don't know that much, but I can notice, because here (points at the first letter) it went: A *dona simone*...I think here it should be *voltei* is one (word), *terminar* is another, *saudade* is another, and...
*T*: How do you know, now?
*S*: Now, because I'm here, aren't I? I know because you're like, telling me, look it' not like that, so now I already know how, sort of, how it's like, how it starts, what a name is like, but I still make some stupid mistakes.
*T*: They're not stupid mistakes. You're...
*S*: But I'm doing better than in the first letter because (...) not any more. Now I know more or less how to separate: Each word has to be a little separated.

In the last version, the genesis of paragraphing can be noticed: A negative indentation separates blocks of sentences (linked by subject) into paragraphs.

Brasilia...
Luis eu recebi a carta que você mandou. Eu fiquei
muito alegre.
Eu peço par favor que você me mande sempre
carta pra eu ficar correspondendo.
Eu pergunto se você Já tirou os documentos.
Depois de resolver os problemas na minha
Casa eu vou mandar buscar você.
Aqui a pessoa que tem estudo é fácil de arrumar
emprego. Eu peço que você não fala para ninguém
eu quero que fique em segredo.
Luis eu vou te pedir um favor se for passivel
peço que você tente consegeir o número do
telefone da Deuza com minha prima Célia.
Eu espero que na próxima correspondência. você
tenha conseguido. Reginaldo

**FIGURE 10.5. Letter C—third version**

There is more lexicalization of information and the use of indirect discourse (such as "I ask you to..."). The tone is more formal than is common in oral interaction. Complex structures like "I hope you try" and "I hope you will have managed" appear. There is greater use of intralinguistic reference to eliminate redundancies and extend information. An example is the expression "someone who has studied," which refers to the addressee, avoiding the repetition of "you." In "I hope you will have tried to get it..." there is new intralinguistic reference, avoiding the repetition of "the telephone number."

***Semiotic activity***

The manipulations with the means of representation go beyond the level of grapho-phonic equivalence and basic text mechanics; the subject engages in an activity devoted to the choice of lexicon (an example is the elimination of talking and its exchange for corresponding, more adequate to the written medium) and the reorganization of the text to aid comprehension.

The motives for writing the letter are two: answering a letter which pleased him and solving a problem. It is specifically this latter motive that leads him to re-elaborate the whole last paragraph, which in the end reads: "Luis, I'm going to ask you a favor. I ask you if possible to try and get Deuza's phone number with my cousin Célia. I hope that by the next letter you will have got it." It is interesting to note that this correction was initiated by the student himself.

In the editing procedures, the subject engages in an imaginary dialogue with the addressee and invites the tutor to monitor the development of this dialogue. These aspects, linked to the high degree of lexicalization of information, reveal this to be a letter with a high degree of psychological contiguity (or dialogicality) with the receptor of the information. Besides, the use of indirect discourse reveals a distancing from dialogic discourse, and takes on a more distanced stance. The letter begins to consolidate itself as a mediational device.

**Letter D** (see Figure 10.6)

Brasilia, 05/11/89
Dear Mother how are you all right.
I hope you are in health and happiness.
Mother I would like to know the result of the exam you had.
I would like to say that we won't be able to send the money.
Dalva got a piece of land and she can't build because it is very expensive.
We are going to help because she only has a month to build.
Mother in a month we are going to send for you. Father I managed to open my savings account it was my dream the day I got here I told the girls. Mother I got a set of twenty plates.
Father I would like to know whether you fixed the canoe.
I feel a lot of saudades of you.
Here are in health.
Zuleide and Berenice send a hug and Adam.
I send my nephews and my sisters a hug
Reginaldo.

***Text structure***

In the original version of this letter, all words are treated as units. Sentences are consistently marked by capitalization and punctuation. It

Brasilias 05/11/89
Querida mãe Como vai a senhora tudo bem-
espero que estejam com saude e felecidade.
mãe eu queria saber o resultado do-
exame que a senhora fez.
Eu queria dezer que não vai dar para
nós mandar o dinheiro.
A Valtra ganhou um lote e ela não está
conseguindo fazer porque é muito caro
nós vamos ajudar porque ela só tem um-
mês para construir.
mãe da qui um mês nós vamos mandar.
buscar a senhora-
Pai eu conseguir abrir a minha cadeneta
de poupança era o meu sonho no dia.
que eu chegeui aqui eu falei para as-
menias. mãe eu ganhei um conjunto de-
vinte peças de pratos.
Pai eu queria saber si você consertou
a canoa.
Eu estou com muitas saldade de vocês.
A qui nós estamos com saúde.
A Inledi e a Berenice manda um abraço e
o Adão. Eu mando um abraço para os.
meus sobrinhos e para as minha-
irmãs.

Reginaldo

**FIGURE 10.6. Letter D**

is interesting to note that in this letter, a hypothesis arises for the use of the hyphen. Instead of being used for the separation of words in between lines, sentences that did not fit into a line are concluded with a hyphen. Paragraphs are marked by a negative indentation and spaces between one and another.

As to lexical choice, one can note the extension and the avoidance of redundancies. For example, so as not to repeat "well," the author extends the information and writes "...in health and peace." One can note explicitation of information, for example, in the question about the exam, the explanation of why he cannot send the money and the explicitation of the personal significance of opening a savings account.

Sentence syntax is elaborate in comparison to the first letter, with the use of subordinated sentences, for example. The topics are well organized, ranging from opening greetings and report on the subject's well-being, an inquiry into his mother's well-being, and the question of the money order, onto general news and closing greetings.

***Semiotic activity***

Consolidating a tendency that had been pointed to in the previous letter, the subject presented to the tutoring situation a text that had already undergone several editing procedures, in which the subject used the aid of friends, relatives, a dictionary, and reference to other texts. This can be seen in the "clean copy" format of the version presented and in the construction of the hypothesis, for example, that a sentence, when interrupted, should be separated by a hyphen. This is undoubtably constructed on the basis of the observation of hyphens in other texts, and the active attempt to use them adequately. This growing autonomy of the subject in relation to the tutor can be read as a greater insertion in the interaction with social others and their cultural products.

The text indicates that its elaboration involved conscious operations on the concept of word (it must be noted that the notion is not yet fully consolidated as in later texts, not presented here; equivocate separations and junctions still occurred). Additionally, the concept of the unit of a sentence seems to have been consolidated, as well as the need to organize the text into idea units marked by paragraph separation. All of this results from an effort of previous planning and editing. Orthography seems to have been automated in most cases, and the resource to a dictionary is used in cases presenting difficulty.

Vocal mediation is still necessary while writing and reading; however, it is practically inaudible: A moving of the lips and whispers accompany text elaboration, suggesting the transition to its extinction.

There is a great level of intralinguistic reference, and extralinguistic reference is appropriately explicited and marked, revealing a consolidation in the consciousness of the need for psychological, as opposed to physical, contiguity in the organization of the text.

## DISCUSSION

What developmental tendencies can we point out in the texts being produced by the subject and what semiotic activity does this movement rest upon? In this discussion, we shall attempt to build a hypothesis that may explain the movement observed in this constitution of discourse.

Initially, we can state, based on this and former, more extensive analyses (Fávero and De Lima, 1989, and De Lima, 1993), that the presence of the prototypical characteristics of written monologic discourse increases as the texts are written. This is a nonlinear process, with developmental regressions and leaps. In order to try to interpret the data and integrate it to our original hypothesis, we could perhaps observe the development of some of the parameters longitudinally.

The organization of the text in the graphic space, with the separation of words, sentences, paragraphs, and lay-out, is a gradual achievement. The genesis of paragraphing, for example, suggests it is linked to an increase in the organization of idea units, an organization that we believe lies in the communicational function of the text. This means that this organization is not a mere convention, but a mediational, communicative device.

The same can be said of the separation of words and sentences into discrete units. The concept of sentence is consolidated before that of word. The mastery over the concept of sentence is mediated by the notion of meaning unit. It therefore requires planning and conscious reflection. In a previous stage, this concept is heavily mediated by orality. The concept of word, being a more arbitrary unit, emerges only later.

It is interesting to note that in the sociogenesis of alphabetic writing, one can note that the separation of words arose late in history, in the Renaissance. The lack of separation, according to Illich (1987), limited severely the access to texts and obliged the few proficient writers to mediate their reading with vocality.

We can thus note that the main obstacle to the reading and previous editing of the first letters was the faulty text mechanics. In other words, the potential socio-communicative function of the text was gradually increased by the growing consciousness of organization in the graphic space and of spelling procedures, which in turn are a result of the communicational demands imposed on the text.

As to the vocal mediation of the text, one can note that, although the need for it decreases, it is still present (although in a subvocal manner) until the end of the tutoring sessions. This disturbed the subject: His school teacher had said this was not real reading: "She said you've got to read with your eyes only, you know? But I can't! I cannot read with my eyes only, I have at least to speak low, or else...she said that's not real reading!"

His struggle shows the force of the Vygotskian proposition, later restated by Luria, that writing originates as the representation of another representation (oral language), and only gradually becomes independent.

The orality that still mediates writing marks the text. This suggests that part of the difficulty in text production by adults learning to write is the lack of familiarity with written discourse. Urban children who have been exposed to written monologic discourse through storytelling, for example, are at an advantage in relation to those to whom writing is an alien land.

The progress observed in text elaboration is not, we believe, a mere question of the passive absorption of a written model. During the work, the suggestions given by the tutor focused questions relative to text mechanics and grapho-phonic equivalence. We observed how these suggestions are internalized, as in the dictation to oneself of certain basic instructions and rules. It is interesting to note, however, that the subject goes beyond these suggestions and amplifies the process of conscious reflection on the text. His attention frees itself from mechanical problems and focuses on those of communication. This construction of novelty—novel concerns when writing, novel uses of writing, novel association with words—is a result of the communication processes with heterogeneous texts (his home town, his relatives and friends, the tutor, other cultural texts). In Vygotskian terms, we can say that writing is initially objectified and later assumes a mediational function. Written language, initially the object of consciousness, becomes a medium of communication.

We believe this amplification is linked to the dialectics of communicative restrictions and potentialities of a written text. Initially a means to communicate well-being, the letters begin to constitute also a problem-solving instrument, a messenger of essential information, and an instrument of political influence (Letter 11, analyzed in De Lima, 1992).

This experimenting with textual functions, allied to the high level of affective significance he deposits in the letters, demands a reorganization of the communication/means-of-communication relation.

Going back to Lotman (1988b) and his propositions of socio-communicative processes present in a text, we note that the subject starts off with a letter with very little socio-communicative role, in the sense that the subject himself and the tutor could not decipher it, and develops to texts that allow not only communication between the writer and the reader, but also a vehicle of communication between the audience and the cultural tradition, and between the text itself and culture. This happens as texts acquire a structure and content that allow them to inform on the cultural context from which they originated and to which they are headed. The kind of explicitation of information makes it clear, for example, that the letters are headed to an area that is different from the urban, literate-oriented area from which it comes (cf. "Here somebody who has studied can get a job easily," Letter C: the explicitation of a different system of values related to education in the rural and urban areas). The texts are thus contextualized: They are texts of a time and space. Due to the possibility that a written text can be fixed graphically and constitute a physical object, it assumes the capacity to survive over time and be at any time re-read and interpreted, taking on the function of a collective memory.

With the building of a consciousness that, in the media of letters, addressant and addressee do not share spatial and temporal contiguity, extralinguistic reference is reorganized in order to "point to" a reality that is now shared. More decontextualized explanations are required. Besides, the links established in the text in intralinguistic reference constitute the means through which the subject learns to use the text (and not the spatial-temporal context) as context. This is what Wertsch (1985) has termed the decontextualization of mediational means: "the process whereby the meaning of signs becomes less and less dependent on the unique spatial temporal context in which they are used" (p. 33). In this use of writing, then, we were able to observe the inauguration of a new contextual space, previously unknown to the subject. A space that becomes an instrument of interlocution with the subject and himself, with the reader and the text.

In the process of elaboration of texts, we were able to observe that the reading of the subject's own text leads him to re-elaborate his metacognition, his perception of his capacities, and his perception of the addressees of the information. This new space allows for the creation of novel, abstract concepts and novel insights into language:

*S*: (Looking at what he has just written.) Morros da Mariana (His hometown, translated as Hills of Mariana)...what a horrible name! (Sounding surprised)
*T*: Not horrible. I've always thought it was beautiful!
*S*: No, because Morro ... MORRO (morro means hill, but also [I] die). (Someone) will die there, because there no one makes any money!

We can see how the contemplation of a word in its fixed, graphic state may lead to previously unthought of associations—the basis of poetic activity, for example. In the monologization of written discourse the text becomes an intellectual instrument. The contact with the text, and especially, with its elaboration, allows an internal dialogue that reorganizes the subject. We have previously discussed the constitution of this internal dialogue in De Lima (1992) and rejected the interpretation that the constitution of written monologic discourse represents the closing of the subject upon himself. Contrariwise, we have attempted to show that the mastery over this kind of discourse yields an increment in internalized dialogicality, which involves the writer in intense interaction with the virtual addressees and in the counterposition of the varied cultural contexts involved. It is in this sense that the external, observable discourse is monologized, at the same time as we can observe an increase in internal dialogism, which, according to Wertsch (1991), characterizes higher mental processes.

In the analysis of the initial interview, it became clear that processes such as abstraction, analysis, and the establishment of relations were used by the subject before the start of the tutoring sessions. We could not, therefore, reach the conclusion that literacy is a necessary and sufficient condition for mental development, or that any literate use of the language has, *per se*, consequences in terms of the decontextualization of mediational means. We restate the capital importance of considering the heterogeneity of such means: Even in the limited universe of our study, focusing letter production, a wide variety of functions and dialogic potentials are involved, all loaded with socially constituted meaning.

We can, however, based on the former analysis, affirm that while working with significant reading and writing, the subject engages in a reflection process that creates internal instruments of amplification and organization of information through letters, the intersection of two desires—becoming literate to communicate with his homeland and making his mother happy. In this process, the subject communicates not only with his homeland, but with himself, and thus amplifies his interaction with the universe of literate representations. The disclosure of such a new world is described by the subject himself, in one of his last sessions:

> I think it's really different, because I think I'm making progress, I'm getting where I want (...) Everything I see I read (...) I'm even surprised at myself, because (...) everything I see I pick up. The newspaper, I pick up the book in the drawer we keep our clothes in (...) Full of books, you know? Schoolbooks. 2nd year, 3rd...Then I read, every day I read a lesson. I read about the sun, about the planets, about...Then I understood everything...I didn't even use to understand what it was like, and now I already know more or less...how many planets there are, how (...) Many things I don't know, I think I'm managing (...) Emotion, wow, I think I'm...I'm developing fast. I really think I'm even making it.

## NOTES

[1]The first version of the original letters are presented, along with translations. In the translations, words that appear mistakenly connected or separated in the

original have been kept so in the translation. Bold letters indicate spelling mistakes.

[2]"To feel *saudade*" means, approximately, to deeply miss. I have maintained the original noun as there is no such noun (with the exception of the roughly equivalent term, nostalgia) in English.

## REFERENCES


Cagliari, L. C. (1985). O principe que virou sapo [The prince who turned into a frog]. *Cadernos de Pesquisa, 55,* 50–62.

Carraher, T. N., Carraher, D. W., & Schliemann, A. D. (1985). Mathematics in the streets and in schools. *British Journal of Developmental Psychology, 3,* 21–29.

Collins, J., & Michaels, S. (1991). A fala e a escrita: Estratégias de discurso e aquisição da alfabetização [Speech and writing: Discourse strategies and the acquisition of literacy]. In J. Cook-Gumperz (Ed.), *A construção social da alfabetização*. Porto Alegre, Brazil: Artes Médicas.

Cook-Gumperz, J. (1991). Introdução: A construção social da alfabetização [Inroduction: The social construction of literacy]. In J. Cook-Gumperz (Ed.), *A construção social da alfabetização*. Porto Alegre, Brazil: Artes Médicas.

De Lima, S. G. (1992). *The voices in letters: A case study.* Paper presented to the I Conference for Socio-Cultural Research, Madrid, Spain.

De Lima, S. G. (1993). *A mediação semiótica na produção de texto: Um estudo de caso da alfabetizacão de um adulto [Semiotic mediation in text production: A case study].* Unpublished Master's dissertation, University of Brasilia, Brazil.

Fávero, M. H., & De Lima, S. G. (1989). *A produção de texto por um migrante da zona rural: Um estudo de caso [Text production by a rural zone migrant: A case study].* Paper presented to the XIX Annual Meeting of Psychology of the SPRP, Ribeirão Preto, Brazil.

Fávero, M. H., Tunes, E., & Marchi, A. (1991). A representação social da matemática e desempenho na solução de problema [Social representation of math and problem solving performance]. *Psicologia: Teoria e pesquisa,* 7(3), 225–262.

Ferreiro, E., Navarro, L., Vernon, S., Loprena, M. L., Taboada, E., Corona, Y., Hope, M. E., & Vaca, E. (1983). Los adultos no-alfabetizados y sus conceptualidades del sistema de escritura [Illiterate adults and their conceptions of the writing system]. *Cuadernos de Investigaciones Educativas* (10). Mexico, D.F., Mexico: Departamento de Investigaciones Educativas, Centro de Investigación y Estudios Avanzados del I.P.N.

Finnegan, R. (1988). *Literacy and orality. Studies in the technology of communication.* Oxford: Basil Blackwell.

Francis, H. (1987). Cognitive implications of learning to read. *Interchange, 18*(1/2), 97–108.

Freire, P. (1981). *A importância do ato de ler [The importance of the act of reading].* São Paulo, Brazil: Cortez.

Gee, J. P. (1988). The legacies of literacy. From Plato to Freire through Harvey Graff. (*Review of The Legacies of Literacy: Continuities and Contradictions in Western Culture and Society*). *Harvard Educational Review, 58*(2), 195–212.

Gould, S. J. (1991). *Wonderful life.* London: Penguin.

Greenfield, P. M. (1972). Oral or written language: The consequences for cognitive development in Africa, the United States and England. *Language and Speech, 15,* 169–178.

Holland, D. C., & Valsiner, J. (1988). Cognition, symbols and Vygotsky's developmental psychology. *Ethos, 16,* 247–273.

Holquist, M., & Emerson, C. (Eds.). (1986). *Speech genres and other late essays.* Austin: University of Texas Press.

Illich, I. (1987). A plea for research on lay literacy. *Interchange, 18*(1-2), 9–22.

Kulick, D., & Stroud, C. (1990). Christianity, cargo and ideas of self: Patterns of literacy in papua New Guinean village. *Man (N.S.), 25,* 286–304.

Lotman, Y. M. (1988a). The semiotics of culture and the concept of a text. *Soviety Psychology, XXVI*(3), 52–58.

Lotman, Y. M. (1988b). Text within a text. *Soviety Psychology, XXVI*(3), 32–51.

Luria, A. R. (1981). *Language and cognition.* J. Wertsch (Ed.). New York: Wiley.

Oliveira, M. K. (1982). *Cognitive processes in everyday life situations: An ethnographic study of Brazilian urban migrants*. Unpublished PhD thesis, Stanford University, California.

Oliveira, M. K. (1992). Analfabetos na sociedade letrada: Diferenças culturais e modos de pensamento [Illiterates in literate society: Cultural differences and modes of thought]. *Travessia: Revista do Migrante, 12,* 17–20.

Olson, D. R. (1977). Oral and written language and the cognitive processes of children. *Journal of Communication, 27*(3), 10–26.

Olson, D. R., & Astington, J. W. (1990). Talking about text: How literacy contributes to thought. *Journal of Pragmatics, 14,* 705–721.

Parmentier, R. J. (1985). Signs' place in Medias res: Peirce's concept of semiotic mediation. In E. Mertz and R.J. Parmentier (Eds.), *Semiotic mediation: Sociocultural and psychological perspectives.* Orlando, FL: Academic Press.

Rockwell, E. (1985). Os usos escolares da língua escrita. *Cadernos de Pesquisa, 52,* 82–95.

Scinto, L. F. M. (1985). Text, schooling and the growth of mind. In E. Mertz & R. J. Parmentier (Eds.), *Semiotic mediation: Socio-cultural psychological perspectives* (pp. 203–218). New York: Academic Press.

Scribner, S. (1985). Vygotsky's uses of history. In J. V. Wertsch (Ed.), *Culture, communication and cognition* (pp. 119–147). Cambridge: Cambridge Univeristy Press.

Scribner, S., & Cole, M. (1978). Literacy without schooling: Testing for intellectual effects. *Harvard Educational Review, 48*(4), 448–461.

Scribner, S., & Cole, M. (1981). *The psychology of literacy.* Cambridge, MA: Harvard University Press.

Tfouni, L. V. (1988). *Adultos não alfabetizados: O avesso do avesso [Illiterate adults: The reverse of the reverse].* Campinas, Brazil: Pontes Editores.

Torrance, N., & Olson, D. R. (1987). Development of the metalanguages and the acquisition of literacy: A progress report. *Interchange, 18*(1/2), 136–146.

Tulviste, P. (1987). L. Levy Bruhl and problems of the historical development of thought. *Soviet Psychology, XXV*(3), 3–21.
Tulviste, P. (1989). Education and development of concepts in adults with and without schooling. *Soviet Psychology, XXVII*(1), 5–21.
Tulviste, P. (1992). On the historical heterogeneity of verbal thought. *Journal of Russian and East European Psychology, 30*(1), 77–88.
Valsiner, J. (1988). *Developmental psychology in the Soviet Union.* Brighton: Harvester Press.
Valsiner, J. (1989a). *Human development and culture.* Lexington, MA: Lexington Books.
Valsiner, J. (1989b). How can developmental psychology become "culture-inclusive"? In J. Valsiner (Ed.), *Child development in cultural context* (pp. 1–8). Toronto: Hogrefe and Huber Publishers.
Vygotsky, L. S. (1929). The problem of the cultural development of the child. *Journal of Genetic Psychology, 36,* 415–434.
Vygotsky, L. S. (1962). *Thought and language.* Cambridge, MA: The MIT Press.
Vygotsky, L. S. (1960/1977). The development of higher psychological functions. *Soviety Psychology, XV*(3).
Vygotsky, L. S. (1925/1979). Consciousness as a problem in psychology of behaviour. *Soviet Psychology, XVII*(4), 3–35.
Vygotsky, L. S. (1987). The development of scientific concepts in childhood. In R. W. Rieber & A. S. Carton (Eds.), *The collected works of L. S. Vygotsky* (Vol. 1, pp. 167–241). New York: Plenum Press.
Wertsch, J. (1985). *Vygotsky and the social formation of mind.* Cambridge, MA: Harvard University Press.
Wertsch, J. (1991). *Voices of the mind: A social-cultural approach to mediated action.* Cambridge, MA: Harvard University Press.

# Author Index


**A**

Adams, M. J. 87, *101*
Ahuja, G. K. 150, 151, *159*
Ainlay, S. C. 175, *180*
Akinnaso, F. N. 169, 173, *180*
Alegria, J. 152, *159*
Allen, J. 140, *142*
Astington, J. W. 250, *278*
Austin, J. L. 109, *121*
Azenha, M. G. 9, *11*

**B**

Bakhtin, M. 111, 118,*121*
Barton, D. 186, *222*
Beck, I. 155, *159*
Becker, G. 175, *180*
Bell, L. 155, *159*
Berger, M. 171, 174, *180*
Bertelson, P. 152, *159*
Bever, T. G. 147, *157*
Bissex, G. L. 171, *180*
Boag, S. T. 131, *142*
Bohannon, J. N. 147, 149, *158*
Borel, M. J. 193, *222*
Bottéro, J. 2, *11*
Bourdieu, P. 197, 208, 210, 211, 215, *222*
Bowey, J. 147, *160*
Branscombe, A. 126, *141*
Braslavsky, B. P. 80, 84, 96, 99, 100, 101, *101, 102*
Brody, G. H. 126, *142*
Brown, J. D. 177, *182*
Bruner, J. 89, 90, *102,* 110, *121,* 124, *143,* 174, *180*

**C**

Cabral, L. S. 151, *159*
Cagliari, L. C. 248, *277*
Cahnman, W. 175, *180*
Caldeira, A. 151, *159*
Carey, S. 228, *244*
Carraher, D. 188, 191, *222*
Carraher, D. W. 248, *277*
Carraher, T. 188, *222*
Carraher, T. N. 248, *277*
Carroll, L. 123, *141*
Carter, B. 91, *103*
Carton, A. 229, *245*
Cary, L. 151, 152, *159*
Castorina, J. A. 8, *11*
Cazden, C. 124, 125, *141*
Chafe, W. 189, *222*
Clark, E. V. 147, *158*
Clark, M. M. 171, *180*
Clark, R. 188, *222*
Cochran-Smith, M. 169, 172, 173, 174, *181*
Cole, M. 76, *77,* 82, *102,* 145, 146, *158, 160,* 168, 173, *181,* 190, *225,* 229, *244, 245,* 248, *278*
Coleman, L. M. 175, *180*
Collins, J. 253, *277*
Coll Salvador, C. 85, 88, *102*
Cook-Gumperz, J. 3, *11,* 253, *277*
Corona, Y. 250, *277*
Custro, M. J. 151, *159*

**D**

Dalgado, R. 151, *159*
Damon, W. 140, *141*
Danielewicz, J. 189, *222*
Dash, U. N. 145, *158*
Decker, S. N. 171, *180*
DeFries, J. C. 171, *180*
Dehant, F. 151, *159*
DeJong, W. 175, *180*

DeLima, S. G. 252, 255, 256, 259, 261, 273, 274, 275, *279*
Descardeci, M. A. 207, *222*
de Villiers, J. G. 147, *158*
De Villiers, P. A. 147, *158*
Donaldson, M. 148, *158*
Downing, J. 87, 90, *102*
Duranti, A. 136, *141,* 169, 173, *180*

**E**
Edwards, D. 110, *121*
Ehri, L. C. 148, 149, 152, *158*
Elkonin, D. B. 91, *102*
Emerson, C. 255, *278*
Evan, J. S. 147, 148, 149, *158*

**F**
Fairclough, N. 201, *222*
Fairclough, N. L. 188, *222*
Fávero, M. H. 250, 252, 255, 259, 273, *277*
Ferguson, C. A. 199, *222*
Ferreiro, E. 9, *11, 12,* 61, 62, 64, 65, 66, 67, 68n, 69, 70, 72, 73, 74, 75, 76, 77, 81, 82, 83, 84, 85, 86, 87, *102,* 250, *277*
Festinger, L. 175, *180*
Filmus, D. 88, *103*
Finnegan, R. 253, *277*
Fisher, F. W. 91, *103*
Fitzgerald, K. 171, 173, *180*
Flavell, J. H. 148, *158*
Fontana, R. A. C. *12*
Foucambert, J. 217, *222*
Foucault, M. 111, 118, 120, *121*
Fraenkel, B. 2, *11*
Francis, H. 250, *277*
Freeman, H. E. 169, *180*
Freire, P. 168, *180,* 183, 208, *222, 277*
Frost, J. 91, *103*
Fulker, D. W. 171, *180*

**G**
Galda, L. 126, *142*
Gallimore, R. 85, *103*
Gay, J. 146, *158*
Gee, J. 189, 190, 204, *222*
Gee, J. P. 247, *278*
Geertz, C. 221n, *222*
Gelb, I. 74, *77*
Geva, E. *158*
Gimeno-Sacristán, J. 84, 85, *103*
Ginzburg, C. 3, *12*
Gleitman, H. 147, *158*
Gleitman, L. R. 147, *158*
Glick, J. A. 146, *158*
Góes, M. C. R. 108, 110, *121*
Goffman, E. 175, 177, *181*
Goodman, K. S. 95, *103*
Goodman, Y. 140, *141*
Goodman, Y. M. 95, *103*
Goody, J. 167, 168, *181,* 190, *222,* 229, *244*
Goody, J. S. 2, *12,* 145, *158*
Gould, S. J. 249, *278*
Graff, H. J. 195, 196, *222*
Graham, S. 140, *141*
Greenfield, P. M. 134, *141,* 145, *158,* 247, *278*
Grodzinsky, Y. 156, *158*
Gumperz, J. 203, *223*
Gurd, J. 151, *159*

**H**
Habermas, J. 196, 205, *223*
Hagell, A. 176, 178, *181*
Hakes, D. T. 147, 148, 149, *158*
Hamel, R. E. 199, *223*
Heath, S. B. 126, *141,* 173, *181,* 188, 197, 199, 217, *223*
Herrenschmidt, C. 2, *11*
Herriman, M. L. 148, *160*
Heubner, T. 167, *181*
Hildyard, A. 187, *224*
Hohepa, M. 137, *141*
Holland, D. C. 250, *278*
Holquist, M. 255, *278*
Hope, M. E. 250, *277*
Hughes, C. 155, *159*

**I**
Illich, I. 273, *278*
Infante, R. 3, *12*
Ivanic, R. 188, *222*

**J**
Jokubvitz, R. 151, *159*
Joshi, R. M. 154, *160*
Junqueira, M. S. 151, *159*

**K**
Ka'ai, T. 130, 131n, 136, *142*
Karanth, P. 149, 150, 151, 152, 154, 155, 156, *158, 159, 160*
Karmiloff-Smith, A. 147, 149, *159*

Karmann, D. 151, *159*
Kassebaum, G. G. 169, *180*
Kato, M. A. 183, *223*
Kessen, W. 135, *142*
Kleiman, A. B. 185, 192, 193, 195, 197, 200, 202, *223*, *225*
Knijnik, G. 188, 201, 207, 210, *223*
Koda, K. *159*
Koehler, W. 17, 18, *56*
Kozol, J. 170, *181*
Kozulin, A. 108, *121*
Kudva, A. 151, *159*
Kulick, D. 253, *278*

**L**
LaBuda, M. C. 171, *180*
Langer, K. 173, *181*
Lapacherie, J. 2, *11*
Laplane, A. L. F. *12*
Lave, J. 126, 138, 140, *142*
Lecours, A. R. 151, *159*
Lemos, C. T. G. 59, *77*
Levine, K. 165, 168, *181*
Liberman, I. Y. 91, *103*
Londono, L. O. 3, *12*
Loprena, M. L. 250, *277*
Lotman, Y. M. 252, 254, 255, 274, *278*
Luckman, T. 174, *180*
Lundberg, I. 91, *103*, 148, *159*
Luria, A. 94, 95, 99, *103*
Luria, A. R. 58, 60, 62, 63, 64, 65, 66n, 67, 71n, 72, 74, 75, 76, *77*, 146, *159*, 190, *223*, 229, *244*, 252, 253, 268, *278*

**M**
Maingueneau, D. 111, 114, 120, *121*
Malcolm, C. B. 178, *181*
Marchi, A. 250, *277*
Martin-Jones, M. 188, 199, *222*, *223*
Mason, J. M. 140, *142*
Matencio, M. L. M. 195, *223*
McLane, J. B. 173, *181*
McNamee, G. D. 173, *181*
McNaughton, S. 124, 127, 130n, 131n, 136, 138, 139, 140, *141*, *142*
Mead, G. H. 175, *181*
Medin, D. L. 228, *244*
Mehler, J. 151, *159*
Metge, J. 135, 136, 137, *142*
Mey, J. 212, *224*
Michaels, S. 253, *277*
Miéville, D. 193, *224*
Milanez, W. 192, *224*
Moll, L. C. 88, *103*
Morais, J. 152, *159*
Moreira, T. M. 192, *224*
Morrison, K. 2, *11*
Moscovici, S. 174, *181*
Murphy, G. L. 228, *244*

**N**
Nagaraja, D. 150, 151, *159*
Natali, N. 99, *102*
Navarro, L. 250, *277*
Needlman, R. 171, 173, *180*
Nesdale, A. R. 148, *160*
Nigam, R. 152, 155, *160*
Ninyoles, R. L. 199, 200, *224*

**O**
Obler, L. 156, *159*
Ochs, E. 136, 138, *141*, *142*, 169, 173, *180*
Ogbu, J. U. 173, *181*
Oliveira, M. K. 59, *77*, 187, *224*, 248, 249, *278*
Oliveira, M. K. de 9, *12*, 229, *244*, *245*
Olson, D. 170, *181*, 187, *224*
Olson, D. R. 148, *159*, 187, 190, *224*, 247, 250, *278*
Ong, W. J. 189, 194, 195, 210, *224*
Orlandi, E. 111, *121*
Osoria, Z. 151, *159*

**P**
Palacio, M. G. 61, *77*
Pandit, R. 150, 151, *159*
Parente, M. A. 151, *159*
Parmentier, R. J. 251, *278*
Passeron, J. C. 197, *222*
Patel, P. G. 154, *159*
Payer, M. O. 211, *224*
Pecheux, M. 111, *121*
Pellegrini, A. D. 126, *142*
Perez Gomez, A. 85, *103*
Perfetti, C. A. 155, *159*
Perlmutter, J. C. 126, *142*
Peters, A. M. 131, *142*
Petersen, Ole-P. 91, *103*
Petit, J. C. 120, *121*
Phillips, G. 127, 130n, *142*
Piaget, J. 60, *78*, 109, *121*
Pino, A. 108, 110, *121*

Polatajko, H. J. 178, *181*
Potter, J. 110, 114, *121*
Prakash, P. 152, 154, 155, *160*
Pratt, C. 147, *160*
Putnam, S. E. 166, *182*

**R**
Rama, A. 199, *224*
Rama, G. W. 80, *103*
Rangamani, G. N. 156, *160*
Ratto, I. 195, 210, 211, 212, *224*
Reid, J. F. 95, *103*
Rekha, D. 152, 155, *160*
Resnick, D. 167, 170, *181*
Resnick, L. 167, 170, *181*
Ribeiro, D. 200, 211, 218n, *224*
Rieber, R. 229, *245*
Robinson, J. L. 172, 179, *181*
Rocco, M. T. F. 9, 70, *78*
Rockwell, E. 250, *278*
Rogoff, B. 124, 125, 138, 139, 140, *142*, 174, *181*
Rosen, N. 99, *102*
Ross, G. 124, *143*
Rutter, M. 171, *180*
Ryan, E. B. 147, *160*

**S**
Santos, S. L. 191, *222*
Sasanuma, S. 156, *160*
Saxe, G. 8, *12*
Schieffelin, B. B. 169, 172, 173, 174, *181*
Schiffman, H. F. 155, *160*
Schliemann, A. D. 248, *277*
Schliemann, A. L. 188, *222*
Scholl, D. M. 147, *160*
Scinto, L. F. M. 250, 253, *278*
Scribner, S. 145, 146, *160*, 168, 173, *181*, 190, *225*, 229, *244*, *245*, 249, *278*
Setúbal, M. A. 9, *12*
Shankweiler, D. 91, *103*
Sharp, D. W. 146, *158*
Shivashankar, N. 150, 151, *159*
Sierra, M. T. 199, *223*
Signorini, I. 192, 210, 213, 214, *225*
Simons, J. 178, *181*
Smith, G. H. 137, *141*
Smith, L. T. 137, *141*
Smolka, A. L. B. 6, *12*, 87, *103*, 108, 110, *121*
Soares, M. 195, 217n, *225*
Sommerville, C. J. 7, *12*
Soper, H. V. 154, *159*
Spratt, J. E. 139, *142*
Srivastava, R. N. 146, *160*
Srividya, R. 156, *160*
Steinhouse, L. 85, *103*
Street, B. 168, *181*
Street, B. V. 184, 186, 190, 216, *225*, 229, 230, *245*
Stroud, C. 253, *278*
Suchitra, M. G. 149, 150, *159*, *160*
Sulzby, E. 83, *103*, 124, 125, 126, 127, 138, 139, 140, *142*

**T**
Taboada, E. 250, *277*
Taylor, S. E. 177, *182*
Teale, M. H. 83, *103*
Teale, W. 124, 125, 126, 127, 138, 139, 140, *142*
Teberosky, A. 9, *12*, 62, 64, 65, 66, 67, 68n, 69, *77*, 81, 82, *102*
Tfouni, L. V. 187, 207, *225*, 248, *278*
Tharp, R. 85, *103*
Torrance, N. 250, *278*
Torrey, J. W. 171, *182*
Toulmin, S. E. 213, *225*
Trevarthen, C. 174, *182*
Tudge, J. R. H. 166, *182*
Tulviste, P. 3, *12*, 166, *182*, 229, *245*, 248, 249, *279*
Tunes, E. 250, *277*
Tunmer, W. E. 146, 147, 148, 149, *158*, *160*
Turman, M. C. 167, *182*

**V**
Vaca, E. 250, *277*
Vaid, J. *160*
Valsiner, J. 2, *12*, 108, *121*, 127, 136, 139, *142*, *143*, 166, *182*, 229, *245*, 248, 249, 250, *279*
Vandermeersch, L. 2, *11*
Van Der Veer, R. 108, *121*, 139, *143*, 229, *245*
Van Kleek, A. 147, 149, *160*
Vellutino, F. R. 95, *103*
Vernon, M. D. 87, 95, *104*
Vernon, S. 250, *277*
Vijayan, A. 151, *159*

Vygotsky, L. S. 28, *56,* 62, 73, *78,* 79, 89, 90, 91, 92, 93, 94, 95, 98, *104,* 166, *182,* 229, *245,* 251, 252, 255, 256, *279*
Vygotsky, S. 109, 110, *122*

**W**
Wagner, D. A. 139, *142,* 173, *182*
Watt, I. 145, *158,* 229, *244*
Wells, G. 148, *160*
Wendt, A. 123, *143*
Wenger 126, 138, 140, *142*
Werner, H. 47, *56*
Wertsch, J. 248, 249, 252, 256, 275, 276, *279*
Wertsch, J. V. 6, *12,* 90, 92, *104,* 108, 110, *122,* 166, *182*
Wetherell, M. 114, *121*
Williams, R. 167, *182*
Winterhoff, P. A. 166, *182*
Wolfgramm, E. 132, 133n, 136, 138, *143*
Wood, D. 124, 125, *143*

**Y**
Yule, W. 171, *180*

**Z**
Zilberman, R. 83, *104*